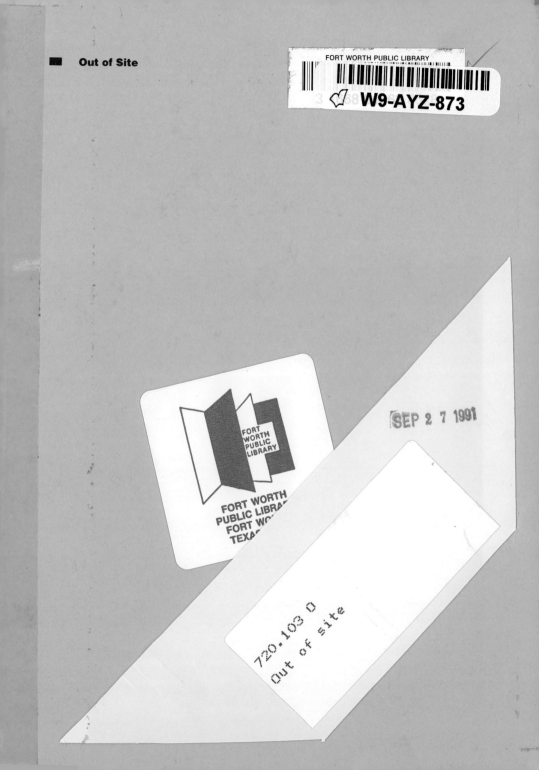

Out of Site

A

Social

Out of Site

Criticism

of

Architecture

Edited by Diane Ghirardo

Bay Press Seattle 1991

Published in 1991.
Printed in the United States
of America.
First Printing 1991.

Bay Press
115 West Denny Way
Seattle, Washington 98119
USA

Designed by Katy Homans
Set in Helvetica
Printed by BookCrafters

Rosalyn Deutsche's essay originally
appeared in *October* 47 (Winter
1988) and is reprinted here with the
permission of *October* and MIT
Press.

Kenneth Frampton's essay was
originally presented at the annual
meeting of the east central region
of the Association of Collegiate
Schools of Architecture, at the
University of Michigan, October
1989, and is published here in a
revised form with the permission of
the organizers of the conference.

Diane Ghirardo's essays originally
appeared in a slightly different form
in *Architectural Review* (June 1990).

Tony Schuman's essay originally
appeared in *The Journal of Architectural Education* 40/1 (Fall 1986)
and is reprinted here with permission of the *Journal*.

**Library of Congress
Cataloging
in Publication Data**
Out of Site: a social criticism of
architecture /
edited by Diane Ghirardo.
   p. cm.
Includes bibliographical references.
ISBN 0-941920-19-4 (pbk): $16.95
1. Architecture and society.
2. Architects and community.
I. Ghirardo, Diane Yvonne.
NA2543.S609   1991
720' .1'03—dc20
90-48948
CIP

■ Acknowledgments

This book grew out of a paper I presented at the conference "Criticism and Beyond" in Seattle, Washington, November 1988. Parts of my introduction derive from the paper I presented there. I am grateful to Thatcher Bailey for the opportunity to develop some of those arguments with this group of distinguished scholars. Cathy Johnson edited this diverse group of texts with care and sensitivity, and Katy Homans beautifully designed the book.

To my parents, Margaret Madden Ghirardo and Joseph Ghirardo

Contents

Diane Ghirardo

"Any hack . . . can build a dumb box," a New York architect recently remarked.[1]
He went on to assert that real architecture should contain ideas about society and express "the cosmology of the culture." Indeed, buildings do express
ideas about our culture or, at the very least, its values—commodity fetishism
being the predominant value expressed in contemporary society. But that is
not what he meant: instead, his remark articulates widely held views about
Architecture—in contrast to architecture and building—and about the capacity
of the designer to imbue a building with lofty and critical ideas about society.

At a 1989 conference entitled "Postmodernism and Beyond: Architecture as the Critical Art of Contemporary Culture," architecture was defined in
precisely those terms.[2] The definite article *the,* dropped just so in the conference title, tells us that architecture is "the"—meaning *only*—critical art. We
are thus led, by the title alone, effortlessly and from the onset, out of the
world of social practice and into the realm of art. Conference panelists projected slide after slide, leaving the audience to conclude that the pictures
told architecture's story, that the artfully contrived interiors bereft of people—
but often cast in striking shadows or glowing marble surfaces—constituted
all there was to know about these architectures.

The implicit premise of the conference was that the architect could
engage critically with contemporary problems through formal manipulation:
in other words, that through form alone, one could contest such things as
the commodification and consumption of culture. Such a premise has a pedi-
gree, though not a very ancient one. It constitutes a contemporary version of
Robert Venturi's playful response to the condition of contemporary housing
in his Vanna Venturi house of 1962 or his search for ironic juxtaposition of
design elements in subsequent buildings. Following Venturi's lead, architecture came to be seen as the silent witness to all of the weaknesses, indul-
gences, and self-absorption characteristic of modern culture.[3] As disengaged
voyeur, architecture first and foremost came to be understood as an exercise
in meaning, meaning that issued from the architect and emerged in the archi-

tecture, for example, in the form of witty comment upon earlier conventions (such as that found in the work of Charles Moore, Robert Stern, or Michael Graves) or what is held to be comment upon a current social situation (Peter Eisenman or Bernard Tschumi).

In the long run, this understanding of architecture constitutes a radical shift: instead of being understood as interventions into the environment that bear social, economic, and political programs, and that in turn affect all of these realms, architecture oscillates uneasily between self-expression and some form of effete cultural commentary. Multiple and complex reasons underlie this shift—Margaret Crawford's essay in this book explores many of them from the perspective of the history of the profession—but there is no mystery about what sustains this view of architecture: architects and critics work together to set forth a rubric for evaluating buildings. Clear aesthetic standards are proposed, and then architects and critics explain how a project originated, how the design team approached the problem, how the building fits into its environs, and depending upon the size of the building, what the nature is of its structural system, its materials, its formal relationship to neighbors, and so forth.

Even in the best of cases, and despite the interest of each of the above issues, this mode of assessing architecture—essentially a formal analysis— works within the institutional confines of architecture. By this I mean that architecture's conceptual framework is set out in such a way as to define what is relevant to the discourse on architecture and to exclude that which is deemed irrelevant. This essentially self-serving scheme for determining what is legitimate and pertinent operates to mystify architecture, with direct consequences in at least two fundamental categories of analysis:

I. the selection of buildings that may legitimately be considered Architecture: as things now stand, the overwhelming number of constructions erected annually are not considered Architecture.

2. the relation of Architecture to the wider nexus of social, political, economic, and ideological institutions: as set forth in the paradigm outlined above, Architecture remains autonomous from the range of ideological,

political, social, and economic roles that it is designed to fulfill and that collaborate in generating the conditions for building.

On the first point, my initial observation is that to the degree nonarchitect or builder designs enter into the architectural discussion, it is as the objects of thoroughgoing condemnation: from subdivisions, to mini-malls, to tract houses. In the current orthodoxy, such building production lacks the virtue of design, both as individual objects and as objects in the landscape; that is to say, the buildings lack the artistic qualities associated with architect-designed structures. Whereas fervent debate animates discussions about most architect-designed buildings—because no clear standard that guarantees merit exists—there is tacit and often explicit professional agreement that nonarchitect-designed buildings cannot be considered Architecture. Such a view refers back to a general belief that Architecture is an art, and that art in turn has a high moral purpose in the formation and transmission of culture. And, as John Ruskin suggested in the nineteenth century, the artist (or architect) owes an allegiance to Beauty, which Ruskin in turn equated with Truth: only the artist was peculiarly suited to illuminating this equation, to being the standard bearer for this demanding, complicated, "high" architecture. More specifically, in this view the architect is trained to design aesthetically pleasing forms and poetic spaces, in other words, to realize his or her creative potential and thereby bring Beauty and Truth to the untutored spectator. Alberto Perez-Gomez, for example, claims that "architecture is the re-creation of a symbolic order, deployed in the most immediate and concrete universe of essences . . . [it] is not the embodiment of information; it is the embodiment of meaning."[4]

This viewpoint and, indeed, disagreements over the merits of architect-designed buildings depend upon a hierarchy of taste that excludes more than it includes. Such issues are not trivial, for the architects' claims to special authority in formal matters rest on the shifting grounds of taste. To the layman, no obvious difference distinguishes a Michael Graves design in which the Seven Dwarfs festoon the cornices from the smaller, nonarchitect design for the Snow White restaurant—replete with Disney characters—in Hollywood, but to the architectural cognoscenti, the former is legitimate (highly debatable on formal grounds, but sufficiently legitimate to merit publication in professional magazines) whereas the latter is simply building.

Part of the problem with what is defined as nonarchitecture is that it caters to what is variously called mass, low, or popular culture.[5] That Graves would employ an unabashedly pop icon does not significantly complicate matters: the power to recuperate low culture remains within the purview of arbiters of high culture, and until so recuperated, an artifact of mass culture remains merely an artifact of mass culture. This represents what is called a mandarin view of culture, which does have its merits, chiefly, that of shoring up the status of those who assert mandarin prerogatives.

The reverent views of architecture and architect that underlie the distinctions noted above depend in part upon the belief that the architect enjoys some special access to a world of spirit and meaning. Although there is no gainsaying the fact that architects are more likely to be able to assemble interesting forms, devise rich spaces, or sheath elevations with arresting façades than the average person might be, the corollary assumption that they are uniquely gifted with some special contact with 'transcendental essence' is more difficult to swallow. The insistence upon architecture as art and the resulting exclusion of large categories of buildings—those in the overwhelming majority—from discussion, not to mention from architectural attention, precisely parallel the thesis of Allan Bloom in *The Closing of the American Mind* (1987) with respect to works of literature: in both cases, a canon is held up as the model, not open to debate or modification except from within, according to the standards established by a small group of self-appointed professionals. For the architect, this serves the very specific purpose of attaching architecture to relatively high social and cultural status. Even if one accepts all of these conditions, at best one concludes by assessing buildings as "art" and as carriers of high culture, which is to say that a certain strata of society and a certain group of architects decide to evaluate a limited body of buildings according to a set of standards that they then define. Eliminate any claims to truth, let alone relevance.

To return to the issue of architecture's critical capacity and its relation to wider society, it seems obvious to me that formal critique, directed as it invariably is to those already in the know, has as much to do with criticism or critique as a placebo does with curing cancer. To continue the parallel, it is worth observing that a placebo is not harmless: the patient operates under the illusion that a medicinal agent is at work battling the disease, whereas no such thing is going on at all. So, too, with the fiction of critically engaging social and cultural problems by means of form: one operates under the complacent illusion that something is being changed. Criticism, in my view, can neither exclude a certain class of construction from consideration nor apply those traditional "high art" standards to it; nor can it permit architecture to evade the political, social, economic, and ideological nexus from which it springs and in which it plays a role. Whatever problems, flaws, or weaknesses one might discern in nonarchitectural building—or "low art"—ignoring them, dismissing them out of hand, or failing to analyze the relationship between high and low art in effect means that one is not engaging in the act of criticism, but rather acting to preserve a particular status quo.

Beyond the large class of buildings excluded, there is an equally large class of questions that is not allowed. In fact, the institutional production of architecture itself must be called into question. What do I mean? One could ask a range of questions about the institution, for example: what does it reward, what does it penalize, whom does it include and exclude, what mechanisms are operative to exclude or discount certain questions, and so on.

We might ask, in addition, who profits from the exclusions? When architects dismiss as nonarchitecture the production of nonarchitects, or of pedestrian or mediocre architects, they enhance their professional status, in particular by claiming that their work is of higher worth because of its artistic qualities: ours is good; theirs is bad. I find it hard to identify an absolute good or an absolute bad here, only things that are good and bad in different ways for different groups.

One recent example concerns the enlargement of Rome's Olympic stadium to outfit it for the 1990 World Soccer Cup games. The addition of several rows of seats and a partial cover gave rise to heated polemics among architects, but only one (Franco Purini) challenged the decision to enlarge the stadium on the grounds of its urban impact: specifically the consequences on Rome's expansion, traffic congestion, pollution, and so forth.[6] The other participants in the debate almost exclusively argued about the aesthetic appeal of the additions. The persistent degradation of Rome's urban environment (see Ferruccio Trabalzi's essay) doesn't seem to elicit similarly heated indignation from Rome's architects. The profession's symbolic capital here as elsewhere is invested exclusively in formal appearances.

Excluding a certain class of questions and buildings also means not facing up to the whole range of problems they present. Andres Duany of Miami is fond of pointing out that more well-educated, Ivy League design talent is spent designing doorknobs for lofts in New York City than is spent on entire suburban housing and shopping center projects in the rest of America. This allows an architect a certain sense of complacency. In effect, it permits the architect to perceive his or her tasks as different from—and of course better than—those of the builder or contractor.

But is this a true perception? I find it difficult to make categorical distinctions between those who tart up the inside of a building and those who tart up the outside, between those who design for suburbanites who want revivalist styles and those who design for upper-class clients who want the latest "Po Mo" or "decon" fad. With skyscrapers, for example, program, site, size, and so forth, have already been set down before the architect ever appears. Profile, materials, formal resolution are guided—but not controlled—by the architect, since by and large even the structural and infrastructural systems are handled elsewhere. The critic assesses the project precisely where the architect is likely to have had some say: façade, materials, profile, occasional interior spaces. What has been excluded here is a whole range of questions regarding land use, profits, and financing—for example, taxpayers paying basic land development costs in order to provide "incentives" for developers to build. Since when did developers need incentives? How, in the most fundamental ways, can one distinguish the task of the 'art' architect from that of the builder here?

The most fundamental questions address *what is built for whom:* expenditures for museums, skyscrapers, concert halls, and other objects of bourgeois gratification come at the expense of important and necessary social services, not to mention adequate housing at modest prices. Architects quietly design for the very same public-private partnerships that are responsible for razing masses of low-income housing, especially single-room-occupancy hotels in urban downtowns. Such destruction, however, is not simply the casual by-product of urban development: it is the direct consequence of a whole series of related actions issuing from a particular set of economic and social arrangements. What has happened is that an ideological mask has been provided for developers, real estate interests, and government officials at all levels.

Let me put it another way: developers and real estate interests, in their wildest dreams, could not have come up with such an intellectually credible screen for their activities, an intellectually and academically respectable and viable means of diverting attention away from the toughest issues in land development and the building process toward trivial matters of surface. But not only that: the work of the big name 'art' architect not only masks but legitimates the project by virtue of the power of art, rendering any other questions pointless.

This book is directed in open polemic to the notion of architecture as critique, as well as to the kind of criticism that allows the belief in architecture as art to take precedence over other, more important issues. The essays here have been developed by the authors in order to engage the issue of a social criticism of architecture from several perspectives. Kenneth Frampton, Margaret Crawford, and Vincent Pecora address the predilection for conceiving of architecture as an autonomous entity with no necessary or important connection to any other issues related to building. Frampton sets out the problematic as it is defined in architecture, and Crawford analyzes the history of the profession's transformation over the last century. Pecora's study of the publication *Oppositions,* which claimed to be the avant-garde in architecture in the 1970s and early 1980s, serves as a bridge between the more theoretical essays and the case studies. In the latter group, the authors examine specific cities or buildings: Mike Davis on downtown Los Angeles, Diane Ghirardo on the Wexner and Getty centers, Ferruccio Trabalzi on the history of low-cost housing in Rome, Rosalyn Deutsche on homelessness and public space in New York, and Tony Schuman on a low-cost housing project in France. Analyses range from the most humble buildings to those with the highest architectural stature, from the perspective of the entire city to that of a single building. The intention is to undertake a broad-based critique that directly challenges the formalist assumptions currently dominating both teaching and practice, and to direct attention to the institutional practice of architecture and the larger community involved in the building process.

1. The comment is from Peter Eisenman, quoted in John Taylor, "Mr. In-Between," *New York Magazine,* 17 October 1988, p. 46.
2. "Postmodernism and Beyond: Architecture as the Critical Art of Contemporary Culture," symposium at the University of California, Irvine, 26–28 October 1989.

3. These ideas have recently been promulgated chiefly by deconstructionists such as Eisenman, Bernard Tschumi, and Daniel Libeskind.
4. Alberto Perez-Gomez, "Architecture as Embodied Knowledge," *Journal of Architectural Education* 40 (Spring 1987), p. 87.
5. Any number of essays in *The New Criterion* propose such a view, but see especially Hilton Kramer, "The Whitney's New Graves," *The New Criterion* (September 1985), pp. 2–3.

6. The exchanges occurred in May and June 1990 in *La Repubblica,* one of Rome's dailies, and included articles by Giuseppe Strappa, Enzo Pinci, Giorgio Muratore, Tommaso Longo, and Luca Zevi, among others. Purini's article "La città dello sport—occasione mancata," appeared 14 June 1990.

■ **Reflections on the Autonomy of Architecture:**

A Critique of Contemporary Production

Kenneth Frampton

Save for the axiom that nothing can be regarded as autonomous in an absolute sense, it is difficult to know how to initiate a discourse on the topic of architectural autonomy. Among the many aspects of the cultural enterprise, it may be claimed that architecture is, in fact, the least autonomous, compelling us to admit to the contingent nature of architecture as a practice.

It is one of the paradoxes of everyday life that although reality presses in on us from every side, we tend to overlook its effects, particularly when they do not happen to suit our ideological prejudices. Few architects care to remind themselves that only 20 percent of the total built output in developed societies is subject to the advice of the profession, so that the greater part of the man-made environment escapes our creative intervention. This disturbing fact means that we have to acknowledge the limited domain in which we are asked to operate, and in so doing we should recognize that there is a world of difference between architecture as a critical act and building as a banal, almost metabolic activity.

As is well known, the emergence of architecture as a self-conscious individual practice is inseparable from the rise of the burgher class in the last half of the fifteenth century. Our notion of architectural design as a specifically modern, innovative, nontraditional procedure cannot be traced back beyond this moment in history, when the first signs of divided labor and the dissolution of preliterate guild culture are discernible in the methods by which Brunelleschi erected the dome over Santa Maria del Fiore in Florence. We are indebted to Giulio Carlo Argan for his observation that this is precisely the moment when the so-called *artes liberales* gain their ascendancy over the *artes mechanicae* and when the rise of the individual architect/artist, as a protoprofessional, brings about a corresponding fall in the stature of the *maestri* or the master-craftsmen. This condition is reflected in the fact that although the generic cathedral and the everyday shed were markedly different undertakings within guild culture, there seems to have been a symbiotic continuity in the medieval worldview that served to unify the entire production of an agrarian-based civilization. This continuity is evident in the fact that the barn and the temple emerged from the same genre of craft production.

It is hardly an accident that the two schisms that concern us here should occur at the same time, that is to say that labor should become divided at precisely the moment in which it becomes possible to distinguish between architecture and building and when it becomes necessary to discriminate between the architect, on the one hand, and the master mason on the other. It is important to note that this schism is accompanied by the process of secularization. This seems to have been one of the preconditions, so to speak, for the emergence of empirical science and for the rise of the new technocratic-cum-mercantile class. The nineteenth-century Gothic revivalist A.W.N. Pugin was surely justified in his polemical view that the Renaissance represented exactly the point at which exclusively economic and productive values began to usurp the place of the spirit; the moment, that is, when *homo economicus* replaces *homo religioso.* Self-conscious and schizophrenic, the Renaissance barely believed in its own ideology. It is already historicist in its dependency on the spiritual authenticity of the antique world.

The hypothetical autonomy of any given practice is relatively delimited by the sociocultural context in which this practice unfolds. That this societal limitation is apparently greater in architecture than in any other art suggests that we should distinguish precisely between the province of architecture and the province of art. It is necessary to note that, unlike all other forms of so-called fine art, architecture mixes with that which the phenomenologist Edmund Husserl identified as the "life-world," and it is this irreducible condition that sets obvious limits on the autonomy of the field. That is to say, architecture is both a cultural discourse and a frame for life. One might say, to stretch the Marxist terminology, that it is both superstructure and infrastructure. This last means that architecture is appropriated by the society in a way that is categorically different from that of art. In its appreciation of art, society seeks to preserve the intrinsic, inalienable essence of the artwork in its mint condition. Moreover, after the medieval period, society covets the individual signature. (It is an interesting coincidence that the terms for business [*firm*] and signature [*firma*] come from the same root.) In architecture, on the other hand, society tends to transform the subjective originality of the work through the process of appropriation. Architecture in any event does not have the same iconic or fetishistic status as art, nor despite the emergence of the star architect, is it possible to give comparable artistic status to the "signature building."

The idea of appropriation returns us to the unfashionable doctrine of functionalism, although it is removed from the idea of a perfect ergonomic fit or any notion that there is a directly causal relationship between form and behavior or that a building will accommodate only one absolutely fixed pattern of use. The Dutch architect Herman Hertzberger does not intend such a fit. His idea of what is appropriate and open to appropriation is generic and institutional rather than reductively functional.

Aside from the disturbing schism that obtains in all postguild culture between the projection and the realization of built form, architectural practice has been slowly and surreptitiously undermined in the course of this century by the increasing privatization of society. Architecture has been hard-pressed to sustain its proper discourse in a society in which the public realm hardly exists and in which the continuity of the life-world as a repository of values becomes increasingly unstable. It is obviously difficult to sustain the legitimacy of architecture in a society that is constantly being overwhelmed by the innovations of technoscience, by demographic change, and by the ever-escalating cycles of production and consumption that constant modernization serve to sustain.

Lacking a collective *raison d'être*, architecture has turned first this way and then that in an effort to legitimate itself and to bring its practice into line with the dominant discourse, be it applied science as the reality principle or applied art as a psychosocial compensation. The first of these impulses no doubt partially accounts for the rise of ergonomic-cum-logarithmic design methods in the early 1960s and for the rather drastic attempts to convert architecture itself into a form of technoscientific practice. I am referring, of course, to the way in which leading British and American schools of architecture—the Bartlett School at London University, in the first instance, and the faculty of architecture at the University of California at Berkeley, in the second—changed their respective names in the sixties from schools of architecture to schools of environmental design, thereby implicitly abandoning the old bourgeois, elitist, hierarchical connotations of architecture and pretending instead to the wider scope of addressing the supposedly scientific design of the environment as a whole. It says much about the pendulum of ideological fashion and the intrinsic resistance of architecture as a craft that the Bartlett School has since reassumed its former denomination as a school of architecture.

Anxiety and envy have accompanied such pendulum swings as architects have attempted to justify their *modus operandi* by appearing to be scientists or, alternatively, by representing architecture as though it were fine art, writ large. One may speak, perhaps, of "science envy" in the first instance and of "art envy" in the second. We may regard the late Buckminster Fuller as a characteristic case of science envy, and any number of contemporary architects, from Frank Gehry to Peter Eisenman, seem only too happy to have their work classified as art. Indeed both of these legitimating ploys may be detected in Eisenman's career, in which there is a noticeable shift from the science envy of the early theory, with its dependency on structural linguistics, to the art envy of the later work, where the justifying critique has recourse to literature and philosophy. It should also be noted that there is a semiotic thread that unifies Eisenman's career, although this hardly changes the nature of his attempt to justify his idiosyncratic practice through extra-architectural references, be they scientific categories such as fractal geometry or the supposedly subversive aims of late avant-gardism. Either way, the possibility of architecture being an essentially tectonic or institutional discourse is largely denied.

One may claim that, unlike either science or art, architectural practice favors stasis rather than process and that it tends, however weakly, to resist the fungibility of the industrialized world. In this regard, latter-day appeals to science and art may be seen as subtle efforts to accommodate architecture to the dominant categories of a totally privatized and process-oriented world.

This state of affairs has produced strange convergences. For a latter-day radical like Daniel Libeskind, the institutions of the contemporary life-world are to be eschewed on the grounds that they are contaminated by a totally destitute political and ethical reality. A similar sentiment may be detected in the stance of Leon Krier, even if Krier's recent flirtations with practice seem to deny the total negativity of his earlier claim that "I do not build because I am an architect: I am an architect therefore I do not build." Today, while Libeskind projects neo-avant-gardist works as though they are nothing more than colossal pieces of sculpture, Krier invites us to return to a petrified neo-Biedermeier manner, as though only such a low-key, classical order still embodies the essence of a strictly architectural culture.

It is symptomatic of the times that both architects owe their ascendance in some way to the revival of drawn representation, for although drawing has always played a fundamental role in architectural practice, there is convergence today between the revival of drawing and the assertion of architecture as though it were a branch of fine art. The socioeconomic crisis attending architecture in the seventies was overcome in part by the proposition that quality architecture could still be pursued as drawn representations that would be readily appreciated and consumed by the art market. The salon mannerism that attended all this is very revealing. One is reminded, by the way of our example, of the Institute for Architecture and Urban Studies exhibition entitled *The Idea as Model,* for which Eisenman produced a three-dimensional, isomorphic, axonometric model of one of his houses in which the axonometric, like the skull in Holbein's painting *The Ambassadors,* could be perceived only from a particular viewpoint. These subtly interrelated gestures, stimulated by the pervasive rise of the media, evade, in my view, the issue of architectural autonomy in a more fundamental sense: that is to say, the question as to what belongs intrinsically to architecture and not to the other arts.

Clearly architecture cannot be reduced to architectural representation at any level, nor can it be passed off as large-scale sculpture. In attempting to advance a hypothetical model of architectural practice that lies beyond the idiosyncrasies of any specific style, one may say that the autonomy of architecture is determined by three interrelated vectors: typology (the institution), topography (the context), and tectonics (the mode of construction). It should be noted that neither the typological nor the tectonic are neutral choices in this regard and that what can be achieved with one format and expression can hardly be realized with another.

On balance, the formal *parti* is of greater import than the tectonic, for obviously the selection of the type as the basic spatial order has a decisive impact on the result, however much the constructional syntax may be elaborated in the course of development. The primacy of the type perhaps makes itself most evident in the basic difference between building and architecture: for where building tends to be organic, asymmetrical, and agglutinative, architecture tends to be orthogonal, symmetrical, and complete. These distinctions would not be so crucial were it not for the fact that building and architecture tend to favor the accommodation of different kinds of institutional form.

The organic architecture pursued in various ways by such architects as Frank Lloyd Wright, Richard Neutra, R. M. Schindler, Erich Mendelsohn, Eileen Gray, and Alvar Aalto affords us sufficient evidence as to the potential of what Neutra termed the *biorealist* culture of building. By a similar token, a modern architecture largely inspired by the classical can be found in the work of Ludwig Mies van der Rohe, Giuseppe Terragni, and Le Corbusier. It is obvious that our traditional institutions of power have been so frequently embodied in classical form that only with difficulty can classicism be brought to represent and embody more informal and hypothetically more democratic kinds of civic agencies. In this regard Aalto's town hall in Säynätsalo, Finland, may be seen as housing a seat of government in a particularly informal way, so that it presents and re-presents the institution in an intimate and accessible manner.

Architecture is fundamentally linked to institutional form in ways that are little understood today because contemporary society has become so privatized. From the micro to the macro scale, we have become poorly skilled as a society at discriminating between private, public, and semipublic space, and this lack of a common perception in hierarchical terms has had a brutalizing effect on contemporary architecture. The aestheticization of late modernism as a compensatory strategy becomes patently evident at this point, since irrespective of whether the stylistic affinities are neotraditionalist or neo-avant-gardist, the outcome tends to be the same, namely that architecture is increasingly reduced to a matter of superficial appearance: that is to say, it is valued solely as a convenient situation-setting rather than as a cultural value in itself. In other words, late modern building seems often to be totally divested of any articulated sociosymbolic substance, even if all the necessary functions are provided for. The fact that the civic institution has become a fragile entity in the late twentieth century is made all too clear at the level of architecture, particularly when the museum emerges as the last public building of our time. As surrogate temple or simulated *res publica,* the museum has become the compensatory realm of our totally secular, suburbanized spirit; the last depoliticized vestige, so to speak, of that which Hannah Arendt once called "the space of public appearance."

It is a sign of our times that aesthetic display has come to be used as a form of packaging to such an extent that architecture is often called upon to provide nothing more than a set of seductive images with which to "sell" both the building and its product. And while the aesthetic may well be regarded as the abstract, autonomous, self-referential quantum of late modern form, the vernacular returns us to the anthropological origins of building and to that moment in the mid-nineteenth century when the German architect Gottfried Semper formulated a new theoretical basis for architecture on the grounds of its anthropological origins. Through his transcultural worldview, Semper sought to construct a theoretical framework that would be capable of transcending the idealistic impasse of eclecticism.

Semper's quadripartite theory as contained in his essay *The Four Elements of Architecture* (1852) still constitutes a valid model with which to adumbrate the relative autonomy of architecture today. To the extent that Semper's four elements constitute a categoric break with the classically humanist Vitruvian triad of "firmness, commodity, and delight," his categories may be used as means for delineating the scope of contemporary practice. I am alluding, of course, to his reworking of the paradigm of the primitive hut, in the terms of an anthropological exhibit that he saw at the Great Exhibition of 1851. Semper was prescient in realizing that the generic hut comprised the following components: (1) an earthwork, (2) a hearth, (3) a framework and roof, and (4) a screen wall. He was particularly susceptible to the last component because of the etymological connotations of the word *wall* in German, wherein a light, basketlike wall, known by the term *die Wand* is to be distinguished from a heavy, masonry wall, indicated by the term *das Mauer.* Semper's four elements give rise to a whole discourse that may be said to express itself in terms of heavy versus light. Thus the framework, roof, and enclosing screen are light structural elements tending toward the immaterial, whereas the earthwork and hearth together encapsulate the rudimentary institutional nexus of the work.

In the Greek *megaron,* consisting of a single cellular space with a door at one end, the earthwork may be seen as raising itself up in the form of *heavy,* load-bearing masonry, wherein the *light* correspondingly withdraws, as it were, to form the beams spanning the walls, supporting a flat or low-pitched roof. The hearth is contained within the *cella* of the megaron. Meanwhile the outriding walls establish the place form of the dwelling; where this *temenos* contains a temple, the boundary serves to separate the cella from the profane world beyond the walls.

The interaction of nature with culture in architecture manifests itself first and foremost through the effects of gravity and light. The structure both resists and reveals the impact of gravity on its form, wherein light discloses, as it were, the intrinsic nature of the structure. Even more important, from an institutional point of view, light may assume a hierarchical significance, in which darkness is associated with the privacy of the megaron and light comes to be associated with the space of public appearance—the *agora.* Both temenos and agora depend primarily upon the topographical context, that is, on the "marking of the ground" that for Italian architect Vittorio Gregotti is the first world-creating act, coextensive, so to speak, with Semper's primordial knot as the first tectonic joint. The deepest roots of architectural autonomy lie here, one might say: not in the Vitruvian triad of classical lore but in the far deeper and more archaic triad of earthwork (topography), construction (tectonic), and hearth (type) as the embodiment of institutional form. These three aspects permit the structured articulation of the work as it passes from public to private and from sacred to profane, or of nature as it is mediated by light, gravity, and climate within the tectonic of the realized form.

Since around 1750, the species has been overwhelmed by the all too rapid transformation of basic material and ethical conditions and by the ever-escalating impact of technoscientific technique. These two interrelated processes have shaped the modern myth of progress. Since the turn of the century, the juggernaut of technology has been mediated if not mitigated in a number of ways. From the sculpture of Brancusi to the theater of Appia, from the philosophy of Heidegger to the architecture of Barragan, the archaic came to be reasserted as a foil to the idea of progress. This critical qualification does not depend however upon a categoric rejection of technology or on the acceptance of any particular expression. However, unlike futurism, the self-consciously archaic refuses to see advanced technology as transcendental in itself. Perhaps this complex double qualification has never been more succinctly expressed than by Aldo van Eyck when he wrote that that which antiquarians and technocrats have in common is a sentimental attitude toward time, the antiquarian being sentimental about the past, and the technocrat sentimental about the future. Van Eyck's insistence on the priority of the present does not entail some fictitious return to the past or presuppose a categoric repudiation of modern technique. It amounts instead to a critical view in which both modern and archaic technologies may be accepted and mixed together without being fetishized.

Such an attitude does not necessarily entail a reactionary cultural stance, for it seeks an appropriate elaboration of present conditions in a way that is capable of sustaining the life-world in all its richness, without wishing to preempt the significance of this world through the maximization of either technology or aesthetics. Such an attitude challenges all our received ideas of creativity to such an extent that we will be compelled to acknowledge that much that passes for originality in our time comes into being not so much out of poetic exuberance as out of competitiveness.

Behind our preoccupation with the autonomy of architecture lies an anxiety that derives in large measure from the fact that nothing could be less autonomous than architecture, particularly today when because of the domination of the media we find it increasingly difficult to arrive at what we want. Under such skeptical circumstances, architects often feel constrained to perform acrobatic feats in order to assure attention. In so doing, they tend to follow a succession of stylistic tropes that leave no image unconsumed, so that the entire field becomes flooded with an endless proliferation of images. This is a situation in which buildings tend to be increasingly designed for their photogenic effect rather than their experiential potential. Plastic stimuli abound in a frenzy of iteration that echoes the information explosion. We drift toward that entropic state that Lewis Mumford once described as a new form of barbarism. In the meantime, the ideology of modernity and progress disintegrates before our eyes and the imminent ecological disaster of late industrial production is manifest everywhere. There is no logical imperative, however, that these conditions demand an artistically fragmented, over-aestheticized expression in the field of architecture. On the contrary, one may argue that such a level of disjunction needs, even demands, an architecture of tranquility, an architecture that lies beyond the agitations of the present moment, an architecture that returns us, through the experience of the subject, to that brief illusive moment touched on by Baudelaire, to that instant evoked by the words *luxe, calme, et volupté.*

██ Can Architects Be Socially Responsible?

Margaret Crawford

As individuals, most American architects sincerely assert that they are deeply concerned about issues of social and economic justice. Yet, over the past twenty years, as a profession they have steadily moved away from engagement with any social issues, even those that fall within their realm of professional competence, such as homelessness, the growing crisis in affordable and appropriate housing, the loss of environmental quality, and the challenge posed by traffic-choked, increasingly unmanageable urban areas. What accounts for this enormous gap between individual concern and professional indifference? The answer to this question can be found in the nature of the profession itself. Modern professions, rather than simply existing as the sum of the professional interests of their individual members, instead are complex social constructs that structure their autonomous identities in relation to the specific configuration of the economy and society in which they operate. Successful professional identities depend as much upon devising convincing ideological representations of professional practices as on the actual practices themselves.

The architectural profession's attempts to operate within both economic and social constraints and to fashion a successful identity have been complicated by a series of contradictions unique to the profession. Even a superficial examination of American architecture's professional structure over the past one hundred years reveals a history littered with an accumulation of unresolved contradictions, as virtually every observer of the field has noted.[1] This suggests that the current gap between individual concern and professional inertia represents a contemporary reformulation of a persistent barrier between the needs of professional identity and the demands of social responsibility. Recognizing this, the current impasse needs to be addressed as much as a historical legacy as a contemporary dilemma. Only by untangling this web of contradictions can the profession start to address and formulate a professional identity compatible with the social and economic needs of American life.

◼ The Professional Problem and the Ideological Solution

During the late nineteenth century, American architects fresh from European educations undertook to restructure the ancient activity of building into a modern profession able to meet the social and economic requirements of an advanced capitalist economy and a liberal state. The efforts of architects were part of a much larger American movement toward professionalization, in which an educated middle class increasingly established a "monopoly of competence" by claiming exclusive rights to previously unregulated activities. This professional project depended on two separate but closely linked goals: first, the definition and control of a protected market for professional services, and second, the assurance that membership in the profession would provide both social status and visible economic advantages.[2]

Architecture followed medicine, law, and engineering in pursuing these goals through institutional structures. The American Institute of Architects (AIA), founded in 1857, provided the organizational basis for professionalization efforts. Significantly, it was initially constituted as a gentlemen's club, where shared cultural conventions rather than techniques served as the initial means of separating "architects" from others in the building field. The diploma and the license created exclusionary competencies requiring formal education and a credentialing process. Professional schools, such as the ones at the Massachusetts Institute of Technology (1868) and Cornell University (1871), defined and standardized knowledge. A legal definition validated by the state was provided through a licensing requirement based on a professional examination, instituted first in Illinois in 1897 and subsequently in other states. Licensure, however, did not allow architects to control all building: their domain was limited to large buildings such as churches, apartment houses, and public structures.[3]

By the beginning of the twentieth century, architecture existed as a profession, a credentialed elite legitimized through conventional procedures established by other professions. In spite of these institutional achievements, architecture, unlike other professions, failed to satisfy many of the underlying social assumptions necessary for successful professionalization. Exclusive control of professional territory depends on achieving social distance from other groups who provide similar services, a process that involves two crucial legitimization strategies: first, competency and superiority based on technology, rationality, and efficiency, and second, an ethical claim of detachment from any particular class or business interest. In both these areas, the American architectural profession's claims have historically been much weaker than those of other professions.[4]

Unlike engineering and medicine, which draw authority from science, or law, which receives it from the state, the architect's professional authority rested on an inherently contradictory base: combining the inherited identity of architecture as artistic creativity (reinforced by the powerful influence of the French Beaux-Arts system) with a more recent ideal of technical rationality. The already uneasy balance between these two components was complicated by the professional imperative for distance from competing groups. Architecture's claims to the technical monopoly of building activity were already circumscribed: on one side by the technical superiority of engineering and on the other by the empirically established efficiency of the building industry.

The profession responded to these competing claims by creating even more contradictory identities. The introduction of the division of labor and specialization into office practice (particularly the inclusion of engineers into architectural firms, as in the famous partnership of Adler and Sullivan) rationalized design and production, promoting greater efficiency while undermining the synthetic integration allowed by more purely artistic methods. On the other hand, the profession's artistic pretenses allowed architects to easily disengage themselves from the spheres of technique and building construction, thus effectively separating them from the material bases on which their professional activities rested.

Because it could not claim possession of its own technical competencies, the profession's claims increasingly invoked superior aesthetics rather than superior building. At the same time, however, its aesthetic claims were not fully liberated. Unlike artists, who have never been formalized into a profession, but rather produce for a specialized market that generates a huge "reserve army" of unsuccessful practitioners, architects do not operate freely, but require clients. The contrast was not lost on nineteenth-century architects: Mariana Van Rensselaer observed in 1890, "Fancy a painter unable to make pictures except when someone says to him: Paint now, paint this or that, and paint it thus and so. . . . Imagine this, and you will realize the architect's actual position and the contrast between his life and that of other artists. The difference is the natural result of the fact that architecture is not an art pure and simple. Its products . . . cannot be spun out of the artist's brain, but must cost a great deal of money."[5] Architecture's expensiveness inevitably binds it to the sources of finance and power, making it very difficult to achieve the autonomy from bourgeois standards that art had fought for since its emancipation from aristocratic patronage.[6]

Even so, the need for patronage constituted only a partial barrier between architecture and the large heterogeneous mass clientele other professions, such as medicine and law, had developed. Because licensing had legally established a monopoly over only certain types of building, unlicensed contractors and speculative builders continued to dominate residential and commercial construction. The professional necessity to define themselves as an elite caste of builders required licensed architects to remain aloof from these activities, and by and large, the leaders of the profession scorned the vast potential market for middle-class houses. By distancing themselves from contractors and builders with economic control of the field, they also effectively repudiated the interests of moderate-income clients. Instead, the profession linked its professional identity to large-scale monumental commissions requiring wealthy patrons.[7] This left architects dependent on the restricted group of clients who could afford to support their ambitions: the hoped for, but only occasionally awarded, patronage of the state (far less active than in Europe), but more often, the backing of large business and corporate interests.

Thus architecture's apparent professional success actually rested on provisional and contradictory grounds. Of the dual aims of the professional project, architecture achieved only the second—status and economic advantages; in the absence of the more significant goal of control over the professional market, even this achievement remained tentative. Their inability to control their own professional marketplace left architects at the mercy of the larger market economy. As a result, architecture, a luxury rather than an indispensable service, remained within a premodern model of elite patronage, its provision of services primarily dictated by economic power. Moreover, the profession's single advantage—status and economic power—could be maintained only by keeping a social distance from surrounding groups. This entailed the loss of considerable technical and economic control over building activity, further restricting the architect's ability to engage issues in the larger social arena autonomously. Paradoxically, the architect's status depended equally on pursuing an ethics of disinterest, establishing an equivalent social distance from the capitalist market and its profit motives.[8]

Architecture's tradition as a liberal art, though weakening its strength in the modern professional marketplace, provided it with intellectual weapons that could offset this weakness and address these contradictions in the ideological arena. An already established theoretical discourse, inherited from Vitruvian times and considerably enriched by recent contributions from the École des Beaux-Arts, could be strengthened by new constructs to address its current dilemmas; its dissemination through new institutions such as universities and professional journals and through adjunct professions such as architectural history and criticism was integrated into the professional project. Ideological claims served multiple roles: they buttressed the status of the profession as well as acted as a substitute for economic control over the built environment, thereby allowing the profession to claim in the intellectual realm what it could not accomplish in the material world.

Faced with these conditions, architecture has managed to survive as a profession by constructing a series of identities tenuously balanced between actual practices and ideological representations. At several critical historical junctures, the profession has been forced to restructure itself to sustain its professional autonomy and legitimacy. Architects, to avoid the ever-present danger of incorporation into the dominant economic and political structure, created powerful myths that directly addressed the inherent dilemmas of professionalization; they structured these myths around the two main actors in the professional project, the architect and the client.

■   Act 1: May 1, 1893.

Daniel Burnham Opens the World's Columbian Exhibition

The World's Columbian Exhibition constituted the profession's first great public achievement. The "White City" itself, a temporary plaster representation of
an ideal architectural realm, functioned more as an ideological statement
than as a potential urban reality. The fair's enormous success transformed its
organizer, Daniel Burnham, from an architect who served Chicago's commercial and real estate interests into a charismatic hero, "a resourceful and in-
domitable planner, the real Titan, the Emperor of architecture," according to
one of his contemporaries. Burnham's commanding slogan, "Make no little
plans, for they have no magic to stir man's blood," claims power that largely
exists in the ideological realm. Although Burnham's major public successes,
such as the replanning of Washington, D.C., were accomplished through political rather than architectural means, their ambition and scale heightened the
image of the architect's absolute control. This belied the actual fragmentation of the profession into a hierarchy of specialized roles, a development
most evident in the nearly corporate organization of Burnham's own office.[9]

   Perhaps more significant, the fair provided an opportunity for the profession to identify two clearly separate clients, one the actual purchaser of
architectural services, the other, the "ideal" client, an ideological construct
that allowed the profession to focus on the group the profession hoped to
serve and that established the claims of ethical disinterest required for professional legitimization. Although the fair was actually sponsored by Chicago's
corporate elite, its ideal client was the larger public as user of urban space.
The aesthetic unity of the fair defined a public realm that countered the
chaos, greed, and squalor evident in laissez-faire American cities. The device
of the ideal client permitted the profession, although still financially dependent on elite patronage, to acquire legitimacy through ideological means that
were denied them by the economic necessities of patronage. This allowed a
professional critique of the narrowly economic aims of their real clients, commercial investors seeking speculative profits in the city. At the same time,
the exclusively ideological and aesthetic nature of this critique made it vul-

nerable to a higher level of co-option, and the fair's ideals were soon employed in "imperial" city planning and, through piecemeal application, the
realization of even larger speculative profits through urban development.[10]

Act 2: January 11, 1937.
Walter Gropius Arrives at the Graduate School of Design at Harvard

The modern movement appeared in the United States almost forty years after
the World's Columbian Exhibition, bringing with it a powerful new set of answers to architecture's persistent professional dilemmas. Forged in the heady
climate of the Weimar Republic, the Bauhaus, under Walter Gropius's direction, had negotiated a somewhat halting path through the plethora of modern-
isms to arrive at a new definition of the tasks of the architect. Although this
role had to be radically readjusted to fit into the framework of the American
profession, even in its truncated version, it offered a new scope and vision for
professional ambitions. From his beginnings under the thrall of the Werkbund
slogan "from the cushion to the city" to his later book, *The Scope of Total
Architecture,* Gropius consistently affirmed modernism's tasks as the restructuring of the entire environment according to an unvarying set of principles.
Although the conditions of American practice rapidly dismantled Gropius's
vision of a collaborative method in which minimalist forms derived from technical analysis and functional criteria would be successfully applied to a broad
range of social needs, it succeeded as an ideology. Modernism, a minority
position in the profession at the beginning of Gropius's tenure at Harvard had
become dominant by the time he left in 1952.

The rapid acceptance of modern movement architecture in the United
States owed much to its self-presentation as the application of scientific
rationalism to the field of building. By the mid-thirties, actual achievements in
large-scale housing construction then taking place in Germany and Holland
as much as rhetorical slogans such as Le Corbusier's "machine à habiter"
lent credence to these claims. Modernism's visual imagery of functionalism
and objectivity appeared even more convincing in comparison to the pallid
aesthetics of the waning American Beaux-Arts movement. Ironically, how-

ever, the real achievements of the *siedlungen* were jettisoned in their passage across the Atlantic in favor of Hitchcock and Johnson's exclusively aesthetic definition of the international style. Thus, curiously, modernism's acceptance on an artistic level effectively undermined the technical claims it needed to legitimize itself on a professional level.[11]

In spite of their claims to the *Zeitgeist* and the mastery of the new needs and building types generated by modern life, modernists were no more successful than their academic predecessors in competing with adjacent professional competencies. The biggest failure was with engineering, architecture's main rival for control of the realm of industrial production, whose systems, materials, and image lay at the heart of modernism's self-definition. Already effectively incorporated into an industrial structure dedicated to expanding productivity, American engineers barely noticed the architect's pretensions.[12] That doomed architectural attempts to engage with industrialized building production, such as Gropius and Wachsmann's experiments with manufactured housing and the magazine *Arts and Architecture*'s Case Study House projects, to an inevitable failure.[13] Instead, the profession satisfied its industrial dreams with brilliant symbolic gestures—such as Mies van der Rohe's skyscrapers, which celebrated the steel frame without altering either its structural or building technology—while actually delegating many technical areas of design and construction to engineering expertise.

Modernism's ideal of industrial production helped to perpetuate the profession's already profound separation from the construction industry and the building trades. Although architects often accepted conventional construction for economic reasons, this went counter to the ideology of modernism, which scorned the vernacular practices of the building industry because of an infatuation first with industrial and then with naturalistic materials, both of which required expensive and skilled craft techniques. While architects kept the professional distance necessary to maintain their separate status, large-scale builders organized housing construction into a virtually mass-produced system, along the way providing vast amounts of conventional housing at cut-rate prices.

Failure to reestablish connections with the technical and economic bases of building also undermined modernism's social ideals, closely linked to its technical abilities. Modernism brought with it a very specific ideal client, the masses, a nonpejorative social category that included both workers and the less affluent ranks of the educated middle class. European experiences with large-scale housing and institutional projects sponsored by the state suggested that by adopting the state as patron—serving as mediator for the masses—the profession could resolve the conflict between real and ideal client. During the 1930s, the New Deal's support of public building and housing, although often clothed in traditional styles, initially appeared to offer a similar resolution. The Housing Act of 1949, promoted by the construction industry and lending institutions, eliminated this possibility by establishing a new ideal: owner-occupied single-family houses available to the masses. Since architects had already ceded the mass market in housing to speculative builders, this effectively severed their connection to large numbers of ideal clients. Although architects continued to pursue government housing commissions, the needs of their real clients dominated architectural production: their clientele was split between large-scale corporations, which needed office towers, and members of the upper middle class, who wanted distinctive homes.

That division reflected a growing stratification in the profession between large offices that dealt with corporate clients and small offices that provided single houses. Office organization inevitably reflected those clients: Skidmore, Owings and Merrill became the model of a corporate firm, a huge national organization with identical regional offices vertically integrated to offer complete design services. The complex hierarchy of the firm's structure was necessary to ensure maximum efficiency and productivity from more than a thousand employees. Even within this type of firm, a tendency toward greater specialization generated new professional categories that increasingly challenged the architectural domain: industrial designers, interior decorators, landscape architects, and urban and transportation planners. At the other end of the spectrum, small offices concentrating on domestic commissions proliferated. If large offices controlled the profession economically, small offices dominated numerically.[14]

Alternative ideologies of practice, even assuming modernism's assertions of total architectural control, were not adequate to counter this reality. In 1945, Walter Gropius attempted to restructure professional practice into a more socially useful form by establishing a new firm, The Architects' Collaborative (TAC), founded on a cooperative model emphasizing teamwork with allied disciplines such as sociology, economics, and art. These idealistic goals floundered from the beginning, and as the office became successful, it inevitably fell back on a corporate model of specialization.[15] However, a more powerful compensatory myth had emerged with the publication of *The Fountainhead* in 1943. The novel's hero, Howard Roark, established a new definition of raw architectural ego: armed only with talent and integrity, Roark triumphs over a corrupt profession, venal clients, and hostile critics. This image of uncompromising individualism, loosely based on the career of Frank Lloyd Wright, firmly lodged itself in the subconscious of the profession, for it appealed far more to American sensibilities than did Gropius's self-effacing position.[16]

As Gropius's career drew to a close, the disparities between his actual practices and their ideological representations encapsulated the contradictions of the American profession. By the mid-fifties TAC produced the massive Pan-Am building, which set a new record for rentable square feet in a single building, demonstrating Gropius's nearly complete capitulation to the demands of economic and political power. Even when they did not lower construction costs, modernism's reductive forms appropriately mirrored the homogenizing tendencies of multinational business and the bureaucratic state. In the real world of practice, success was achieved only at the cost of a profound architectural and philosophical retreat from Gropius's previous ideals. At the same time, Gropius's greatest professional achievement was to establish architecture as an academic discipline with sound theoretical and pedagogical premises. This gave architecture a new level of status and prestige and allowed the university to become the primary base for addressing the persistent technical and ethical problems of the profession.

■ Act 3: July 15, 1972.
The Dynamiting of Pruitt-Igoe Housing, St. Louis

The successful appropriation of modernism's forms by the dominant political and economic order made the gap between theory and practice too large to contain within the existing modernist ideology. The destruction of Pruitt-Igoe's high-rise housing blocks symbolically culminated more than a decade of attacks on the premises of modernism, which initiated the beginnings of the first new theoretical discourse since the thirties. Every aspect of modernism's theory and practice was subjected to criticism, effectively undermining the continued relevance of not only modernism but the American profession itself. In terms of professional significance, three critiques were particularly meaningful, and each implied a solution, even if it was only applicable to the questions addressed by that critique. Throughout the 1970s, the critiques provided a series of provisional reformulations of professional roles, new definitions of both architect and client that could undergo testing in practice.

The Technological Critique

The proto-postmodern critique of modern architecture began with Reyner Banham's definitive refutation of modernism's functional and technological aspirations. In his influential study, *Theory and Design in the First Machine Age,* Banham argued that early modernism's engagement with technical and industrial issues was confined to the realm of the symbolic and aesthetic. Although Banham exhaustively examined both buildings and texts, his most powerful evidence against architecture's failures was the counterexample of Buckminster Fuller. Banham cited the Dymaxion house and car of the thirties to demonstrate that genuinely technological solutions to the problem of modern living had to be grounded in the realities of engineering principles and industrial production.

Banham and a whole generation of alternative architects, from Archigram to contributors to the *Whole Earth Catalog,* failed to understand that Fuller's technocratic approach asserted a largely mythical ideal. Fuller's claims that social and ecological problems could be solved through the rational application of technology ignored the realities of existing economic and political structures. Exposure to the realities of the corporate economy, the building industry, mass production, and democratic consensus rapidly clarified the fundamentally idealistic and illusory nature of this alternative model. Fuller's disciples and other advocates of unrealizable technological solutions retreated to architecture schools, which, protected from the realities of professional practice, functioned as experimental venues for ideas that could not survive in the architectural marketplace. There, in spite of their alienation from the profession, the technological utopians' activities legitimized essential facets of the professional identity—an avowed seriousness in addressing global concerns and continuing pursuit of technical and scientific goals.

The Social Critique

Another line of attack focused on the failure of modernist solutions to resolve social problems. Here the gap between theory and practice separated European theories formulated in the 1920s and 1930s from the practical experiences of postwar America. Radical architects and planners used a populist notion of democracy to attack the generalized application of modernism's universal forms to social needs such as housing and community development. Its uniform geometries, rather than offering an egalitarian order, were seen as imposing an alienating social regimentation. This posited a modernist architect who was not only an elitist by birth and training but also an oppressor who forced an unwelcome vision of modern life on unwilling users. Similarly, the postwar welfare state that implemented these visions was no longer perceived as a benign mediator operating on behalf of the masses, but as an authoritarian and dehumanized bureaucracy. In many cases, reality justified these accusations: for example, rather than addressing housing needs, 1960s federal housing programs simply provided holding cells for a permanent underclass. Worse yet for modern architecture, given a choice, the tenants usually rejected modern architecture, as in the drastic remodelings at the Pessac housing estate designed by Le Corbusier.[17]

In order to serve the cultural and social needs of society, radical architects proposed solutions ranging from participatory design to advocacy and self-help architecture. All of these strategies required a profound transformation of the nature of the professional structure, inverting the traditional relationship between architect and client to allow previously excluded users a democratic voice in the design process. Similarly, in slums or squatter settlements, architectural norms were reevaluated, allowing social needs to take precedence over formal order. In this way design was envisioned as part of a larger and liberating social project. The apparently total social and professional transformations radical architects called for, however, actually constituted an incomplete negation, which simply reversed the already fictional roles of the all-powerful architect and the ideal client, the masses, while accepting the ideological assumptions on which they rested.[18]

Put into practice in the real world of architecture, these principles ran into trouble. The radical architect's sacrifice of professional power to democratic principles failed to empower the masses. In the face of the economic and political forces that construct the built environment—the architect's control was primarily ideological, and the client was merely "ideal," not an actual purchaser of architectural services—both were relatively powerless to effect social changes. In response, radical architecture increasingly focused on mere opposition to the dominant aesthetics of modernism. This led them to identify the masses' needs primarily in terms of "taste cultures," defending the user's preference for colonial styles or bright patterns as meaningful social opposition.[19] Even these limited claims to architectural decision-making were illusory, since without the mediation of the state, users did not command the power or money to affect architectural products. Thus, unwittingly, radical architects replaced modernism's welfare state with a marketplace, in which, unfortunately, their ideal client did not have the means to purchase architectural services.[20] Defeated in their efforts to restructure professional roles, the radicals also retreated to the universities, where like love beads and student demonstrations, they served as reminders of the unfulfillable social hopes of the sixties. Like the technological utopians' position, radical architecture's critical stance against the profession paradoxically reinforced the profession's claims of ethical disinterest and social concern.

The Formalist Critique

Robert Venturi's attack on modernism, unlike the failures of the technological and the populist critiques, profoundly affected both architectural theory and professional practice. Venturi acknowledged and incorporated both previous critiques with one significant alteration: he stripped them of their ideological underpinnings, defining the architect's professional role according to its actual material power and practices. He designated "platitudinous architects who invoke integrity or technology as ends in architecture, the popularizers who paint 'fairy stories over our chaotic reality'" as specific targets. Venturi's unflinching realism led him to eliminate any possible technical and social aspirations in architecture since they appeared to be practically unrealizable under existing conditions. Acknowledging the powerlessness of architects to change the world, Venturi suggested in his preface to *Complexity and Contradiction in Architecture* that architects instead narrow their concerns and concentrate on their own job. Accepting architecture's inherent limitations, he claimed, might ironically reverse "the architect's ever diminishing power and his growing ineffectualness in shaping the whole environment."[21]

As defined by Venturi, the architect's "own job" was an essentially formalist task, based on an enlargement of modernism's circumscribed formal vocabulary to include both historical elements and, as proposed in *Learning from Las Vegas,* lessons from the commercial landscape. The "decorated shed," Venturi's conceptual answer to the modernist "duck," was essentially an architectural billboard on buildings already structured by the market's lowest common denominator—economy. Venturi continues to practice what he preached: although his successful firm operates at the higher level of institutional commissions, its participation in architectural projects is typically limited to exterior design. Collaboration with specialized, technically oriented firms confines Venturi's role to the surface decoration of complexly programmed buildings, as in the Lewis Thomas Laboratories at Princeton, where the architectural credits are listed as Robert Venturi, architect for the exterior of the building, and Thomas Payette, architect for the interior.[22] Venturi's successful attacks on modernism, by eliminating the profession's ideological protections of technical and ethical claims, resulted in the further separation of building from architecture and, by emphasizing the marketplace of taste, allowed the dominant economic tendencies to become the final arbiter of architectural form.

■ Epilogue: June 20, 1986.
Michael Graves Begins Designing for Disney World

Venturi's work was influential in restructuring the postmodern profession. Effectively abandoning its claims to technical rationality and rejecting the social ethics of disinterest, the profession largely staked its claim to status on aesthetics. This was an almost inevitable choice since, of the Vitruvian triad of firmness, commodity, and delight, only delight was not claimed by professional rivals.[23] If the original formulations of postmodernist aesthetics made much of the socially progressive nature of its expanded vocabulary of imagery, these sources were quickly forgotten once the rewards of corporate patronage became clear. Rather than drawing on popular and vernacular sources considered congruent with the cultural codes of the masses, imagery became more explicitly elitist. Classicism, an ideology of form invoking historical precedents, provided the prestige necessary for the profession's continuing distance from more pragmatically oriented professional groups. If the architect's economic privileges derived from the same patronage as before, status came from a new source—the past.

What remained was the marketplace, the actualities of the building industry, and the limits set by the client paying the bills. The expanding economy and culture of consumption incorporated postmodernism's emphasis on surface and readable imagery as a useful form of packaging essentially identical structures into more compelling products, subsuming architectural style into a brand-name marketing strategy. Recognizable personal styles and signature forms, such as those of Michael Graves, in effect constitute designer labels, which raise the price of the product and the prestige of the consumer, a logic used by developers such as Gerald Hines, who spends considerable amounts developing skyscrapers with architecturally self-conscious forms. Postmodernism's adaptability to the marketplace allowed its rapid and nearly total assimilation for commercial purposes, an architectural trickle-down effect that has made postmodernism the style of choice for the cheapest and most expedient building types: motels, shopping malls, and fast food restaurants.[24]

If postmodern style functions as packaging, the buildings it clothes have become increasingly large and complex, requiring sophisticated solutions to programming and structural requirements and demanding many separate environmental control systems. These needs have generated even more rival competencies impinging on the architectural domain: as many as twenty-five consultants may be required on a single building. Building practices have also changed to meet these needs, with construction firms becoming larger and more concentrated and often acting as developers. New supervisory positions, such as construction managers, now rival the architect's claims to manage the construction process. Clients are also playing an increasingly significant role in the building process. Large organizations construct buildings as important capital assets, which need to produce income and profit as well as provide an efficient working environment, leading them to make much more specific demands on architects. A new professional specialization, facilities manager, acts for the client in establishing the program, overseeing construction, and supervising the completed building. All of these changes have reduced the profession's connection with building even further, as Robert Gutman warns, turning the architect into a design subcontractor, whose decisions are limited to aesthetic arbitration.[25]

The narrowing of architectural practice has been balanced by an expanding architectural avant-garde, who, opposing the corruption of architecture by business, take on roles closer to that of the artist. Avoiding the inevitable "contamination" of the professional world of building, these architects survive through teaching, publication, competitions, and the growing niche in the art market for architectural drawings and models. The gap created by the absence of building has been filled by complex theoretical constructs that render architecture untouchable by the demands of modern life. A range of postmodern stances, heavily informed by poststructuralist thinkers such as Michel Foucault and Jacques Derrida, have emerged: Peter Eisenman's moderate position extends the formalist claims of late modernist art to create an autonomous architecture, which need only relate to the internal conditions posited by its maker. In the more extreme case of Daniel Libeskind, architecture is completely disengaged from any analogy with building in favor of metaphysical operations undertaken through drawing and object-making.[26] In both cases, in spite of their claims to decentered subjectivity, the result is the same: the role of the ideal client has now been subsumed by the architects themselves, a stance not that different from that of Howard Roark.[27]

Given this situation, the answer to the question "can architects be socially responsible?" is, as the profession is presently constituted, no. Both the restricted practices and discourse of the profession have reduced the scope of architecture to two equally unpromising polarities: compromised practice or esoteric philosophies of inaction. After nearly a hundred years of professional existence, architects have almost completely surrendered both the tools and the ideological aspirations that might allow them to address the economic, political, and social concerns posed by modern life. Clearly, given both the inherent contradictions of the profession and the historical legacies of its struggle to maintain professional autonomy and status, altering this situation will be difficult. At the same time, a growing demand from individual practitioners and students to reconnect architecture to social and economic questions demands a thorough reformulation of both theory and practice in order to avoid repeating the well-intentioned but mistaken strategies used by modernist reformers and sixties radicals.[28]

First of all, the architectural profession must establish new connections with the existing technical and economic practices of building, since aesthetics alone cannot solve the difficult problems of current housing and urban conditions. These connections should be based on an analysis of existing material conditions rather than on idealistic projections of future technical capabilities. Focusing on social concerns can establish a professional base from which architects can claim more control over building and challenge professional rivals who occupy even narrower areas of competence.[29] In spite of its reduced ideological claims, the architectural profession is expanding: the growing demand for its services is demonstrated by both an overall growth in profits and an increase in the architect's share of the construction dollar. The AIA's sanctioning of forms of practice such as design/build and design/development opens up new possibilities for expanding the limits of the profession.[30] Both developments suggest that considerable room to maneuver still exists within the profession if architects can lift themselves from their lethargy and seize the possibilities that now are opening up for them.

In order to maneuver successfully, the profession needs to give some serious thought to renewing and refashioning its ideological premises. Unlike "realist" readings that reify the status quo, deconstructed poetics that justify disengagement, or idealist mystifications of real practices, ideology can also serve as a positive fiction, telling a story about a larger vision of professional aspirations.[31] By creating compelling stories about social needs, the architectural profession can envision a new set of ideal clients, not the generic masses of modernism, but specific groups whose needs are not being served by the architectural marketplace. There is no shortage of possible subjects: the homeless; individuals and families excluded from the real estate market; communities threatened by decay or development; elderly, poor, and minority groups with inadequate housing. Identifying these ideal clients is an important first step toward creating a discourse adequate to the enormous tasks faced by the architectural profession if it accepts the challenge of reshaping society and the built environment.

1. A growing literature on the American architectural profession includes the following: Bernard Boyle, "Architectural Practice in America, 1865–1965—Ideal and Reality," in *The Architect*, ed. Spiro Kostof (New York: Oxford Univ. Press, 1977), pp. 309–44; Andrew Saint, *The Image of the Architect* (New Haven: Yale Univ. Press, 1983); Magali Sarfatti Larson, "Emblem and Exception: The Historical Definition of the Architect's Professional Role," in *Professionals and Urban Form*, ed. Judith Blau, Mark La Gory, and John Pipkin (Albany: State Univ. of New York Press, 1983); Robert Gutman, *Architectural Practice: A Critical View* (Princeton, N.J.: Princeton Architectural Press, 1988).

2. Larson, "Emblem and Exception," pp. 60–61. An enormous literature addresses the emergence of American professionalism, both conceptually and historically. For general discussions, see the following: Magali Sarfatti Larson, *The Rise of Professionalism* (Berkeley: Univ. of California Press, 1977); T. J. Johnson, *Professions and Power* (London: Macmillan, 1972); descriptions of American professions can be found in Burton Bledstein, *The Culture of Professionalism* (New York: Norton, 1976); Daniel Calhoun, *Professional Lives in America: Structure and Aspirations* (Cambridge, Mass.: MIT Press, 1965); Samuel Haber, *Efficiency and Uplift* (Chicago: University of Chicago Press, 1964); Robert Wiebe, *The Search for Order* (New York: Hill and Wang, 1967).

3. Gwendolyn Wright, *Moralism and the Model Home* (Chicago: Univ. of Chicago Press, 1980).

4. Sibel Bozdogan, "The Rise of the Architectural Profession in Chicago, 1871–1909" (paper delivered at the Society of Architectural Historians Annual Meeting, Chicago, April 1989).

5. Quoted in Larson, "Emblem and Exception," p. 49.

6. Alan Colquhoun, "Postmodernism and Structuralism: A Retrospective Glance," in *Modernity and the Classical Tradition* (Cambridge, Mass.: MIT Press, 1989), pp. 244, 245.

7. Wright, *Moralism and the Model Home*, pp. 53–4.

8. Larson, *The Rise of Professionalism*, pp. xii, xiii.

9. Thomas Hines, *Burnham of Chicago* (Chicago: Univ. of Chicago Press, 1974), pp. 268–71.

10. Mario Manieri-Elia, "Toward an Imperial City," in *The American City from the Civil War to the New Deal*, ed. Giorgio Cuicci, et al. (Cambridge, Mass.: MIT Press, 1979), pp. 76–104.

11. Reyner Banham, "Actual Monuments," *Art in America* (October 1988), p. 175.

12. Edwin Layton, *The Revolt of the Engineers* (Cleveland: Press of Case Western Reserve Univ., 1971).

13. See Gilbert Herbert, *The Dream of the Manufactured House* (Cambridge, Mass.: MIT Press, 1984) and Elizabeth Smith, ed., *Blueprints for Modern Living* (Cambridge, Mass.: MIT Press, 1989).

14. Boyle, "Architectural Practice in America," p. 318.

15. Ibid., pp. 335–38.

16. See Andrew Saint's discussion of *The Fountainhead* in *The Image of the Architect*, pp. 1–18.

17. Philippe Boudon, *Lived-in Architecture* (Cambridge, Mass.: MIT Press, 1972).

18. See Marco Cenzatti, "Marxism and Planning Theory," in John Friedmann, *Planning in the Public Domain* (Princeton, N.J.: Princeton Univ. Press, 1987), p. 440.

19. This concept, developed by Herbert Gans in *Popular Culture and High Culture* (New York: Basic Books, 1974), was adopted by Robert Venturi for use in *Learning from Las Vegas* (Cambridge, Mass.: MIT Press, 1972).

20. A more thorough discussion of the failures of "populist" architecture can be found in Laine Lefaivre and Alexander Tzonis, "In the Name of the People," *Forum* 25, no. 3 (1976), pp. 291–303.

21. Robert Venturi, *Complexity and Contradiction in Architecture* (New York: Museum of Modern Art, 1966), pp. 20–21.

22. Gutman, *Architectural Practice*, p. 41.

23. Larson, "Emblem and Exception," p. 72.

24. Steven Kieran, "Theory and Design in a Marketing Age," *The Harvard Architectural Review* 6, pp. 102–13.

25. Gutman, *Architectural Practice*, p. 45.

26. Diane Ghirardo, "The Deceits of Postmodern Architecture," *After the Future: Post-Modern Times and Places*, ed. Gary Shapiro (Syracuse, N.Y.: Syracuse Univ. Press, 1990), pp. 236–37.

27. Ibid., p. 244.

28. Robert Gutman, "Taking Care of Architecture," *Progressive Architecture* 71 (April 1990), p. 120.

29. Kenneth Frampton has advocated the reconnection of architecture and building in "Towards a Critical Regionalism," *The Anti-Aesthetic: Essays on Postmodern Culture*, ed. Hal Foster (Port Townsend, Wash.: Bay Press, 1983), pp. 16–30.

30. Gutman, *Architectural Practice*, pp. 46–49.

31. Stanford Anderson developed this concept in "The Fiction of Function," *Assemblage* 2 (November 1987), p. 19.

■ Towers of Babel

Vincent P. Pecora

For most of its history, architecture has been a profession dependent upon close ties to wealth and power, even in realizing its minor dreams. Primarily, this is simply owing to the cost of unique, specialized construction, and it has always been so. The elite citizen, the corporation (whether religious or commercial), and the state have generally been the architect's patrons. And the practical interests of the patron have been adopted in turn as the supposedly autonomous principles of the profession itself. The Vitruvian ideals of solidity and permanence, the emphasis on monumentality, the age-old capacity of building to represent man's dominion over (or reconciliation with) the earth, the belief that significant form expresses something otherwise hidden about human being, about the spirit of a people, about the character of an individual—even the term *architecture* itself, with its implications of rule, mastery, and origin—all conspire equally in the production and conceptual reproduction of the discipline. Such notions serve first as the motive behind patronage; and they immediately serve again, more or less unchanged, as architecture's second nature, as the story it tells itself about its own independent sensibility and standards.

At its most paradoxical (modern) point, such doubling means that the same quality—for example, the value of significant form in building—will be used simultaneously to signify both the exchange or commercial value of the architect's skills *and* the architect's ability to renounce all mere exchange value. This paradox does not mean that architecture loses its way in ideology. On the contrary, it means that architecture, precisely because of its intimate ties with wealth and power, easily becomes the perfect expression of the collapse of all ideology into things themselves—the service of and resistance to social power prove to be indistinguishable and interchangeable. It is important to remember, however, that this interchangeability cannot be avoided (paradoxically) as long as architecture insists on a substance, and a mission, achieved by being true to itself. Only by actually altering its relationship to its social bases, rather than by signifying a "critical" attitude toward other kinds of built form, would architecture become something other than an advertisement for itself. And to do this, architecture would have to become seriously involved in those increasingly specialized areas supposedly external to it—urban and regional planning, the need for affordable housing, relations between commercial and consumer interests, oligarchic control of public policy—that allow specialized architects in turn to imagine that they really do possess a substance and mission of their own. In short, architecture would have to address the array of institutional apparatuses that, through their control of the built environment, help to maintain inequity in the present distributions of power and wealth. But then, the architect will say, what remains of architecture?

This response is itself more than a little paradoxical. If, as is commonly asserted today, architects are responsible for only a small part of the built environment, it is hard to see what architecture gains by sustaining its independent role under present conditions, which more or less exclude all those (builders and dwellers alike) without ready access to capital. Of course, what it does gain, though many would say this is a rather Pyrrhic victory, is the preservation of the myth—along with the history, traditions, and aesthetic (or epistemological, or ontological) aura—of its own proper substance and mission. Thus, while only a very small stratum of the profession materially benefits from the self-preservation of its aura, all architects, of whatever degree of success and prestige, hope to share in the symbolic capital Architecture bestows. Even this slice of the pie may soon shrivel: "The architecture profession is still some distance from encountering the image and identity problems of interior designers, but in the case of some firms, not very far removed."[1] There is no way, however, that such conditions can be salvaged by "raising standards," or by a return to the fundamentals of "good practice." For it is precisely this recurring fetishization of a "substance which is absoutely one's own" that is indeed the mystifying alibi of all modern, capitalist rationalization of labor.[2] Do your job, and leave the rest to those who know better—in this is the true impoverishment of architecture, the sign of its willing submission to a state of things it pretends to abhor. In fact, architecture as autonomous art and science, as a discipline in possession both of some historical experience in solving practical problems and of a progressive vision of how things unchained from existing social hierarchies might look and feel—*this* architecture is doomed precisely to the degree it refuses to recognize that its autonomy is nothing more than a specific effect of social relations. By insisting on the irrelevancy of such relations, architecture finally succeeds in making itself irrelevant.

I.

Some would of course say that such problems begin with the initial separation of exchange from use value wrought by the eighteenth-century division of labor between architect and engineer. Others would point out that this division itself accompanies industrial capitalization. Surely, the modernism of Le Corbusier and Mies van der Rohe and the Bauhaus only heightened the contradictions: if what was useful was by definition beautiful, the architect's specialized and programmatic relation to art—a style that dismantles the category of style itself, as it were—need never appear to contradict the claim of practical, social redemption. But the category that allowed all discrepancies to be magically overcome—technology—was keenly double-edged. To the extent that architecture domesticated technology as the true aesthetic, it could only display its own inadequacy to the social tasks it set for itself. In the face of that inadequacy, modernism instead settled for the autonomous expression of technological values, for the aestheticization of society rather than the socialization of aesthetics. The postwar, post-Auschwitz reaction against modernism's false transcendence was oddly prefigured when the last incarnation of the Bauhaus under Mies tried to negotiate a separate peace with the new Nazi regime. "The new era is a fact," a resigned Mies had said in a speech from 1930; "it exists, irrespective of our 'yes' or 'no'. . . . Let us accept changed economic and social conditions as a fact. . . . All these take their blind and fateful course."[3] By 1933, of course, such pragmatism was already anachronistic, and the Bauhaus remained closed.

Certain sentiments, however, are not simply local expressions. One might have expected that, by the 1960s, architecture would have found a more persuasive response than Mies's to the bad totalities of modernism. But Robert Venturi, who saw complexity and contradiction inside the house of architecture, was perfectly clear and unambiguous about what he found outside: "The architect's ever diminishing power and his growing ineffectualness in shaping the whole environment can perhaps be reversed, ironically, by narrowing his concerns and concentrating on his own job. Perhaps then relationships and power will take care of themselves."[4] When he writes a note to the second edition of *Complexity and Contradiction in Architecture* eleven years later, Venturi's faith is undiminished; all that is missing for him from the earlier edition is a treatment of architectural symbolism, the vogue of the 1970s, as if symbolism represented something truly challenging for form. Venturi's polemic is plain enough, targeting modernism, city planning, "platitudinous architects who invoke integrity," anything that might "suppress those complexities and contradictions inherent in art and experience." Venturi is so convincing here that one wonders how he achieved the sublime simplicity of a vision in which "relationships and power will take care of themselves." Undoubtedly, something like this had occurred to Mies, too. Venturi would seem to have forgotten how wrong his predecessor had been.

Even more than the later *Learning from Las Vegas,* Venturi's book delivers the first great salvo against the ideological hegemony of modernism. But like other apparently basic conflicts between rationalism and realism, between context and tradition, between inherent meaning and historically determined meaning, even between the great modernist problems of form and narrowly defined function, the oppositional pose Venturi strikes primarily guarantees one thing—that the architect remains safely insulated from all those "complexities and contradictions" outside the boundaries of the discipline, a discipline increasingly defined precisely by such insulation. His later juggling with the terms *form* and *symbolism* only thickens the walls. Venturi himself posits architecture as a necessarily critical activity, but what he means by this is largely what the early T. S. Eliot meant about poetry: first, that the critical analysis of architecture in terms of its constituent parts is "a process present in all creation"; and second, that this critical process takes place more or less in the autonomous realm of a great tradition, which in turn manifests itself in the individual artist. In Eliot's words: "This historical sense, which is a sense of the timeless as well as of the temporal and of the timeless and temporal together, is what makes a writer traditional, and it is at the same time what makes a writer most acutely conscious of his place in time, of his own contemporaneity."[5] Thus, Venturi is able to add one more polarity to the discussion, that between the naive modernist obsession with novelty and difference, and his (and Eliot's) postmodern sense of the classical tradition *in* the individual talent. Clearly, Venturi was catching up on literary criticism at this time: the notions of paradox and contradiction within unity are taken from Cleanth Brooks, the value of ambiguity from William Empson.[6] With such allies, Venturi is able to imply that his polemic emphasizes the complex richness of an architectural practice interwoven with real history and real experience as opposed to the simple and reductive totalizations of high modernism.

Venturi turns out to be a rather curious reader of literary criticism, however. For, of course, Eliot and Brooks and Empson are veritable high priests of modernism for the literary establishment. It is possible that Venturi means to imply here an early version of the "Modernism never really happened in architecture" thesis, a notion taken up briefly by Peter Eisenman in the 1970s. But even Eisenman seems to have been unwilling to go very far with the idea, and such an anachronism is belied by Venturi's larger polemic. What Venturi does not explore is crucial: that the emphasis on irony, paradox, ambiguity, contradiction, and, perhaps most of all, the immanent presence of the entire tradition in the work of the truly classic artist—that all of this is in itself only one more aesthetic program no closer to history and experience than any other. The relation between the ideals of purity, geometric clarity, revolutionary unmasking of calcified truisms, and concentration on absolute essences on one side and those of paradox, ambiguity, complexity, and tradition on the other is much closer within literary modernism—and, I would suggest, in modernist art and architecture as well—than Venturi seems to imagine.

Both sets of ideals resolve themselves in supposedly unified works of art. More important, every potential opposition, like that between an absolute essence beyond time and a historical tradition, turns out to be not only a complementary pairing, but an intimate relationship of supplementarity as well. A modernist poet like Ezra Pound could cry "Make it new" and note that "utter originality is of course out of the question" without contradiction. Such juxtapositions are precisely what will allow an autonomously conceived tradition to work in the first place. They make up the necessary machinery projecting the appearance, like the Wizard behind the curtain in Oz, of an ongoing conversation among great creative minds. Simplicity, for example, is in fact raised to a higher prominence by Venturi, precisely because of the complexity it must overcome. Venturi does not really negate Louis Kahn, only his less talented ephebes: "Aesthetic simplicity which is a satisfaction to the mind derives, when valid and profound, from inner complexity. The Doric temple's simplicity to the eye is achieved through the famous subtleties and precision of its distorted geometry. . . ."[7] Venturi's complexity is of course meaningless to him without the sublating order and unity imposed by the creative architect. Like Schiller's romanticism, or Eliot's modernism, what Venturi actually wants is that sublime moment when freedom and necessity come together, where the truth of aesthetic contradiction becomes embodied "in its totality or its implications of totality."[8] When Schiller spoke of the aesthetic as that "representation of the Infinite" in which the conflict between anarchic sensuality and formal rationality merge, he could have had Venturi in mind.[9]

And the creative mind of the artist that achieves such sublime moments is itself only an element in something larger. In a passage from Eliot's essay which, perhaps wisely, Venturi omits, one reads that the artist "must be aware that the mind of Europe—the mind of his own country—a mind which he learns in time to be much more important than his own private mind—is a mind which changes, and that this change is a development which abandons nothing *en route*. . . ."[10] One would only half-facetiously discover *Learning from Las Vegas* emanating from such a sentiment; for on the strip that quite literally abandons nothing along the way, one discovers the universal significance behind the vernacular. It would in any case be difficult to see how, given the ultimately organic, monolithic, and totalizing scope Eliot grants "the mind of Europe," his early remarks on tradition could in any way serve to subvert Frank Lloyd Wright's vision of simplicity and "building harmonies" that "would change and deepen the thinking and culture of the modern world."[11] In fact, Venturi and Wright, like Venturi and Le Corbusier, or Venturi and Mies, or Venturi and Kahn, are engaging in the meeting of minds that, in Matthew Arnold's wonderful phrase, yields "sweetness and light."

The formalist transformation in aesthetics that took place in St. Petersburg and Moscow around the time of the Bolshevik Revolution—one which had clear parallels with the linguistics of de Saussure some ten years earlier, and which was itself revised by an Anglo-American tradition including Eliot and Brooks and Empson—was in no sense a real threat to older notions of an autonomous history of culture to be found in Hegel, Burkhardt, Arnold, or Taine. What formalism actually provided was an internal mechanism that could be used to explain the ongoing dialogue between artists, movements, and generations, a mechanism that relied on what later structuralists called intertextuality rather than on any other cultural relations. As Boris Eichenbaum noted in his apology for the Russian movement, history and the formal method were hardly opposed; they could be related, however, only through a most stringent rationalization of the disciplines that further emphasized their autonomy from the social bases of their production. "We studied literary evolution insofar as it bore a distinctive character and only to the extent that it stood alone, quite independent of other aspects of culture."[12] And the mechanism propelling that evolution was what Victor Shklovsky, in one of the seminal documents of the movement, called *ostraneniye*—"making strange": "Habitualization devours works, clothes, furniture, one's wife, and the fear of war. . . . And art exists that one may recover the sensation of life; it exists to make one feel things, to make the stone *stony*. . . . The technique of art is to make objects 'unfamiliar,' to make forms difficult, to increase the difficulty and length of perception because the process of perception is an aesthetic end in itself and must be prolonged. *Art is a way of experiencing the artfulness of an object; the object is not important.*"[13] Venturi's "complexity and contradiction" is merely one version of this technique; but Shklovsky's perspective makes it plain that such gestures are indeed as basic to the reductive simplicity of modernism as they are to his entire conception of aesthetic evolution. Venturi does not take his readers *back* to architectural history after modernism's failure—he fulfills the requirements of disciplinary independence no less than his modernist adversaries had.

There is, nevertheless, an essential difference to be observed between a strict formalism applied to literature and one applied to architecture. Shklovsky's notion of literary ostraneniye contains an often ignored but crucial ambiguity, one that would be relevant to later attempts, such as that of Julia Kristeva, to make the device do the work of sociopolitical critique. For Shklovsky, as the previous quote indicates, art is that which is able both "to make objects 'unfamiliar,'" *and* "to make forms difficult." That is, Shklovsky's notion implies a twofold estrangement: (1) of familiar objects, or *referents* (such as the stone) by unfamiliar perspectives; (2) of familiar forms, or *signifiers* (such as a literary style) by unfamiliar ones, a category under which one can include Boris Tomashevsky's notion that new art "lays bare the device" of older art.[14] Shklovsky himself uses the term in ways difficult to decipher, perhaps because of the revolutionary situation in which he wrote. When he illustrates defamiliarization, for example, he chooses a passage from Tolstoy's story "Kholstomer," in which the narration emerges from a horse's point of view and the matter discussed is the strangeness of private property when looked at from the point of view of the property. What is being estranged here? Is it an object that Tolstoy's readers would have found familiar enough—private property? Or is it an earlier set of narrative conventions (those limited to conscious human subjects) that is being questioned by introducing a horse's-eye view to literature?

Referents, such as private property, are clearly already socially embedded in beliefs and ideologies; literary styles appear to be far more autonomous. The ambiguity in Shklovsky was never really clarified by the earlier Russian formalists, but one can at least understand why it would have been important. If literary referents (like stones, but even more like private property) are truly being violently yoked from the automatism of established perspectives, defamiliarization could perhaps be theorized as a critical, even revolutionary project. When it is earlier form or style per se that is being subverted, it is far less easy to define the sociopolitical vector art describes.

Much of continental formalism (including Tomashevsky and, later, the work of Prague linguists like Roman Jakobson) came to rely on the latter device—the defamiliarizing effect of new form on old. Whatever other issues are at stake here, it should be clear that any conception of the critical power of architecture that relies on its defamiliarizing potential is stuck with the latter device of formal estrangement. Unless architectural analysis decides to emphasize the iconographic within built form—as in constructivist agitprop, or as in images of Lenin or Mussolini or the swastika hung from balconies—any notion of referent in the literary sense will be impossible. Such things are useful to remember when architects refer to the power of built form to upset cultural conventions; for in the main, this can never mean anything more than the conventions of earlier architectural form. What, precisely, architecture opposes through such supposedly critical gestures of formal estrangement will be the crux of the issue facing architectural criticism.

■ II.

Many of course will immediately object that expecting Robert Venturi to produce the needed critique of modernism is simply setting up a straw man; even Vincent Scully, they will say, in his introduction to *Complexity and Contradiction,* pointed out how close Le Corbusier and Venturi were under the skin. Where one needs to turn, the argument might continue, is to those analyses of built form that rigorously question the very boundaries of the profession itself. In many ways, *Oppositions,* the house organ of the Institute for Architecture and Urban Studies in New York from 1973 to 1984, would appear to be the place in which such criticism could be found.[15] *Oppositions* was an avowedly critical journal that defined itself in terms of its adversarial relationship not only to existing architectural discourse, but also to the larger trajectory of high modernism, and even to those more recent statements— like Venturi's—pretending to ground architecture anew. Further, the journal explicitly linked these more traditional discourses and practices to the existing social relations supporting them, and reinforced by them. In a joint editorial for the journal's first issue, cofounders Peter Eisenman, Kenneth Frampton, and Mario Gandelsonas make clear their intention to provide a forum for discussion of "the nature of architecture and design in relation to a man-made world."[16] Their ultimate goal was "the evolution of new models for a theory of architecture," a project that entailed more than reaction to recent work. *Oppositions* was supposed to question the larger history of architecture, as well as those conventional models explaining how such a history held together. Moreover, there would be no univocal editorial position; the journal would itself reflect different concerns "for formal, socio-cultural and political discourse." And that first issue, with essays devoted to modernist neoclassicism, contemporary urban housing projects, industrialization, and ideological consumption in architecture, appears to fulfill expectations. This will *not* be *Progressive Architecture,* as Gandelsonas himself would note elsewhere.[17]

But a third of the way into the journal's eleven-year run, the oppositional project that began as a critique *of* architecture had "evolved" into the analysis of architecture *as* critique. With *Oppositions* 9 (1977), the editors—now including Anthony Vidler, an Eisenman protegé—"re-assess" the journal's "intital aims and format" and provide a "renewed statement of intent." Here, it appears, opposition is embodied not so much in the critique of architecture as a discipline, but instead refers to "the critical practice of architecture."[18] And in that subtle shift, I would suggest, can be read much of the development of postmodernism as a self-proclaimed "deconstruction" of an earlier and monolithic humanist tradition. For it is at such a moment, in the very act of defining itself against this tradition, that architectural thinking once again reveals where the primary critical values are always already to be found: in the defamiliarization of built form by built form, in the autonomous dialogue of architecture with itself. Thus, although the ninth editorial still affirms a plurality of intentions, among which are "the nature of ideology" and "the problematic nature of architecture and urbanism," it is also obvious that such issues will prove almost impossible to address from outside the parameters of architecture's auto-affective practices.

Perhaps this should have been obvious right from the start. In the second joint editorial, heading the list of objectives is "the critique of built work as a vehicle for ideas."[19] And the third joint statement explicitly announces a tension among the editors concerning the importance to be attached "to the relationship of architecture and society."[20] Clearly, Frampton's interests in social questions, Gandelsonas's semiotics of ideology, and Eisenman's focus on undoing humanism were only tenuously matched, and a series of independent editorials would follow, at least until number 9. But within the supposed divergence of views in this third editorial, there is also a curious level of agreement. First, the editors seem resigned to the idea that "the dominant mode of production and consumption has little use for architecture in any profound sense." Second, the editors explicitly declare their alliance on two fronts: "a faith in the importance of architecture as a poetic manifestation"; and "a belief in the importance of criticism as a necessary force set in perennial opposition to the established values of an empirically oriented society." Even if one assumes that the phrase "empirically oriented society" is a euphemism for utilitarian capitalism, the linking of these two articles of faith immediately raises a question concerning the location and aim of the critical act demanded here. In the third of the four points for subsequent debate that conclude the editorial, one perhaps finds the expected answer: "We will also attempt to establish *the essence of the nature of architecture as a critical agent* and the degree to which this critique is affected by an opposition between the human lifeworld and the idea of 'progress.'" While one can hear Frampton's specific echoes of Habermas and the Frankfurt School in the latter clause, the italicized phrase already sets the grounds of the debate.

My point here is a relatively simple one: that in the course of establishing an adversarial position from which to critique the truisms of an older, humanist, ideologically determined, and conceptually reductive architectural tradition, *Oppositions* largely (though not entirely) reconstitutes that tradition—and does it precisely along the formalist lines of defamiliarization and autonomous generic evolution outlined above. Eisenman's introduction to *Oppositions* 6 (1976) is a classic example. In an essay titled "Post-Functionalism," Eisenman reiterates a position that was in fact visible in the opening essay of the journal's first issue, Colin Rowe's "Neoclassicism and Modern Architecture."[21] There, Rowe (not unlike Venturi before him) had redefined modernist functionalism, especially the Miesian variety, as a *"cul-de-sac"* of magnificent "single-mindedness." For Rowe, the reductive "simplicity" of a project like Mies's Crown Hall was, ironically, only persuasive in spirit; in it, reality was less accommodated in the flesh than "transcended" by a vision "probably too pure to be useful."[22] Rowe's altogether justifiable critique of the reified functionalism of much modern architecture is further extended in Eisenman's later editorial, where the attempted "modernist" synthesis of function and form is now understood to be indistinguishable "from the 500-year-old tradition of humanism."[23] Indeed, the "oscillation between a [functionalist] concern for internal accommodation. . . . and a concern for the articulation of ideal themes in form" becomes for Eisenman *the* ideological dialectic in Western architecture.

Like Rowe, Eisenman would seem to be on to something here, on the verge of that step outside of age-old hegemonies—including the falsely (because autonomously) conceived utility of modernism—that the journal as a whole has promised. But Eisenman's argument takes a surprising turn, one which paradoxically responds to the editorial board's conviction that the "dominant mode of production and consumption has little use for architecture in any profound sense" by a wholesale retreat into the autonomous profundity of architecture alone against an unfeeling world. For Eisenman argues that the "oversimplified form-follows-function formula" of so-called modernism is itself only a continuation of traditional humanism's "idealist ambition of creating architecture as a kind of ethically constituted form-giving." That is, modernism as a received program failed, *not* by settling for a technocratic reduction of the practical social functionality and utility implicit in its claims, but rather by having been "humanistically" weak enough to make such claims in the first place. Eisenman's radical gesture then is to oppose that "*moral* imperative" grounding not only received modernism but also the whole of a humanist tradition behind it, as an idea "no longer operative within contemporary experience." What Eisenman calls for is a *truly* modernist rejection of all humanist (that is, functionalist) moralism, a radical break that had not yet been achieved by contemporary "eclecticism, post-modernism, or neo-functionalism." What Eisenman wants is the dismantling of the form-function dialectic that, because it is only culturally based, is supposedly the naturalized ideology a critical architectural practice should oppose.

Why this agenda should be understood as constituting a genuinely modern and critical practice of architecture, however, is only awkwardly spelled out. First, there is the demand imposed by "contemporary experience," circa 1976—but this demand seems to be answered rather anachronistically for Eisenman by the authentically antihumanist modernism (again, one which did make it into architecture) of Malevich and Mondrian, Joyce and Apollinaire, Schönberg and Webern, Richter and Eggeling. But beyond such particular figures, Eisenman discovers the essence of the modern sensibility, and it is this essence that for him a contemporary critical architecture must articulate: man, displaced "from the center of his world . . . is no longer viewed as an *originating agent*. . . . In this context, man is a discursive function among complex and already-formed systems of language, which he witnesses but does not constitute." Behind genuine modernity, that is, Eisenman discovers Lévi-Strauss's structuralism and Foucault's notions of *épistème,* discourse, and genealogy. Or rather, he discovers a strangely flattened version of them. For the antihumanism of someone like Foucault was, in its fullest elaboration, an attempt to demystify those hegemonic social powers that ritually invoked a unified subjectivity and history—both terms Europocentric, heterosexual, originary, organic, progressively liberating, progressively more knowing, progressively more truly human—in order to legitimate their own existing and exclusive authority. For Foucault, demonstrating that an established order was culturally based, and not natural, would serve to reclaim (like a "counter-memory") all those unacceptable voices repressed by a dominant historiography, marginalized by discursive authority. Foucault's work is filled with its own contradictions; he often seems stuck amid the discourses he would dissect. But the social and political (even ethical) motors driving his project are clear enough.

For Eisenman, Foucault's radical antihumanism means something else entirely, and how it means what it does for him is in itself an object lesson about the way "theory," from the mid-1960s on, was to be reappropriated by an aestheticist (or antiaestheticist, since such terms will prove to be interchangeable) rhetoric. What radically destabilizing, Foucaultian, antihumanist postfunctionalism in architecture means for Eisenman turns out to be something far less alien than the blustering rhetoric suggests. Indeed, it turns out to be our old friend, the autonomous, perennially defamiliarizing, self-propelled evolution of form. "This new theoretical base," Eisenman concludes, "changes the humanist balance of form/function to a dialectical relationship within the evolution of form itself." Now, it would appear, architecture must recognize only two formal tendencies in supposedly dialectical relation—tendencies which could easily be mistaken for Nietzsche's tragic dancers, Apollo and Dionysus. Form as a unifying recollection of "simple geometric condition" (a "humanist relic") is always opposed by, yet linked to, form "as a series of fragments—signs without meaning dependent upon, and without reference to, a more basic condition." But there is no explanation of how this "new, modern dialectic" between unifying and fragmentary, meaningful and meaningless form is any more critical, or any less ideological, than the supposedly monolithic humanist synthesis of form and function.

Indeed, if ideology, humanist and otherwise, can be defined (after Althusser) as "the imaginary relationship of individuals to their real conditions of existence," an imagined relation that (after Marx) allows individuals "to understand all these separate ideas and concepts as 'forms of self-determination' on the part of *the* concept developing in history," then it is hard to discern how Eisenman's "new consciousness in architecture" signifies even a minor break with tradition.[24] "[The formal tendencies] begin to define the inherent nature of the object in and of itself and its capacity to be represented." Like the Russian formalists' "dialectical self-creation of new forms,"[25] within which could be found the essential literariness of literature, Eisenman returns architecture to its inherent, authentic nature. And at this point, it becomes rather difficult to remember that his editorial begins by opposing the conceptual reductions, autonomy, purity, and continuity of a five-hundred-year architectural tradition. There is undoubtedly a certain charm to Eisenman's gesture; "I alone among architects," he seems to declare, "have the courage (or the humility) to admit that architecture can fulfill no higher moral imperatives—it exists for itself alone." But it is merely naive to believe that such a gesture is either new, critical, antitraditional, or even intellectually honest. For, in the end, Eisenman proves himself the most moral of all: unlike the fallen, he remains true to the only great love "real" architects have ever recognized—lady architecture herself. Criticism becomes apotheosis.

■ III.

I have focused on Eisenman's remarks here because, in spite of the visible tension between various theoretical perspectives in *Oppositions* and in spite of the editors' pluralistic intentions, such remarks nevertheless reveal habits of thought that invariably influence architectural discourse, like an intellectual undertow beneath the waves of rhetorical variation. Architecture is transformed into the critical perspective orginally aimed against it, and in that moment every issue formerly lying outside existing practices is reappropriated as if it were merely a question of built form itself. Modernism's fetishization of function is correctly diagnosed as a conceptual reification that ends up deferring actual social restructuring (one need only examine the sad story of Brasilia to see this), but the solution celebrated is then a return to the essential properties of architectural form. What drives this mechanism, in fact, is not so much the desire to adopt a critical perspective on the discipline as a whole, but the desire to reconcile disciplinary claims with the increasingly specialized, rationalized function architects are expected to play in highly developed contemporary societies—that is, with "the architect's ever diminishing power and his growing ineffectualness," as Venturi phrased it. In this sense, Eisenman's career-long rejection of the ineffectual effectivity architects are expected to accept—all that he lumps together in the obviously bankrupt term *functionalism*—is understandable. Unfortunately, the result of such critical rejectionism is generally a more profound retreat into precisely that disciplinary isolation and purity supposedly being denounced. It is as if one were to object to being called a liar by renouncing all claims to truth.

But Eisenman's retreat into a new formalism has at least the merit of clarity. The reader of *Oppositions* will not always be so fortunate. In the essays of two of the journal's editors, Diana Agrest and Mario Gandelsonas, the most deceptive critical prestidigitation is at work, one that makes Eisenman seem refreshing by comparison. For through semiotic theory, Agrest and

Gandelsonas manage to make Eisenman's formalist-inspired "dialectical relationship within the evolution of form itself" resonate with the sound of a politically engaged (vaguely Althusserian) Marxian perspective. Their contribution to the premier issue of the journal, "Semiotics and Architecture: Ideological Consumption or Theoretical Work," in fact requires the most stringent adherence to form—now as an "epistemological" problem—though in the name of the demystification of merely adaptive theories of architecture, which they call "ideology." For Agrest and Gandelsonas, despite their radical political claims, are not as far from Eisenman as they might at first appear.

Architectural ideology, which like all ideology for Althusser functions to hide its true nature, is explicitly defined for them not in terms of Vitruvian ideals, nor in terms of some mystified fetishization of the grand significance (either ontological or epistemological or existential) of built form—not, that is, in terms of the rhetoric that would appear to be most ideologically conditioned to anyone outside the profession. Rather, the true ideology of architecture for them turns out to be quite similar to Eisenman's demon functionalism, and it is just as monolithic: "The summation of Western architectural 'knowledge' in its entire range, from commonplace intuition to sophisticated 'theories' and histories of architecture, is to be recognized as ideology rather than as history. This ideology has explicitly claimed to serve the *practical* needs of society, by ordering and controlling the built environment. Nevertheless, we hold that the underlying function of this ideology is in fact the pragmatic one of both serving and preserving the overall structure of society in Western social formations. It serves to perpetuate the capitalist mode of production, and architectural practice as part of it."[26] Unlike Eisenman, one might say, it would appear that Agrest and Gandelsonas have at least located the problem in a more politically precise way. That is, their essay initially seems to be pointed, finally, toward issues that might justify the critical stance of *Oppositions* as a whole: toward *how* and *by whom* the "ordering and controlling of the built environment" is directed, and toward an architectural practice that might contribute to change in those areas.

But Agrest and Gandelsonas disappoint in rather spectacular ways. First, by ignoring that ideology in Althusser is always embedded in material *practices,* that is, in institutions, Agrest and Gandelsonas treat ideology as if it were reducible to a semiotic code. This is a crucial step: it means that all elements in architecture of any critical importance are embodied as questions of *signification.* And all critical opposition within architecture (like all revolutions of the poetic word in the early Kristeva) will similarly take shape in terms of signifying elements.[27] The new or scientific purchase they believe they have achieved on the old (at least since the eighteenth century) semantic problem of reading architecture as a language is due to the introduction of Saussurian linguistics. That is, since de Saussure has shown that the relation between any signifying element and its significance is not natural but is in fact arbitrarily (conventionally) produced by a linguistic system, architectural significance works in a similar way. The supposedly critical insight this yields is that *"objects* in the environment" (including architectural ones) can be understood to possess significance only by virtue of *"cultural convention"* and not because of any *"inherent meaning."*[28] Thus, the (supposedly) fundamental tenet of architectural ideology from the classical treatises to modernism—that function "is the unique determinant of the form of an object"— can be shown to be no more than an arbitrary imposition of significance. Somehow, Agrest and Gandelsonas have derived a series of reified reductions—architecture becomes signifying code becomes ideology becomes functionalism—that allows them to believe that architectural theory and practice oppose "the capitalist mode of production" only insofar as they question the presumably natural relation between form and function.

Second, by conveniently ignoring that all relatively autonomous ideological struggle in Althusser is always the complement of actual political conflict determined "in the last instance" by basic economic forces, Agrest and Gandelsonas can present the opposition between the "adaptive theories" (that is, ideologies) and their own notion of *theory* "outside ideology" as if this opposition constituted a fully independent (that is, formal) dialectic. What or who will be practically served by their disassembling of ideology is thus an unasked question, and it is unasked precisely because all notions of built form determined by practical service (to anyone whatsoever, it seems) have already been declared *a priori* "ideological."

Third, in comparing their notion of architecture as culturally determined significant code with language, Agrest and Gandelsonas must also confront an obstacle to any notion of ideological critique. That is, while they must maintain the potential of architecture to be a critical project, language as system clearly affords no such opportunities—to criticize the English language, for example, would make little sense. "In language the individual can *use* but not *modify* the system of language (langue). In contrast to language, the architect can and does modify the system, which is fabricated on a system of conventions."[29] *Why* architecture as code should inherently differ from language, since both have been defined in the essay as "fabricated on a system of conventions," is never explained. Worse, left with a definition of significant form that in fact restricts architects to use and manipulation of the system (like a language user), but that thus precludes any viable critical relation to the whole, Agrest and Gandelsonas suddenly unveil the biggest magic trick in their bag: "The model langue/speech does not explain but overlooks creativity in architecture. Creativity in architecture is a complex play of conservation and variation of shapes and ideological notions within certain determined limits."[30] Beyond the fact that to invoke creativity whenever the analysis seems to reach a dead end seems hardly in the spirit of ideological critique, such statements make explicit the vacuity of Agrest and Gandelsonas's contribution to "a more general [nonadaptive] theory of ideology" in architecture. For, as might be expected at this point, and no less than Eisenman's "dialectic," this theory reduces itself to a familiar device: the defamiliarization of old form by new, "the dialectical self-creation of new forms." Agrest and Gandelsonas will insist in their final lines that they are thus outside architectural ideology and that their theory works toward a materialist dialectic. But given even the very brief trajectory visible here in Mies and Venturi and Eisenman, it is rather difficult to tell what they might have meant.

The line of thought Agrest and Gandelsonas present in this first essay is no aberration. It is further developed in Gandelsonas's editorial, "Neo-Functionalism," for *Oppositions* 5 (1976), and in his analysis of Eisenman's work, "From Structure to Subject: The Formation of an Architectural Language," in *Oppositions* 17 (1979); in Agrest's "Design versus Non-Design," *Oppositions* 6

(1976), "Architectural Anagrams: The Symbolic Performance of Skyscrapers,"
Oppositions 11 (1977), and "Architecture of Mirror/Mirror of Architecture,"
Oppositions 26 (1984). One can find related, if equally unarticulated, assumptions about the sociopolitical significance of formal defamiliarization in several essays by Francesco Dal Co (*Oppositions* 13 [1978] and 23 [1981]). And
only occasionally did such a perspective receive a reply: Jacques Guillerme's
very brief critique, "The Idea of Architectural Language," *Oppositions* 10
(1977), and the final pages of Manfredo Tafuri's "The Historical Project," *Oppositions* 17 (1979). In general, it would be fair to say the Agrest-Gandelsonas
approach, however empty it may seem today, remained untouched by serious
appraisal—even Tafuri's quick critique of such a perspective winds up prais-
ing them, albeit sotto voce in his last footnote, for recognizing the importance of creativity. Unsurprisingly, it is of course Agrest and Gandelsonas
who, with Vidler, inherit the journal for its final issue. Joan Ockman attributes
the institute's, and the journal's, "compromise of its orginal mandate as an
antiestablishment institution of progressive architects, planners, and thinkers" to its need to cultivate fashion and patronage, to the "air outside."[31] But
it would appear that no one was checking the air quality inside and that it
was really not much better.

IV.

While the reliance on form as critique provides greater unity to *Oppositions*
than may be apparent at first glance, there were of course essays that did
manage to push the discourse outside its formal cocoon. The work of
Manfredo Tafuri is a notable exception in the journal's pages. For Tafuri's
is perhaps the only critical perspective to maintain, among other things, a
focus on the institutional boundaries by which architecture as a social practice defines itself, a concern for the nature of the division between its socially defined labor and that of others, and a healthy skepticism of all those
"'closed systems,' within which the themes of polysemy and pluralism are
formed and controlled."[32] Tafuri's discussion of the New York Five is to the
point here:

The pleasure which arises from reading the works of Hejduk, Eisenman and Graves is entirely intellectual. I enjoy the subtle mental games which subjugate the absolute nature of the forms (whether they be designed or built, at this point it does not matter). Clearly there is no social value in all of this. And, in fact, is pleasure not an entirely private affair? It is all too easy to conclude that this architecture is a "betrayal" of the ethical ideals of the Modern Movement. On the contrary, it records the mood of someone who feels betrayed and reveals fully the condition of those who still wish to make "Architecture." (If there is a truly arbitrary act, it lies precisely in the choice to make "Architecture.")[33]

Here and in other essays, like his "Giuseppe Terragni: Subject and 'Mask'" in *Oppositions* 11 (1977), Tafuri's work is rather distinct. But even Tafuri is to have a limited effect on the journal's larger trajectory. By issue 17 (1979), he begins surreptitiously to justify the "arbitrary" wish to continue making "Architecture" when he castigates "the transformation of artistic activity into *labor* that is directly channeled into the productive order."[34] With that gesture, Tafuri also abandons any hope of understanding architecture as a specific *kind* of labor, implicated with others in systematic relations serving (at the least) dominant tendencies within an economy, and reinscribes architecture as an art that can only resist a productive order *tout court.*

Tafuri's shift here toward distinguishing the productive economy on one side and an oppositional, because nonproductive, art on the other—though it has obvious precedents in certain Frankfurt School writings—is hardly central to his work.[35] In any case, the distinction never reifies. The same, however, cannot be said of related work in *Oppositions* that at first would appear to complement Tafuri's. Kenneth Frampton's "Industrialization and the Crises in Architecture" in the first issue, an essay heavily influenced by Hannah Arendt, is also a step toward dealing with architecture as a discipline embedded in productive social forces. In that spirit, Frampton begins with the obvious question of labor—the separation of architecture and engineering in eighteenth-century France.[36] And each crisis in architecture thereafter is shown to be related to surrounding technological, economic, and political developments. But even within Frampton's essay, one attentive to just that modern rationalization of labor addressed by the Frankfurt School, the argument takes odd turns. Because he emphasizes that nineteenth-century capitalism "finds itself equipped with a surplus of means over needs," but does not then address the complementary question of the artificial restriction of productive capacity along class lines—so that certain needs would in fact never disappear as might be expected—Frampton ends up focusing instead on one of the cultural by-products of that restriction: kitsch.[37] The effect of this emphasis is to turn the by-product of arrested development, kitsch, into the basis of the social disharmony itself. That is, the real conflict over control of production is put aside in favor of the "depreciation of material"—a phrase quoted from "the German architect and liberal revolutionary" Gottfried Semper—caused by the technology of mass production. Thus, Frampton (again following Arendt) will interpret the primary *social* problem from the nineteenth century on, including the "mass-produced" war of 1914–1918, as the loss of a "culturally viable community," of a "fulfilling socio-cultural arena," in the face of an industrialized world.

To be sure, Frampton gains useful insights with this strategy. Kitsch can be reread as the compensatory bone thrown to a class denied real cultural authority. The nineteenth-century utopian nostalgia for an organic cultural life, as in William Morris, can likewise be understood as an implicit (if misguided) protest against the inhumanity of capitalist industrialization. And, perhaps most interestingly, the fetishization of technology as "value and sign—as the *ding an sich* of human culture" by functionalist modernism can be directly attributed to the Soviet *Proletcult*. But even in the decisive (modernist) crisis of 1918, Frampton's strategy turns on itself. For him, that is, what distinguishes the Proletcult's constructivism from its modernist avatar is not so much that the former (supposedly) arose out of a revolutionary and collectivizing society and the latter out of still divided and hierarchical relations of production, though Frampton does hint at this difference. Rather, and again on Arendt's instigation, the fundamental issue turns out to be one of consumption. What Russian constructivism initially achieved, that is, and later was forced to abandon, was the liberation of objects from the automatic cycle of production and consumption, so that produced objects "now embod-ied the very content of life and its necessary objectification."[38] In effect, by relying on the Heideggerian Arendt and the early Marx, Frampton locates the disalienation of men in the disalienation of objects—a maneuver that turns the struggle over social power into the vaguer, left Hegelian, *cultural* demand that individuals be allowed to fulfill themselves, or recognize themselves, in the objects they make. The obvious shortcomings of such a position as social critique are precisely why Marx more or less abandoned it after 1844.

But it is this return to notions of spiritual and cultural alienation that in fact allows Frampton to hold on to a vision of disalienated objects—and, by extension, disalienated architectural form—even as he recognizes the Hobson's choice modernism left behind. That is, Frampton notes (correctly, I think) that the Proletcult program was simultaneously political, economic, and cultural; if in part constructivism failed because a "rhetoric of technique" was unwilling to give way to real economic struggle, the larger problem was surely the planned productivism of Leninist authority. But Frampton draws a curious lesson from this parable, so that when he turns to modernism, and to the present, it is again a cultural dilemma that emerges, and economic pro-duction *tout court*, rather than just the Leninist variety, becomes the enemy of liberated architecture. Thus, modernism's fracturing between "rigorous modern design" and "the world in which we live" is due to the fact that the former "presupposes . . . a state of scarcity or of homeostasis (where objects are not produced for the purpose of their instant consumption)," whereas the latter "remains in . . . a state where the possibilities of an unalienated culture have been vitiated either by bureaucratic loss of nerve in the East or by 'admass somnambulism' in the West"—that is, either "sterile orthodoxy" or "kitsch." While both choices clearly miss the mark for Frampton, the di-lemma is nevertheless posed as a struggle over *cultural* authenticity. Worse, such authenticity is by its very nature opposed not only to a centralized, au-thoritarian productivism, and a rationalized late capitalism, but seemingly to any notion of material or utilitarian productivity at all.

The real opposition haunting architecture ever since the Proletcult sud-denly reduces itself to this: the desire to produce things *without* a purpose, things *not* made for consumption (what Kant would have called the aesthetic), versus the commitment to "production as some ultimate end."[39] In simple terms, it is an opposition between art and utility, between what in Kant would be purposive without purpose and actually purposeful (if only with a gross simplification of Kant). But Frampton thus forsakes tensions like that between use and exchange value in Marx (tensions that hardly spare culture) for the more metaphysical debate between action as an end in itself (as in art) and "purposeful rational action," in Habermas's words. Somehow, Frampton returns to that atavistic home of architectural discourse (one later elaborated in Eisenman's postfunctional dialectic) where disalienated things valued for themselves alone—the aesthetics of built form again, it would appear—are constantly threatened by material social needs and demands. Having effectively transformed social struggle into the resistance to the degradation of objects, rather than identifying the latter merely as an effect, or sign, of the former, Frampton ends up in the awkward position of the conservative cultural critic. His problem is not, finally, unequal or restricted consumption, but rather too much or too rapid or too easy consumption—and it is here that kitsch returns in a most questionable way. What Frampton discovers at the heart of contemporary social problems is "an ideology of waste," and it is Arendt who again acts as muse: "In our need for more and more and more rapid replacement of the worldly things around us," she writes, "we can no longer afford to use them, to respect and preserve their inherent durability, we must consume, devour. . . ."[40] One can immediately see why Frampton would have been impressed by Arendt's words; she seems to be quoting Vitruvius himself.

Frampton does indeed call for participatory democracy at the end of his essay, but largely so that "our self-consuming ideology of waste will be overcome and architecture redeemed."[41] And in that subtle, perhaps even unnoticed, reversal, all of Frampton's good intentions collapse: it is not so much architectural practice that ought to insist on, and help redeem, participatory goals; it is the redemption of architecture, through the end of waste, that is at stake. Theodor Adorno's diagnosis is a cogent one: "Whenever cultural criticism complains of 'materialism,' it furthers the belief that the sin lies in man's desire for consumer goods, and not in the organization of the whole which withholds these goods from man: for the cultural critic, the sin is satiety, not hunger."[42] Frampton's essay is an important effort to break through architecture's self-conceived protective shell. But by relying on Arendt, and the Heideggerian phenomenology behind her, social conflict is reduced to a struggle over the quality—the "inherent durability"—of man-made goods, and this is in turn further reduced to the fight against indiscriminate consumption, use value, and "cyclical production." It is as if Frampton were actually suggesting that the real alternative to passively instrumental rationality is not a grander notion of historical Reason (as in most Frankfurt School thought), but instead precisely the scarcity that compels greater care (as in Heidegger's *Sorge*) for truly durable objects.

It would perhaps be an unfair exaggeration to suggest that in this essay Frampton only betrays nostalgia for a peasant and agrarian worldview. After all, in other contributions to *Oppositions* on the Ulm curriculum (no. 3) or on constructivism (no. 6), he remains more carefully focused on the ways the aesthetic, however much it may once have embodied a bourgeois *promesse de bonheur,* just as easily becomes a tool of modern repression. But the faint odor of conservative cultural critique in "Industrialization and the Crises in Architecture" should not simply be dismissed, for it in fact registers a more pervasive strain in the journal as a whole. Frampton's editorial "On Reading Heidegger" in *Oppositions* 4 (1974) illustrates the point. As before, Frampton surely frames his statement in terms of the necessary social interface architecture must recognize: in a world where famine coexists with land speculation, building is hardly a politically neutral act. "Autonomous artistic production certainly has many provinces but the task of *place creation,* in its broadest sense, is not one of them." In what would appear to be a progressive step, Frampton thus claims to reject the conventional opposition between artful architecture and mere building by adapting Mies's own synthetic term— *Baukunst,* the art of building—to a contemporary social agenda, to the "activation of the public sphere."

But these apparently positive gestures are embedded in a phenomenological rethinking (and remystification) of the notion of place that Frampton borrows from Heidegger, and with it many of the earlier difficulties return. For of course what finally defines *place* in an existential, rather than merely social, sense is "the act of significant containment." And it is that act that again appears to be the primary cultural value under assault. Hence, "we still indulge in the proliferation of roadside kitsch"; technocratic language testifies "to a fundamental break in our rapport with nature (including our own)"; and merely utilitarian production and waste are demonized anew. The specific social solution proposed—zero-growth "feedback loops of organic metabolism"—thus emphasizes the "rooted ecological nature" of any authentic sense of place. And Baukunst is now defined so that it is fundamentally linked "to that which Aldo van Eyck has already called the 'timelessness of man.'" In the midst of this Green vision of a more authentic relationship with the earth, architecture's mythic links with origins and foundations, with the ontological grounds of human being itself, are restored: "it ministers to the self-realization of man in nature." On such grounds, built form once again assumes its place as the "articulate realm" of "social meaning." Though Frampton may now call it Baukunst rather than autonomous art, architecture thus nevertheless regains its status as the ideal expression of timeless human nature beyond the contamination of degraded contemporary culture. The political arena of a public sphere has been collapsed into the "archetypal aspect" of place, and criticism evaporates into the mists of time.

The return to conservative cultural criticism in these essays, in spite of Frampton's better intentions, would be less troublesome if it were no more than an accidental slippage in his writings. But both Eisenman's brand of formalism, which openly enacts regression within its stated claims of progressive critique, and Frampton's antiproduction ethic, which returns to some atavistic household of the architectural soul at the moment it announces its commitment to a new future, have more troubling implications. The underlying movement of their ambivalent gestures is made explicit in two later and startlingly reactionary essays by Leon Krier: "The Consumption of Culture," *Oppositions* 14 (1978), and "Vorwärts, Kameraden, Wir Müssen Zurück (Forward, Comrades, We Must Go Back)," *Oppositions* 24 (1981). Krier's work here is a rather alarming Heideggerian reawakening of the latent fascism in all agrophilic technophobia. True, Krier's disturbing argument in the latter essay gets a rebuttle: Joan Ockman deftly demystifies a rhetoric of mythic place that makes Frampton's seem innocent. But what Ockman slights, both there and in her later history of the journal, is the degree to which Krier's appearance was unfortunately not inappropriate: it had been in preparation right from the beginning. Krier's title is in fact the slogan of a conservative cultural criticism the journal as a whole subtly promoted even as it labored to renounce the lineage. Ockman notes that "the fate of the avant-gardist magazine in a neo-conservative moment" is neatly allegorized by Phillipe Junod's final essay in the final issue, *Oppositions* 26 (1984), a historical discussion of ruins—"Future in the Past." What Ockman unfortunately fails to point out is that Junod's title accidentally marks more than the journal's fall away from its "revolutionist" beginnings. Implicit in the earlier essays of Eisenman and Frampton, and blatant in Krier's later essays, the avant-gardist rhetoric of *Oppositions* was always already implicated in the rear-guard politics it pretended to denounce.

▪ V.

Of course, there is much more than this to a journal that evolved through twenty-six issues: numerous essays on architectural history, special issues on particular figures like Le Corbusier (two issues, in fact) or topics like "Paris under the Academy: City and Ideology," publication of controversial documents, like essays by Russsian constructivists or by Philip Johnson from the 1930s. Indeed, the penultimate issue 25 (1982), "Monument/Memory," edited by Kurt Forster, seemed to indicate that a historical perspective had taken over by default. As I have implied throughout this essay, however, it was the central theoretical debates of *Oppositions*—as represented by its editors, to a large extent—that gave the journal its claim to difference and that signified its importance to the avant-gardist cultural life of New York in the 1970s and 1980s. Nevertheless, the late concern for a specifically monumentalist historiography (Riegl's work on cult values is reprinted in issue 25), like its periodic interest in cemeteries as the purest form of architectural semiotics, should not be considered an irony. For only rarely and briefly did the journal's critical debates break from the hegemony of traditional architectural history in any case. In *Oppositions* 2 (1974), Rosalind Krauss writes an essay on minimalist art that belongs there largely because it confirms the regressive tendency within the journal's avowedly oppositional perspective. Though she will insist, with no small rhetorical hauteur, on the supposedly radical notion of context rather than on the unity of a Cartesian viewing subject, Krauss predictably manages to reinscribe that context in purely formal terms as a phenomenological "gestalt-formation" that posits "meaning as a function of external space."[43] Krauss's discovery of "the profound reorientation of art and its meanings that begins with Minimalism" depends on the curious notion that something profound occurs when the viewer realizes that the meaning of a trapezoid—which really means whether it is seen as two- or three-dimensional—depends on how the viewer looks at it. One can easily see how profound such a reorientation of art must have appeared to the editors of *Oppositions* in the unsophisticated early 1970s! Krauss's essay, which begins with a discussion of Duchamp's *Fountain* of 1917 but does not mention architecture at all, is titled "The Fountainhead." Is it possible that Krauss, no Ayn Rand to be sure, but one who obviously knows a "profound reorientation" when she sees it, is making an unwitting comment on the false pretense to reorientation in the journal itself?

As long as architectural discourse takes false comfort from the idea that a reorientation of its self-understanding can be achieved through banalities like Kraussian gestalt-formations affecting the meaning of geometric shapes, it will remain trapped in a regressive self-infantilization. And it will seize on any high-sounding intellectual justification to stay in the nursery— indeed, to return, if possible, to the protective walls of the architectural womb (or tomb, which works almost as well) itself. As Daniel Libeskind writes in 1980, at the conclusion of an essay on Aldo Rossi that is a wondrous hodge-podge of most of the critical gestures noted above: "The radically changed milieu of 'modern architecture' is inextricably tied to the fate of abstraction. So different from its predecessors, it resonates with the premonition of a tautologous being: *an escape from things by virtue of going deeper into them."*[44] Although a psychoanalyst would be helpful in fully working through the rhetorical overdeterminations, one is perhaps not really necessary: from Mies's subservience in the Third Reich; to Venturi's inward-turning reaction to his own "growing ineffectualness"; to the parallel crusade in Eisenman, Agrest-Gandelsonas, and Dal Co to defend dame Architecture from the utilitarian, functionalist humanists; to Frampton's battle to preserve some natural place for Baukunst amid the degradation of industry and kitsch; to Krier's wholesale self-interment in the Mother Earth that presumably spawned him—the trajectory is clear enough. Libeskind's italicized phrase is, unfortunately, all too accurate when applied to the supposedly oppositional voices in architecture over the last thirty years. In the end, these voices testify to nothing less than a massive (largely male) fantasy, a ubiquitous fear of sociocultural castration that played itself out in the critical rhetoric of an architectural avant-garde and that hardly seems to have been exhausted. Peter Eisenman's recent discovery of a new critical idea—Gianni Vattimo's *pensiero debole*—promises at least one more round of the same.[45]

In his own complex and difficult attempt to demystify the aura of the aesthetic, "The Work of Art in the Age of Mechanical Reproduction," Walter Benjamin makes a surprising comparison: he likens the new medium of cinema, which for him signifies in itself the destruction of the aura of art, to architecture. For Benjamin, "architecture has always represented the prototype of a work of art the reception of which is consummated by a collectivity in a state of distraction."[46] As such, architecture, that form appropriated both "by use and by perception . . . by touch and sight," is cinema's precursor in the redefinition of art on political grounds. For while "perception" might suggest the old aesthetic ideal of contemplative absorption—"the attentive concentration of a tourist before a famous building"—and hence an auratic presence that Benjamin denounces as latently fascistic, "use" for him is something appropriated only by habit. In habitual use, the cult value of an object recedes precisely because such use, like the cinema, puts the public in the position of the critic, a position which "requires no attention. The public is an examiner, but an absent-minded one."[47] And because use is appropriated only by habit, it can also be appropriated by politics.

Surely, Benjamin was as myopically positive about architecture's past as he would turn out to be about cinema's future. But what did he mean, after all, by architecture's complicity with "reception in distraction," and should it still matter? It is hardly a transparent phrase, but the larger context of Benjamin's essay implies, I think, something like the following: attentive, contemplative perception will always be easily returned to the auratic cult values underlying it and will thereby always contribute to the culturally reactionary project of aestheticizing reality. But what then is the alternative, "reception in distraction"? It is, I would suggest, for Benjamin nothing more than the absent-minded relation of a worker to the tools of a trade—a relationship valuable only in habitual use, a relationship always subject to critical examination, but never contemplative or auratic. The implication is an obvious, if grandly optimistic one. In the midst of a social upheaval that had more or less eviscerated any hope that a worker's consciousness might emerge to save the day, Benjamin looked elsewhere. In the cinema, perhaps, he thought he could see the beginnings of a cultural development that would transform all regressive worship from afar into the "tactile" habits and demands of a collective; the cult of the Führer would be dissipated, simply put, by the right of ordinary people to touch, to use, and yes, perhaps even to throw away when no longer of service.

My claim here is not that architectural discourse should merely embrace Benjamin's perspective. It is in many ways a vision born of the despair that any more practical opposition to existing social tendencies had evaporated. Today, it would be anachronistic, at the very least, to turn to cinema and architecture as if these would be able to "mobilize the masses," in Benjamin's now quaint phrase. In any case, given the recent fate of *Oppositions,* the grand scope of Benjamin's remarks is surely the last thing architectural discourse should be asked to imitate. But there is something crucial in the distinctions Benjamin draws that is still worth reflecting upon. If architecture, as a discipline, ever hopes to cut through the various ideologies that continue to maintain its symbolic capital, its aura, it will have to take seriously the fact that architecture is embedded in the habitual utility of social relations, that it is precisely those social relations that finally give meaning to all built form. Whatever its pretensions otherwise, architecture will *always* serve some function, for someone, and will do so in the context of already existing social struggles among classes, races, genders, and other social groupings over the control of social space and the right to make use of it. It is in the end a rather simple question—who benefits?—that all the avant-garde rhetoric in *Oppositions* never seemed willing to ask.

1. Robert Gutman, *Architectural Practice* (Princeton, N.J.: Princeton Architectural Press, 1988), p. 69.
2. See Theodor Adorno, "Cultural Criticism and Society," in *Prisms*, trans. Samuel and Shierry Weber (Cambridge, Mass.: MIT Press, 1984), p. 23. For a related perspective on contemporary architecture, see Diane Ghirardo, "The Deceit of Postmodern Architecture," in *After the Future: Postmodern Times and Places*, ed. Gary Shapiro (New York: State Univ. of New York, 1990), pp. 231–52.
3. Published in *Die Form* 13 (1 August 1930), p. 406; quoted in Philip Johnson, Mies van der Rohe (New York: Museum of Modern Art, 1947), p. 190. See Elaine Hochman's important discussion of this episode, "Confrontation: 1933. Mies van der Rohe and the Third Reich," *Oppositions* 18 (1979), pp. 49–59, and her more extended treatment of the topic in *Architects of Fortune: Mies van der Rohe and the Third Reich* (New York: Weidenfeld and Nicolson, 1989).
4. Robert Venturi, *Complexity and Contradiction in Architecture* (New York: Museum of Modern Art, 1966; second edition, 1977), p. 14.
5. Ibid., p. 13.
6. Ibid., p. 20.
7. Ibid., p. 17. For Pound's quotations, see *Make It New* (London: Faber and Faber, 1934) and his letter to William Carlos Williams,

21 October 1908, in *Ezra Pound: A Critical Anthology*, ed. J. P. Sullivan (Harmondsworth, England: Penguin, 1970), p. 35.
8. Venturi, *Complexity and Contradiction*, p. 16.
9. Friedrich von Schiller, *On the Aesthetic Education of Man*, trans. Reginald Snell (New York: Ungar, 1983), p. 74.
10. "Tradition and the Individual Talent," *Selected Prose of T. S. Eliot*, ed. Frank Kermode (New York: Harcourt Brace Jovanovich, 1975), p. 39.
11. Venturi, *Complexity and Contradiction*, p. 16.
12. "Teoria 'formalnovo metoda,'" *Literatura: Teoriya, kritika, polemika* (Leningrad, 1927); quoted from "The Theory of the 'Formal Method,'" in *Russian Formalist Criticism*, trans. Lee T. Lemon and Marion J. Reis (Lincoln, Neb.: Univ. of Nebraska, 1965), p. 136.
13. "Iskusstvo, kak priyom," *Sborniki*, II (1917); quoted from *Russian Formalist Criticism*, p. 12.
14. For Tomashevsky's phrase, see "Tematika," *Teoriya literatury [Theory of Literature]* (Leningrad, 1925); translated, in part, as "Thematics," in *Russian Formalist Criticism*, p. 95. See also Kristeva's early essays, such as those collected in *Desire in Language: A Semiotic Approach to Literature and Art* (New York: Columbia Univ., 1980).

15. A brief history of the journal has been provided by a consultant and associate editor from number 7 on, Joan Ockman, in "Resurrecting the Avant-Garde: The History and Program of *Oppositions*," in *Revisions: Papers on Architectural Theory and Criticism, Vol. II: Architectureproduction* (New York: Princeton Architectural Press, 1988), pp. 181–99.
16. *Oppositions* 1 (1973), Editorial Statement.
17. Quoted in Ockman, "Resurrecting the Avant-Garde," p. 194, from the French review *A.M.C.: Architecture Mouvement Continuité.*
18. *Oppositions* 9 (1977), p. 2. K. Michael Hays, in "Reproduction and Negation: The Cognitive Project of the Avant-Garde," in *Revisions, Vol. II*, pp. 152–79, addresses such issues in relation to the complicity between the modernist avant-garde's progressive deconstruction of bourgeois subjectivity and its regressive "affirmation of the structure of totalitarian society" when it remains on "the terrain of architecture" (p. 179).
19. *Oppositions* 2 (1974), Editorial Statement.
20. *Oppositions* 3 (1974), Editorial Statement.
21. *Oppositions* 1 (1973), pp. 1–26.
22. Ibid., p. 23.
23. *Oppositions* 6 (1976), Editorial.
24. See Louis Althusser, "Ideology and Ideological State Apparatuses," in *Lenin and Philosophy and Other*

Essays, trans. Ben Brewster (New York: Monthly Review Press, 1971), p. 162; and Karl Marx and Friedrich Engels, *The German Ideology,* Part I, ed. C. J. Arthur (New York: International, 1977), pp. 6667.

25. See Boris Eichenbaum, "The Theory of the 'Formal Method,'" *Russian Formalist Criticism,* p. 135.

26. *Oppositions* 1 (1973), p. 94.

27. See, for example, Julia Kristeva, *La Révolution du langage poétique* (Paris: Seuil, 1974).

28. *Oppositions* 1 (1973), p. 97.

29. Ibid., p. 98.

30. Ibid., p. 99.

31. Ockman, "Resurrecting the Avant-Garde," pp. 198–99.

32. "L'Architecture dans le Boudoir: The Language of Criticism and the Criticism of Language," *Oppositions* 3 (1974), p. 48.

33. "'European Graffiti.' Five x Five — Twenty-five," *Oppositions* 5 (1976), p. 57.

34. "The Historical 'Project,'" *Oppositions* 17 (1979), p. 73.

35. Tafuri's earlier *Architecture and Utopia: Design and Capitalist Development,* trans. Barbara Luigia La Penta (Cambridge, Mass.: MIT Press, 1976), provides an admirable—and still rather solitary—critique of form and radical architecture in a social context. See also the more recent *History of Italian Architecture, 1944–1985* (Cambridge, Mass.: MIT Press, 1988). For a critique of Tafuri, see Fredric Jameson, "Architecture and the Critique of Ideology," in *Revisions, Vol. I: Architecture Criticism Ideology* (Princeton, N.J.: Princeton Architectural Press, 1985), pp. 51–87.

36. *Oppositions* 1 (1973), p. 59.

37. Ibid., p. 67.

38. Ibid., p. 73.

39. Ibid., p. 78.

40. Ibid., p. 78.

41. Ibid., pp. 79–80.

42. "Cultural Criticism and Society," *Prisms,* pp. 24–25.

43. *Oppositions* 2 (1974), p. 69.

44. *Oppositions* 21 (1980), p. 20.

45. Eisenman's recent discovery of Vattimo and "weak thought" was evident, for example, in his presentation to a conference titled "Postmodernism and Beyond: Architecture as the Critical Art of Contemporary Culture," held at the University of California, Irvine, 26–28 October 1989. See Vattimo's *The End of Modernity,* trans. Jon Snyder (Baltimore: John Hopkins Univ. Press, 1989).

46. *Illuminations,* trans. Harry Zohn (New York: Schocken, 1978), p. 239.

47. Ibid., pp. 240–41.

The Infinite Game:

Redeveloping Downtown L.A.

Mike Davis

On warm evenings, the homeless men who live furtively in the wastelands of Crown Hill like to set up old car seats and broken chairs under the scorched palms to watch the spectacle of dusk over downtown Los Angeles. They have ringside seats to enjoy the nightly illumination of 26 million square feet of prime corporate real estate, half of it built in the last decade. This incomparable light show and the plight of the homeless themselves are the chief legacies of a generation of urban redevelopment. Thanks to over a billion dollars of public subsidies and diverted tax revenues, the "suburbs in search of a city" have finally found what they were looking for.

Despite Reyner Banham's disparaging 1971 "note" (". . . because that is all downtown Los Angeles deserves") that it had become irrelevant, the center has held after all.[1] Indeed, since the arrival of Pacific Rim capital in the early 1980s, downtown Los Angeles has grown at virtual warp speed. The stylized crown on the top of Maguire Thomas's overweening new skyscraper, the seventy-three-story First Interstate World Center, symbolizes the climax of redevelopment in the new financial core from Bunker Hill to South Park. Meanwhile, on every side of the existing corporate citadel, panzer divisions of bulldozers and wrecking cranes are clearing the way for a doubling or tripling of downtown office space in the 1990s. The desolate flanks of Crown Hill itself (the Cinderella stepsister of Bunker Hill, across the Harbor Freeway) will become another glowing forest of office towers and high-rise apartments in a few years. And the homeless, their ranks swollen by the displaced from the redeveloped "West Bank," will probably be watching the nighttime special effects from Elysian Park or beyond.

The terrible beauty struggling to be born downtown is usually called growth, but it is neither a purely natural metabolism (as neoliberals imagine the marketplace to be) nor an enlightened volition (as politicians and planners like to claim). Rather it is better conceptualized as a vast game—a relentless competition between privileged players (or alliances of players) in which the state intervenes much like a card-dealer or croupier to referee the play. Urban design, embodied in different master plans and project visions, provides malleable rules for the key players, as well as a set of boundaries to exclude unauthorized play. But unlike most games, there is no winning gambit or final move. Downtown redevelopment is an essentially infinite game, played not toward any conclusion or closure, but toward its own endless protraction. The Central City Association's fairy-tale imagery of Downtown 2020 as a cluster of "urban villages" offering Manhattanized lifestyles and pleasures is bunk for the hicks.[2] Downtown's only authentic, deep vision is the same as any casino's: to keep the roulette wheels turning.

■ How the Game Started

Certain primordial facts organize the playing of the game. Above all, there is the ghost of sunk capital: a large part of the spoils of the suburban speculations of the early twentieth century—the subdivision of Hollywood and the Valley—were invested in downtown high-rise real estate in the 1900–1925 period. But these investments (including the legendary patrimonies of the Chandlers, Lankershims, and Hellmans) were almost immediately imperiled by the revolutionary tendency of the automobile to disperse retail and office functions.[3] The old-guard elite resisted this decentralization (represented in the 1920s by the rise of Wilshire Boulevard as a "linear downtown") by marshaling an ironic municipal socialism on behalf of the central business district.[4]

The first priority of this "recentering" crusade, led by the *Los Angeles Times* and the Central Business District Association (CBDA) (later Downtown Businessmen's Association, then Central City Association [CCA]), was to reinforce the concentration of civic life within the core. Thus the public-private initiatives that constructed the Biltmore Hotel and Memorial Coliseum in the 1920s were followed in successive decades by the creation of the Civic Center, Dodger Stadium, the Music Center, and the Convention Center.[5]

At the same time, the CBDA also mobilized to ensure the continuing centralization of the region's major traffic flows around downtown. Redistributing

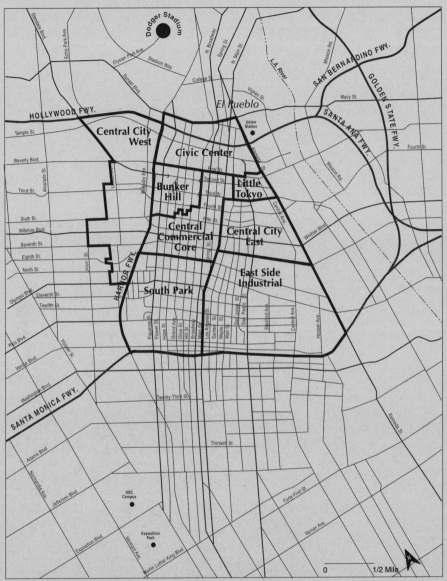

Source: CRA/LA . February 1990

View of Bunker Hill
from Third Street,
Los Angeles, 1963.
(William Reagh)

Same view,
Los Angeles, 1986.
(William Reagh)

tax revenue from the periphery to the center, the city subsidized a heroic program of transportation improvements. The Los Angeles River was bridged by a series of magnificent viaducts (1920–40), downtown streets were widened and tunneled through Bunker Hill, the centralizing Major Traffic Street Plan was adopted (1924), rail commuters were taken underground through Crown Hill in a "Hollywood Subway" (to the profit of the Chandlers and other investors in the Subway Terminal Building at Fourth and Hill) (1925), and the main rail lines were finally persuaded to consolidate in a Union Station (1937–39).[6] Repeated campaigns by downtown business groups to recapitalize and grade-separate the electric railroad and streetcar system (as well as extend it via monorail into the San Fernando Valley) were successfully opposed between 1920 and 1970 by suburban commercial interests.[7] With the support of city engineer Lloyd Aldrich and the Southern California Automobile Club, however, downtown forces were successful in persuading the state highway division to accept a radial freeway grid that minimized "the destructive aspects of decentralization" and eventually made downtown the hub of eight freeways.[8]

The recentering of L.A. is even better envisioned, however, as a succession of social struggles between different interest groups, classes, and communities. If downtown landowners have always been pitted against the developers of Wilshire Boulevard and suburban retail and, later, office centers (now veritable outer cities), there is also a bitter legacy of resentment among San Fernando Valley homeowners, who believe that their tax dollars have been confiscated to improve downtown. But most of all, downtown has been "defended" at the expense of the working-class communities on its immediate periphery. An estimated fifty thousand residents—Chinese, Mexican, and Black—were displaced to make way for such "improvements" as Union Station, Dodger Stadium, the Civic Center, industrial expansion east of Alameda, central business district (CBD) redevelopment on Bunker Hill, city and county jails, and especially, the eight freeways (always carefully routed to remove homes not industry). Chronicling the story of downtown's land grabs and land-use dumping east of the river, Rodolfo Acuna talks about a "community under a thirty-year siege."[9]

For a few years in the early postwar period, however, downtown boosters had to face the challenge of an ambitious housing program that aimed to reconstruct, rather than displace, the working-class neighborhoods next to downtown. Mayor Fletcher Bowron, supported by the Congress of Industrial Organizations (CIO) and civil-rights organizations, signed a contract with the federal government, under the Housing Act of 1949, to "make Los Angeles the first slum-free city in the nation" by building ten thousand public housing units in areas like Chavez Ravine and, potentially, Bunker Hill. The Los Angeles Community Redevelopment Agency was established under state law to assist in the assemblage of land for this purpose. The vision of a stabilized, decently housed downtown residential fringe roused vehement opposition, however, from CBD landowners. Bowron and public housing were defeated by hysterical red-baiting orchestrated by the *Los Angeles Times* and police chief William Parker in 1953.[10] Anything that even smacked of a socialistic rehousing strategy was henceforth excluded from discussions of downtown renewal.

■ Early Game Plans

Infrastructural improvement alone, however—even in tandem with Cold War politics—could not prevent the relative decline of downtown. Postwar Los Angeles continued to trade its old hub-and-spoke form for a new, decentralized urban geometry. Although downtown remained the financial as well as governmental center of Southern California through the early 1960s, it inexorably saw its retail customers emigrate outward along Wilshire Boulevard and eventually toward dozens of suburban shopping centers. Moreover, by 1964, as plans were completed to create Century City—a "downtown" for Los Angeles's Westside—out of an old movie lot, the historic headquarters role of the central business district was suddenly put to question as well.

Embattled downtown landowners were virtually unanimous that the CBD's great competitive disadvantage—even more than the age of its building stock (circa 1900–1930)—was the growing accumulation of so-called blight along Main Street (Skid Row) and in the old Victorian neighborhood of Bunker

Hill.[11] The Hill, in fact, was a double obstacle, physically cutting off the Pershing Square focus of the business district from the Civic Center as well as preventing the district from expanding westward. Public discussion became riveted on images of dereliction, ignoring the simple fact that most of the Hill's eleven thousand inhabitants were, in fact, productive downtown employees: dishwashers, waiters, elevator operators, janitors, garment workers, and so on. The role of city government in the redevelopment of the Hill had already been extensively debated before 1940. In 1925, Allied Architects, denouncing the Hill as "an unsightly landmark . . . blocking business expansion to the west and north," envisioned rebuilding it as a "civic acropolis" of parks and public buildings.[12] In contrast, C. C. Bigelow simply wanted to obliterate the Hill by leveling it to the Hill Street grade, and engineer William Babcock in 1931 proposed a less drastic regrading to buckle the new Civic Center to Pershing Square.[13] Despite considerable political support, both the Allied Architects and Babcock schemes were defeated, and by 1938, the city council threw in the towel to let "the natural forces of economics do the job."[14]

The Bunker Hill debate resumed after World War II with the advent of Greater Los Angeles Plans, Inc. (GLAPI), sponsored by an elite group that included Norman Chandler and Asa Call (often described by his contemporaries as L.A.'s "Mr. Big"). GLAPI actually bought land on Bunker Hill for a music center, but found its plans thwarted by the reluctance of voters to approve the necessary bond issue (even with a sports arena appended). In the meantime, market forces were given a chance to transform Bunker Hill. An early 1950s insurance-company scheme to build upscale apartment towers on the Hill (along the lines of Park LaBrea on Wilshire) never managed to get beyond its directors' anxieties about investing in downtown L.A. A few years later, GLAPI believed that it had convinced Union Oil to build its new headquarters on Bunker Hill, but at the last moment, the corporation instead chose Crown Hill.[15] In light of these failures, piecemeal private-sector redevelopment of Bunker Hill was abandoned.

Instead, the Community Redevelopment Agency (CRA)—in original intention an ally of public housing—became simultaneously the largest developer downtown and the collective instrument of all the developers. Classically, like other regulatory agencies, it was captured by the very interests it was supposed to regulate. Its mayorally appointed board of seven was ideally shielded from direct public scrutiny or electoral responsibility. Moreover, it possessed autonomous financial authority, based on the use of diverted tax increments. After the failure of various private initiatives, the CRA undertook to wrest the entirety of Bunker Hill from its slumlords by invoking eminent domain. The city council approved the final plan for Bunker Hill in spring 1959, and within eighteen months, bulldozers began demolishing the Hill's Gothic mansions and Queen Anne tenements.

The Hill's population, meanwhile, was simply dumped into other downtown areas. Although some ended up on Skid Row, most of the ten thousand ex–Bunker Hill residents were displaced to the west bank of the Harbor Freeway, driving a salient of "blight" and rackrenting across the Temple-Beaudry area well into the fashionable Westlake district. Twenty years passed before the CRA bothered to establish a fund to rebuild the quarter of downtown housing units it abolished in this single stroke.[16]

While the CRA was clearing, regrading, and assembling Bunker Hill into parcels suited for sale to developers, the major downtown stakeholders (organized as the Central City Committee [CCC]) were working for CRA chairman William Sesnon and city planners to create a master plan "to bring about the rebirth of [the entire] Central City." The 1964 plan, titled *Centropolis,* was the first comprehensive design for redevelopment: the product of a series of studies that had begun with an economic survey of downtown in 1960.

Its core vision was the linkage of new development on Bunker Hill with the revitalization of the fading financial district along Spring Street and the retail core along Broadway and Seventh Street. Pershing Square, still envisioned as the center of downtown, was to be modernized with a large underground parking lot, the beginning of Wilshire Boulevard was to be anchored with a dramatic Wilshire Gateway, and El Pueblo de Los Angeles around Olvera Street was to be completed.

The outstanding innovation of the plan, however, was a proposal to link the major structures in the retail core by means of mid-block malls, with pedestrian circulation lifted above the street on "pedways." This superstructure

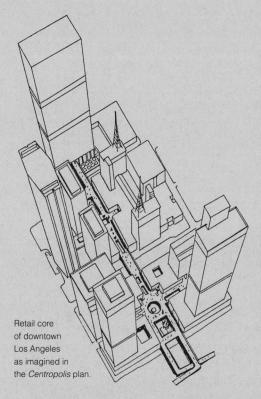

Retail core
of downtown
Los Angeles
as imagined in
the *Centropolis* plan.

would unify prime property, old and new, into a single, vast downtown mall. At the same time, it addressed department store concerns about an enhanced definition of social areas and the insulation of shoppers from "bums." Indeed the "rollback" of Skid Row was one of the plan's major objectives. The idea was to deploy new or augmented land uses, including parking lots, a low-cost shopping precinct, and a light industrial strip along Main and Los Angeles streets, to create an effective buffer zone between Skid Row and the born-again CBD.[17]

Just a year after the premiere of *Centropolis,* the Watts rebellion and the attendant white backlash almost completely vitiated the plan and the seven years of planning that had gone into it. The flames of August 1965 had crept to within a few blocks of downtown's southern perimeter, causing the establishment to lose its nerve. The McCone Commission predicted "that by 1990 the core of the Central City of Los Angeles will be inhabited almost exclusively by more than 1,200,000 Negroes," and the Los Angeles Police Department (LAPD) warned downtown merchants against an "imminent gang invasion" by Black youth ("when encountered in groups of more than two they are very dangerous and armed").[18] Faced with such specters, mortgage bankers and leasing agents started talking about a wholesale corporate defection to Century City and the Westside, even the "death of downtown."[19] As a result, landowners and financiers jettisoned the central tenet of the *Centropolis* plan—the renovation of the historic core—and began to vote with their feet: leaving the Broadway–Spring Street corridor to decline and fall.

■ The *Silverbook* Rules

In the midst of crisis and flight, the Central City Association rallied to save downtown by reinventing it. Rejecting as inadequate the 1969 CBD plan prepared by city planning director Calvin Hamilton, the CCA established its own planning committee, the Committee for Central City Planning, Inc. (CCCP) ("a who's who of business power"), in substantial continuity with the tradition and membership of both Greater Los Angeles Plans, Inc., and the Central City Committee.[20] With the CCCP and the city contributing $250,000 each, an eminent planning firm, Wallace, McHarg, Roberts and Todd of Philadelphia, was hired to create a new urban design for the post-Watts reality.

The firm's *Central City L.A., 1972–1990* became universally known as the *Silverbook* because of its striking metallic cover. Replacing the dead letter of *Centropolis,* it adumbrated the political and design principles that have guided downtown to the edge of the 1990s. For the purposes of analysis, these guidelines can be divided into two orders of importance: "dogmas" and "gadgets."

The dogmas, outlined below, gave new directions to the redevelopment process and established far-reaching goals for public-private cooperation.

1. First, the *Silverbook* categorically reasserted (*contra*-Banham) that downtown was *the center* of the Los Angeles metropolitan area. As Robert Meyers pointed out at the time, this directly contradicted planning director Hamilton's laboriously constructed "Centers Concept"—the keynote of a city master plan emphasizing polycentric development and the equality of major growth poles.[21]

2. The *Silverbook* also proposed a dramatic enlargement of the Community Redevelopment Agency's scale of planning and tax-increment authority to include virtually all of downtown between Alameda Street (on the east) and the Harbor (on the west), Hollywood (on the north), and Santa Monica (on the south) freeways.

3. The defense of the old office core was abandoned in favor of *re-siting* downtown a few blocks further west in the frontier being cleared by the CRA on Bunker Hill and along Figueroa between Fifth and Eighth streets.[22] This was in essence a disguised corporate bailout using diverted tax monies. The

chief role of the CRA was envisioned as *recycling* land value from old to new, as discounts on greenfield parcels (together with rapid appreciation after building) compensated stakeholders for the depreciation of their obsolete properties in the old core.

4. The new *growth axis* (supplanting the Wilshire-Seventh Street-West direction of the last wave of prewar downtown building) was established along Figueroa and Grand, integrated at one end with the Civic Center and pointing toward the University of Southern California (USC) at the other. The luxury apartment community on Bunker Hill was to be counteranchored at redevelopment's prospective southern frontier by a South Park Urban Village. This envisioned southward flow of downtown fortuitously coincided with the personal strategy of CCA president and Occidental Insurance executive Earl Clark, who had erected a solitary skyscraper (today the Transamerica Center) at Olive and Twelfth streets, almost a mile south of the center of new high-rise construction. The *Silverbook* plan, if implemented, would bring downtown and soaring land values to Clark's speculative outpost.

5. Even while rotating the axis of redevelopment ninety degrees from the west to the south, *Silverbook* premised its downtown renaissance upon the coordinated construction of a new rapid-transit infrastructure (Metro Rail) along the Wilshire corridor (with an ancillary line running toward South-Central L.A.—Light Rail). At the same time, the neighborhoods immediately west of downtown, across the Harbor Freeway, were reserved as a periphery for parking and CBD services.

6. *Silverbook* amended the conventional corporate-center vision of *Centropolis* to what might be called the post–Watts rebellion corporate-fortress strategy. Rather than creating a pedestrian superstructure to unify the old and new in a single mall-like configuration as in the *Centropolis* plan, new investment was now massively segregated from old. In the CRA's actual practice—more drastic than the model—pedestrian access to Bunker Hill was deliberately removed, Angels Flight (the Hill's picturesque funicular railroad) was dismantled, and Hill Street, once a vital boulevard, became a glacis separating the decaying traditional business district from the new construction zone.

7. Skid Row, circumscribed and buffered in *Centropolis,* was now scheduled for elimination, thus freeing up "Central City East" for redevelopment as a "joint university communications center and extension school."

In addition to these strategic dogmas, the *Silverbook* unveiled a number of gadgets to make the new downtown cohere in an efficient working order. Most important was the proposed "people-mover" to distribute office workers and shoppers from mass transit terminals, across the broad spaces of Bunker Hill megastructures, to individual buildings, and then, southward, to "South Park Village."[23] Similarly, the elevated, grade-separated pedways of the *Centropolis* plan were reintroduced in Bunker Hill as a preferred option to street-level pedestrian circulation. A second-level plaza and pedway complex ("Bunker Hill East"), again copied from the previous plan, was envisioned as a "five-way, 'pivotal interface'" connecting Bunker Hill, above street level, with the Civic Center, Little Tokyo, "Central City East" (the reclaimed Skid Row), and a corner of North Broadway. Downzoning was proposed throughout the central commercial core (excluding Bunker Hill) to create a "development rights bank" to be allotted or auctioned off according to priorities defined by a prospective Specific Plan. Finally, *Silverbook* had a whole toolchest of miscellaneous gadgets—ranging from a downtown industrial freeway to an intown industrial park—to stimulate new investment in the industrial salient between Los Angeles and Alameda streets.

The political translation of the *Silverbook* concepts into a legally valid blueprint for the CRA—Central Business District Redevelopment Plan[24]—encountered unexpected opposition. Although only Ernani Bernardi opposed passage of the plan through the fifteen-member city council in July 1975, the dissident councilman was soon reinforced by powerful allies, including the county board of supervisors, the county assessor, and state senator Alan Robbins, a mayoral aspirant from the Valley.[25] They joined Bernardi in suing the council to prevent the CRA from diverting billions of dollars of future tax increments (the increase of assessments due to redevelopment) from general-fund uses. As the debate grew increasingly nasty, the CRA and its council supporters (backed by new mayor Tom Bradley) argued that the increments were essential to renewing growth and jobs downtown, whereas the opponents insisted that a handful of large property owners—led by Security Pacific Bank, Prudential Life Insurance, and the Times Mirror Company—stood to reap a windfall at public expense. In the end, before the CBD plan was allowed to take effect, Bernardi and the county forced the CRA (in 1977) to accept a consent decree *capping* the tax-increment bond-issuing capacity of the project at $750 million.

Meanwhile the CRA bureaucracy itself, under commission chairman Kurt Meyer (a well-known L.A. architect) and administrator Edward Helfeld, balked at the CCA's demand that the agency implement the *Silverbook* to the letter. Wallace, McHarg proposals for a large lake in South Park and the university complex on Skid Row were rejected as "unfeasible" (privately, the CRA thought them "preposterous"), and Meyer and Helfeld took a principled stand against a Charles Luckman scheme to move the central public library to Broadway to serve as a buffer between Latino small businesses and the remnant upscale shopping precinct on Seventh Street.[26] Most of all, they railed against the CCCP's attempt to perpetuate itself as the CRA's "shadow government." Although the CCA, under the urging of Franklin Murphy of Times Mirror, ultimately wound down its parallel planning arm, downtown leaders did not forget, or forgive, the disobedience of Meyer and Helfeld. After Meyer resigned (officially to return to his busy architectural practice), he was replaced by a consummate wheeler-dealer and CCA ally, construction trades' spokesman Jim Wood. A few years later, the CCA combined forces with Helfeld foes on the planning commission and city council to purge the controversial CRA administrator.

■ Japan Ups the Ante

Having cleared the initial hurdle of political opposition, however, the central business district plan still had to prove that it could command the requisite levels of investment from private developers. The *Silverbook* had coincided with the epochal transition in city hall from Sam Yorty to Bradley, and the downtown old guard was initially skeptical of what to expect from Los Angeles's first Black mayor with his coterie of South-Central ministers and wealthy Westside liberals. But Bradley, as his biographers emphasize, took great pains from the very beginning to conciliate the powerful downtown interests. Moreover, in the latter part of his first term, a vice arrest—which most insiders believed was set up—led to the dismissal of Maury Weiner, his liberal chief deputy and *bête noire* of conservative critics. Weiner's replacement, to the chagrin of liberals, was a Pasadena Republican, Ray Remy (later head of the Los Angeles Chamber of Commerce). The new deputy mayor was instrumental in consolidating the rapprochement between the mayor and the Central City Association. Indeed Bradley, supported by the powerful building-trades wing of the local labor movement, became an aggressive proponent of the CBD plan and the strategy outlined in the CCA's *Silverbook*.[27]

With city hall (and a city council majority) routinely approving every request of the developers' lobby (or abdicating power to the CRA), new capital was encouraged to flow into downtown's greenfields. If there were just five new high rises above the old earthquake limit of thirteen floors in 1975, there are now fifty. Moreover, as the game picked up pace, purely speculative trading also increased, with perhaps a third of downtown changing hands between 1976 and 1982. Ironically, as the ante has risen, many of the original champions of downtown renewal, including large regional banks and oil companies with troubled cash flow, have had to cash in their equity and withdraw to the sidelines. As Volckerism first created a super-dollar and then destroyed it, the volatile commercial real estate markets around the country favored highly liquid investors and foreign capital.

Downtown simply became too big for local interests to dominate. Thus in 1979 the *Times* reported that a quarter of downtown's major properties were foreign-owned; six years later the figure was revised to 75 percent (one authority has even claimed 90 percent).[28] The first wave of foreign investment in the late 1970s, as in Manhattan, was led by Canadian real estate capital, epitomized by Toronto-based Olympia and York. The Reichmann clan, which owns Olympia and York, collects skyscrapers like the mere rich collect rare stamps or Louis XIV furniture. Yet since 1984, they, along with the New York insurance companies and British banks, have been swamped by a *tsunami* of Asian finance and flight capital.

What the Japanese call *zaitech*, the strategy of using financial technologies to shift cash flow from production to speculation, has radically restructured downtown's investment portfolios and given a new impetus to the realization of the CBD redesign (indeed, become its major motive force). As the super-yen and foreign protectionism slowed domestic industrial reinvestment in Japan, giant corporations and trading companies shifted black ink abroad in search of lucrative foreign assets. The liquid resources of other investors have simply been dwarfed by the sheer mass of the Japanese trade surplus, which has rapidly found its way from U.S. treasury bonds to prime real estate. In the particular case of downtown Los Angeles, the super-yen of the late 1980s put the skyscrapers along Figueroa's "gold coast" at rummage-sale discounts compared to Tokyo real estate. A virtually unknown condominium developer, Shuwa Company Ltd., stunned the downtown establishment in 1986 by purchasing nearly $1 billion of L.A.'s new skyline, including the twin-towered ARCO Plaza, in a single two-and-a-half-month buying spree. As local real estate analysts complained at the time, "the major Japanese companies are borrowing at very cheap rates, usually 5% or less. They borrow in Japan [in Shuwa's case, through ten L.A. branches of Tokyo banks], deduct it from their taxes in Japan, convert it to dollars, and invest in dollars in the United States."[29]

In singing praise to the miracle of the Pacific Rim economy, Los Angeles boosters in the 1980s generally avoided reference to the specific mechanism of the downtown boom. But, to the extent that Japanese capital was now the major player, the downtown economy had become illicitly dependent upon the continuation of the structural imbalance that recycled U.S. deficits as foreign speculation in American assets. In a word, it had become addicted to U.S. losses in the world trade war, and bank towers on Bunker Hill were rising almost in direct proportion to plant closings in East Los Angeles and elsewhere in the nation. The downtown renaissance had become a perverse monument to deindustrialization.

■ The State of Play

But the ironies of international geopolitics were scarcely noted by the Community Redevelopment Agency. Its concern was, rather, that the very success of downtown redevelopment was imperiling the agency's *raison d'être.* By 1989–90, the CRA, working hand-in-glove with offshore capital, had reached the limits of the 1977 Bernardi cap, endangering its hegemony in the central business district and setting off a complex process of plan redesign and political negotiation. Before analyzing this new conjuncture, however, it is first necessary to draw upon a notional balance-sheet of redevelopment in the fifteen years since the creation of the CBD project. To what extent has the grand design, à la *Silverbook,* actually been realized, and how has it been further modified?

First, there have been some strategic setbacks. Skid Row, slated for demolition (or deinstitutionalization, in the Orwellian language of the *Silverbook*), has survived, however infernally, largely as the result of council members' fear of the spillover of the homeless into their districts. This has led Little Tokyo to expand eastward, along First Street toward the Los Angeles River, rather than southward as expected. And despite the deliberate siting of the Jewelry Mart on its eastern margin, the redevelopment of Pershing Square (a subsidiary goal of the *Silverbook*) languishes two decades behind schedule, with street people in occupation of the park and the developers squabbling among themselves. As a result, the Biltmore Hotel, in designing its recent tower annex, rotated its main entrance 180 degrees to face the library—the new focal point of downtown. (The library, in turn, was left in place, *contra* earlier plans, because its air rights were used to add density on the huge Maguire Thomas projects across the street.)

More serious still are the transportation anomalies in the realized downtown design. In the *Silverbook,* the viability of the new downtown depended upon the articulation of Wilshire-axis mass transit with a pedestrian distribution system along the new Figueroa corridor. Although those in the CRA talk wistfully of reviving the scheme, federal funding for the people-mover—a proposed $250-million system of airportlike moving sidewalks—was vetoed by the Reagan administration after heavy lobbying by opponents from the San Fernando Valley. This has marooned pedestrians in the various megastructures downtown and left a useless $30-million people-mover tunnel underneath Bunker Hill.[30]

The fate of Metro Rail has been stranger still. After loud protests from Westside homeowners, Metro Rail was diverted from Wilshire, at Western, to run north through downtown Hollywood and then under the mountains to North Hollywood. This suits some CRA leaders and their developer friends, since it links three major redevelopment projects and creates a continuous corridor of real estate speculation.[31] The environmental impact report of the Southern California Rapid Transit District (SCRTD) forecasts a staggering 50 million square feet of new commercial development (virtually two new downtowns) centered around eleven Metro Rail stations.[32]

But the current alignment also negates the original economic rationale for subway construction, since only the Wilshire corridor currently has the population density to generate an amortizing ridership for Metro Rail. As a result, Metro Rail faces a very likely danger of insolvency, while most downtown commuters (coming from the Westside or, especially, the San Gabriel Valley to the east) will continue to rely on their cars. Metro Rail, at least in its current configuration, will act as an Archimedean lever to increase development densities in the CBD–Hollywood–North Hollywood corridor without mitigating current levels of congestion downtown (but more on traffic in a moment).[33]

In vindication, the CRA and its supporters can claim that, whatever setbacks or anomalies may have occurred, the agency has triumphally achieved the central vision of the *Silverbook*. A new financial district has taken shape on the east bank of the Harbor Freeway, with its skyscraper pinnacle along Grand, focused on the library, and pointing southward toward the expanded Convention Center and USC. Because this successful recentering has been largely fueled by the land rush of Asian and Canadian capital to the central city, it has simultaneously transferred ownership to absentee foreign investors.[34] Yet there is little anxiety downtown that the ultimate economic control panels are thousands of miles away. Although CBD downtown office space remains a surprisingly small fraction of the total regional inventory, more power—in the form of financial headquarters and $400-per-hour firms—is now concentrated downtown than at any time since the 1940s.[35]

▓ Who Wins, Who Loses?

Creating this physical infrastructure for international finance has been un-questionably the chief policy objective—and accomplishment—of the Bradley administration since 1973. More than mere "urban renewal," downtown rede-velopment has also been the city's major economic strategy for creating jobs and growth. In the face of deindustrialization of its older, nondefense, branch-plant economy, the city has gambled on creating office jobs.[36] Has it worked? And, who has benefited?

Certainly the major private-sector players have exploited a real estate bonanza. Speculators and developers have consistently realized large wind-falls from Community Redevelopment Agency write-downs and the equity-raising effects of public investment. For example, the CRA bought sixteen run-down parcels at Fourth and Flower streets in the early 1960s for $3 million; in the early 1970s, despite the explosion in property values, it discounted the combined parcel to Security Pacific Bank for a mere $5.4 million. By 1975, the land alone was worth more than $100 million. In another instance, Richard Riordan, a prominent local speculator and mortgage banker, bought property in 1969 at Ninth and Figueroa for $8 per square foot; within a decade, it had soared to $225 per square foot. (Riordan's successes have attracted unusual attention because he is a major contributor to Mayor Bradley and a member of two city commissions.)[37] A veteran downtown real estate and corporate-leasing expert has "guesstimated" that the $1 billion that the CRA has in-vested in Bunker Hill and the central business district has helped generate "at least one billion, perhaps two billion dollars worth of sheer profit for downtown players, above and beyond their own outlays."[38]

City hall—while in effect promoting downtown redevelopment as "indus-trial policy"—has never bothered to collect accurate figures on the new em-ployment generated by the high-rise boom. Don Spivak, the CRA's manager for the entire CBD project during the 1980s, confessed in an interview that the agency had no idea how many jobs for women or minorities have been created, or what has been their per capita cost-benefit analysis of redevelopment.[39]

Likewise, while city hall has been throwing $90,000 topping-off parties for new skyscrapers, it has paid no attention to the success of outlying areas in capturing the "back-office" jobs ("number crunching" and data processing) that are such vital employment multipliers for entry-level clericals. Thus Glendale (a city that in the last census had 450 Black residents out of a population of nearly 130,000) has managed to snare 3 million square feet of secondary bank, insurance, and real estate investment—becoming as a result the third largest financial center in the state.[40] Other major back-office complexes have grown up in Chatsworth, Pasadena, City of Commerce, and Brea (main base for Security First National). The CRA's indifference to the new geography of service jobs is disturbing since these are precisely the kind of compensatory jobs that East and South-Central Los Angeles—hard hit by plant closings—desperately need, and which presumably might have located there if the city had linked front-office development rights downtown with back-office investment in the surrounding inner city.[41]

The CRA's record in downtown housing has also been considerably obfuscated in agency propaganda. Planners maintain that the creation of a "jobs-housing balance" downtown—both to mitigate traffic congestion and to generate a residential base for a "24-hour downtown"—is one of their major priorities. Yet the CRA, which defines downtown objectives almost exclusively in terms of middle-class populations and needs, ignores the "jobs-housing" equilibrium that exists between the garment industry (downtown's other major industry) and surrounding Latino neighborhoods. It is precisely this existent balance that is now threatened on every side by agency projects (for example, the removal of nearly four thousand people for the recent Convention Center extension) and other public-private initiatives (the potential ten thousand West Bank residents who may be forced out by the proposed specific plan in that area, for example).

The CRA was badly embarrassed in March 1989 when Legal Aid analysts proved that the agency had been deliberately misleading the public by counting cots in Skid Row shelters as "units of affordable family housing." Because neither the agency nor city hall has accurately monitored the destruction of housing by private action downtown, it is virtually impossible to construct an overall balance sheet of the housing record of redevelopment.

A quarter century after the clearance of 7,310 units on Bunker Hill, the CRA claims to have finally constructed their replacements, although most are outside the downtown area and only a quarter are "section 8," or "very low income," like those originally destroyed. Setting aside the rehabilitation of Skid Row hotel and shelter rooms, it would appear from the agency's tangled statistics that it has so far increased the city's net stock of "affordable" housing (after deducting units demolished by agency action) by slightly more than one thousand units. Much of this, however, is actually gentrification—that is, replacing lost "very low income" units with more expensive "moderate income" units (an income differential as great as $21,000). Indeed, in conversations with CRA staff, it has become apparent that they conceptualize "affordable housing" as integrating legal secretaries and school teachers, not garment workers or janitors, into the "new downtown community."[42]

At the end of the day, and in lieu of any official cost-benefit assessment, the redevelopment game yields the following approximate scores:

1. A tripling of land values downtown since 1975, thanks to public action.

2. Zero increment in property taxes available for general-fund purposes (schools, transportation, welfare).

3. Thirty-five to forty thousand commuter office jobs added to downtown (presumably these jobs would have ended up somewhere in the region anyway—the CRA did not create them, but merely influenced their location).

4. A small net increment of "affordable" housing scattered around the city, which would probably be canceled out if statistics on private demolition were available.

5. A series of ineffable and questionable "public benefits" (for example, "downtown culture," "being a World City," "having a center," and so on).

6. The yet uncalculated "negative externalities" generated by redevelopment (that is, the additional traffic load, pollution, neglected investments in other parts of the city, negative tax impact on other services, and so on).

In addition, a full balance-sheet of redevelopment would have to estimate the corrupting impact of "centermania" on city politics. City hall and the downtown development community interpenetrate to such a profound extent that it has become literally impossible to tell where private capital ends and the Bradley administration begins. The resulting trade in influence is a miniature mirror of the military-industrial complex. Just like retired Air Force generals rushing off to fat sinecures on the boards of the aerospace industry, the illuminati of city hall—Art Snyder (ex-councilman), Dan Garcia (former planning commissioner), Tom Houston (former deputy mayor), Fran Savitch (ex–mayoral lieutenant), Maureen Kindel (ditto), and now Mike Gage (another ex–deputy mayor), to give an incomplete list—inevitably seem to end up as lobbyists for bulldozers. With such an extreme concentration of Los Angeles's best minds on moving dirt (and thus creating lucrative second careers for themselves), it is not surprising that lesser priorities—like jobs, safety, health, and welfare in South-Central Los Angeles—have been so neglected.

▪ Disneyfying Downtown South

The social costs of downtown growth will rise steeply in the next decade. But before analyzing the destabilizing impact of emerging "countergames" (the West Bank) and "side-moves" (Central City North, South, and East), let us first consider how the Community Redevelopment Agency proposes to play out the rest of its central-business-district hand. With construction in the new core in the mopping-up stages (including a controversial plan to demolish historic structures on Seventh Street), the focus of the CRA has shifted to the poles of CBD development: South Park and the Third Street corridor between Bunker Hill and Little Tokyo.

South Park, as we have seen, was a coinage of the 1972 *Silverbook*. The idea was to create a mixed-income "urban village" of clericals and professionals to "brighten" the face of downtown around the Convention Center and to extend redevelopment in the direction of the University of Southern California campus.[43] Although the CRA reaffirmed a South Park plan in a 1982 rewrite of development guidelines (eventually extending area boundaries south of Seventh and west of Main to the two freeways), speculators had plenty of time to bid up land values to as much as $300 per square foot before the agency finally acted to assemble parcels. In the face of such land inflation, even luxury units in South Park now require large subsidies.[44]

Indeed South Park's massive need for public financing is probably the major item on CRA's hidden agenda in the struggle to remove the cap on tax increments in the central business district.[45] The CRA sticks obdurately to the dogma that South Park's critical mass (a projected build-out population of twenty-five thousand) is absolutely necessary to transform downtown into a "true community" (poor people evidently do not count) and to shore up street-level leases and overall CBD property values into the twenty-first century. Not surprisingly, housing activists have attacked the premise that the "yuppification" of South Park should be the city's top residential priority.

Thus Michael Bodaken of Legal Aid (now Mayor Bradley's housing adviser), in a 1989 *Times* interview, denounced the $10-million subsidy that the CRA had furnished to Forest City Properties to build $1,200-per-month apartments in South Park. "It is just unbelievable that the city is subsidizing developers with millions of dollars to lure yuppies downtown. This city is the homeless capital of the nation. The money ought to be earmarked for homeless shelters and low-income housing."[46]

Housing advocates have also criticized the relocation of an entire residential community in order to expand the Convention Center, the other major component of the South Park plan. The $390-million expansion—the single largest bond issue in downtown history—is headed for troubled waters as Calmark Holding Co., the developer of an adjacent super-hotel, collapses under the weight of its junk bonds. Without Calmark's $400-million Pacific Basin Hotel—the largest ever planned in Southern California—the expanded Convention Center would be left without a single hotel room within walking distance.[47]

On the rim of South Park (Eighth Street and the Harbor Freeway), a jocular monstrosity called Metropolis is being designed by Michael Graves, current house architect for the Disney Corporation and tongue-in-cheek author of the Disney World hotel, decorated with giant swans, and the Burbank Disney headquarters with its columnar figures of the Seven Dwarfs. Impervious, like most architects, to the social impact of his multi-million-square-foot project on surrounding streets and neighborhoods, his concern is instead focused on making Metropolis a "total experience" for its corporate users. As design critics have appreciated, the arrival of Graves marks a new era downtown, a shift from stern skyscraper monoliths and fortresses to more "livable" and playful environments. He plans colorful glazed bands, "party hat" roof lines, and flashy octagonal pavilions atop some of his towers. A key decorative element will be a six-story base of turquoise terra-cotta—intended, according to Graves, "to show where Daddy works."[48] Indeed.

■ "Reaganizing" the Historic Core

Gentrification is also the municipal objective in the area between Bunker Hill and Little Tokyo. Back in *Silverbook* days, as we have seen, Third and Broadway figured as "Bunker Hill East," a kind of urban universal-gear meshing Bunker Hill, the Civic Center, and Little Tokyo. The fortification of Bunker Hill, however, precluded such interaction, and Broadway became instead the premier Spanish-language shopping street in North America. Now, with the Hill fully secured and almost completely redeveloped, the Community Redevelopment Agency is reviving the idea of a "pivotal interface" (read: yuppie corridor) to allow the free circulation of white-collar workers and tourists in the northern part of the central business district.

The anchor of this gentrification strategy is the new Ronald Reagan State Office Building. The CRA spent more than $20 million in direct subsidies to induce the state to bring three thousand office workers to Third and Spring as the shock troops of the area's "uplift." Both the Broadway Spring Center, across from the state building, and the new *L.A. Times* parking garage, on Broadway north of Third, have been ingeniously designed with CRA and LAPD expertise to provide high-security pedestrian passageways, with surveillance cameras, private guards, and steel-stake fencing, to allay the anxieties of white-collar workers.

The direct beneficiaries of the "Reaganization" of the area are two chief

Bradley backers: Ira Yellin, owner of the Bradbury Building, the Grand Central Public Market, and the Million Dollar Theater Building (all at the corner of Third and Broadway), and his friend and associate, Bruce Corwin, proprietor of various Broadway theaters and largest contributor to the recent defense fund for the embattled mayor. Yellin and Corwin have for a long time been the principal players in the CRA-financed "Miracle on Broadway" association. Now they plan to exploit the captive clientele from the Reagan Building (as well as from the *Times* and Bunker Hill) to create a "Grand Central Square" with upscale restaurants, condos, and offices. Restoration architect Brenda Levin has been hired to "weave together the historical fabric" of the Million Dollar Building with the market and a new ten-story parking garage. The CRA has buttered the way by allowing Yellin to cash in the air rights of the Bradbury and Million Dollar Theater buildings for $12 million (a complex subsidy that after sale to another developer will eventually be costed to the public as further traffic congestion downtown). As Spivack of the CRA put it, the deal-making on Broadway was a "win-win situation," the real "miracle" being the CRA's extraordinary willingness to bankroll Yellin and Corwin.[49]

Another component necessary to complete the corridor between Bunker Hill and Little Tokyo is the removal of the Union Rescue Mission—and its crowds of homeless men—from Second and Main, next door to Saint Vibiana's Cathedral. It is rumored that relocation of the mission is part of the deal that the CRA made with the state to get the Reagan Building. Moreover, Arch-bishop Mahony was reported to have lobbied the CRA (whose chief, John Tuite is an ex-priest) to shift the eyesore away from his doorstep. Still there was some consternation when the CRA suddenly announced in September that it was offering the mission $6.5 million to move—nearly four times the appraised value of the property. Councilman Bernardi (still the hammer of the CRA) decried a new conspiracy of the "moneyed interests," and his Westside colleague, Zev Yaroslavsky, complained about public subsidies to a funda-mentalist body (the mission) that refuses to hire non-Christians. Nonetheless, the council majority (without any debate about the implied subsidy to the other sectarian institution, St. Vibiana's) approved the CRA maneuver.[50]

As a result of the Reagan Building and the other CRA initiatives, land prices have skyrocketed in the Third Street corridor, but the revival of the rest of the Historic Core (as the area bounded by First, Los Angeles, Ninth, and Hill streets is now officially called) remains in doubt. The flight of banks and department stores after the Watts rebellion left millions of square feet of upper-story office space in the core unoccupied. Much of it has sat vacant for twenty years (the city, of course, has never imagined conscripting it for housing for the homeless or other "radical" uses). The CRA has planned to gradually bring this office desert back to life with infusions of restoration money, improved security, the addition of "nightlife" (for example, the old Pacific Stock Exchange transformed into a disco), and so on.[51] Now, however, the fate of the area appears inversely hinged upon the success of a plan to bootleg a second downtown, west of the Harbor Freeway. The emergence of the so-called Central City West has suddenly put the CRA's best-made plans in jeopardy.

■ The Countergame

Certainly, the possibility has always existed of a "countergame." The growing differential between land values in the growth core and its immediate periphery encouraged outlaw developers to gamble on attracting investment across the Harbor Freeway. Indeed, already by the middle 1960s, a diverse group of speculators, large and small, were staking positions west of the freeway (an area that the *Silverbook* had primarily designated for peripheral parking and services). While awaiting redevelopment to come their way, they were permitted, criminally, to demolish entire neighborhoods in the Crown Hill and Temple-Beaudry areas. It was to their advantage to "bank" land in desolation rather than take the risk of tenant organization or future relocation costs.

But the frustrated speculators had to wait nearly a generation before they could compete against the central business district. With the exception of Unocal (a major downtown corporation stranded on the wrong side of the Harbor Freeway), they were either foreigners (overseas Chinese and Israelis) or minor-leaguers outside the mainstream power-structures, opposed by an awesome combination of the old-elite Central City Association and the

Community Redevelopment Agency. Moreover, the notional "West Bank" was balkanized by several city council districts and had no clear "patron."

This calculus of forces began to shift in the mid-1980s. As the Figueroa corridor started to top-out with new development and turn its face away from Pershing Square, the western shore of the freeway suddenly became inviting. Despite the notorious fiasco of the Chinese World Trust building (still half empty today), structures like the new Pacific Stock Exchange (relocated from its magnificent home on Spring Street) proved the viability of the other bank. This led several major-league players—including Hillman Industries and Ray Watt—to migrate west with their awesome financial resources and political clout. Moreover, most of the West Bank became politically consolidated into a new district under Gloria Molina, who was eager to find a resource base for jobs and housing in her crushingly poor constituency.

With Molina's forceful backing, the area's largest stakeholders (organized since 1985 as the Central City West Association [CCWA]), germinated a plan to literally create a second downtown. Despite the dire warnings of former CRA chief Ed Helfand that West Bank competition would undermine the entire logic of downtown renewal, Molina accepted the offer of the CCWA in 1987 to privately fund a "specific plan" for the area. This partnership deliberately excluded the CRA (seen as the custodian of CBD interests) and greatly reduced the role of the city planning commission. In July 1989, after two years of study, the urban-design firm headed by ex-CRA commission president Kurt Meyer submitted a first draft of the plan, detailing transportation and land use for a maximum build-out of 25–30 million square feet of commercial space (that is, roughly equal to all new construction downtown since 1975, or to two-and-a-half Century Cities).

The transportation requirements of such a scale of development are stupefying, especially in wake of downtown's past policy of "starving" the West Bank of transport links in order to make it undevelopable. In the CCWA's conception, the Harbor Freeway, rather than Figueroa, would become the new "Main Street" of a bipolar downtown. Although Caltrans officials staunchly maintain that the freeway—"double-decked" or not—will simply not be able to absorb the new traffic volume from the proposed Central City West, the draft

plan provides for four new off-ramps, as well as an additional Metro Rail station at Bixel and Wilshire, a $300-million "transit tunnel" under Crown Hill,
and a funneling of traffic down Glendale Boulevard that could have nightmar-
ish consequences for the already congested Echo Park area. (Some of the
transport planners involved also argue for the conversion of Alvarado into a
high-speed freeway connector.)

Another breathtaking dimension of the plan is the proposal for twelve
thousand units of new housing gathered in a predominantly affluent "urban
village" similar to the South Park plan, but with a marginally greater inclusion
of low- and very-low-income units (25 percent). Housing advocates, however,
like Father Philip Lance of the United Neighbors of City West, point out that
there is already a housing emergency in the area as the arrival of the big guns
accelerated scorched-earth land-banking: twenty-one hundred units have
been demolished in the last decade.

Moreover, the draft specific plan provides for the replacement of only
three-quarters of the low-income units it proposes to remove for development.[52] Other critics, pointing to the twenty-year timeline of development,
have demanded immediate rehousing of the existing tenants and restitution
for the housing destroyed in recent years.

While the larval Central City West plan gestates through a labyrinthine
process of political negotiation, a land rush of Klondike proportions has broken out on the West Bank. In some cases, land values have increased nearly
4,000 percent in a single decade.[53] Speculators, reinforced by new arrivals
from offshore, are now concentrating on an "underdeveloped" mile-long strip
of Wilshire Boulevard between the freeway and the new Metro Rail station at
MacArthur Park. As CRA planners recognize with some trepidation, this flow
of investment threatens to revive Wilshire Boulevard-westward as the major
axis of downtown growth—in competition to the Figueroa-southward target
of the *Silverbook* strategy.

Meanwhile, with stakes rapidly increasing, developer Ray Watt has
bum-rushed his way ahead of the CCWA pack to break ground. Although the
city planning department's chief hearing examiner opposed the plan for a
1-million-square-foot "Watt City Center" tower on the west side of the Harbor

Freeway at Eighth Street, Watt—in one of the most impressive power-plays in recent city history—ramrodded it through the city council with the help of lobbyist Art Snyder (former East L.A. councilmember) and Molina, chair of the Planning and Landuse Committee. Molina, in liaison with the United Neighbors of Temple-Beaudry, cut a consciously Faustian deal: accepting the Watt Center's additional traffic load in exchange for eighty units of immediate low-income housing.[54]

■ Downtown Every-Which-Way?

To many downtowners, the Watt City Center is a massive symbol that crime (in this case, skyscraper hijacking) does pay after all. But to make matters worse, the West Bank example seems to be spurring other landowners on the central business district's periphery to package megaprojects for sale to interested members of the city council. Venting the Community Redevelopment Agency's anxiety at the dissipation of a downtown focus, the agency's chief, John Tuite, recently outlined the competing vectors of development: "There is the Convention Center (South Park), Union Station, Bob Farrell's [councilmember] ideas for a strategic plan to link USC and the surrounding area to downtown, as well as other CRA areas, City West and City North."

Union Station, especially, is a variable of unknown, perhaps huge, dimension in downtown's future. When Caltrans tried to purchase the station under eminent domain in the early 1980s, its owners (the three transcontinental railroads—Southern Pacific, Union Pacific, and Santa Fe—brought to court a Charles Luckman model showing the site built out to the proportions of Century City. In Luckman's conception, the elegant old station was reduced to minor detail in an overscaled nightmare from the latter-day Hieronymous Bosch, that included two skyscrapers, two mansard-roof Vegas-type hotels, a vast shopping concourse, acres of parking, and a fantastic thirty-story glass "Arc de Triomphe" smiling over twenty thousand office workers and shoppers. Overawed by the model, the judge ruled in favor of the station owners, tripling the value of the site and forcing Caltrans to abandon its purchase attempt.

In following years, as Santa Fe (whose largest shareholder is Olympia and York—the world's largest commercial developers) laboriously negotiated to buy out its partners, the megadevelopment potential of the station became the focus of Councilman Richard Alatorre's attentions. Alatorre, chairing the redistricting of the city council in 1987, allocated to himself the cusp of Union Station and Olvera Street with the specific purpose of making station redevelopment a "financial motor" to drive economic development in his Eastside district's "enterprise zone." Although his idea of linking community development to a rich redevelopment project mimics Molina's strategy on the West Bank, he has collaborated with, rather than excluded, the CRA, in the evident hope of integrating Union Station into the CBD game plan.

Accordingly, in the spring of 1988, the CRA, on behalf of Alatorre and the station owners, completed an in-depth study of the site's development potential (including the vast, nearly empty shell of the neighboring Terminal Annex Post Office). In essence, the CRA analysts endorsed Luckman's 1983 vision of a "new urban center," proposing at least 3 million square feet of mixed-use office, hotel, retail, and residential development, as well as architectural unification with La Placita/Olvera Street across the street. But the study continues to raise as many questions as it answers.[55]

First, it is not clear whether the office potential of the station site can be fully realized in face of the growing competition of Central City West. Second, Olvera Street merchants and East Los Angeles political foes of Alatorre fear that station redevelopment will inundate and destroy the popular character of the old plaza area—a crucial public space for Spanish-speaking Los Angeles. And, finally, Union Station is the fulcrum of competing claims between Little Tokyo (core of an emergent Central City East) and Chinatown (center of a hypothetical City North).

It has become the passion of planning commission chairman William Luddy to unify the area north of the Civic Center—including Chinatown, El Pueblo, and Union Station—as a single planning unit designed to reinforce CBD redevelopment by adding a dynamic, nighttime tourist quarter. Moreover, as the planning department's December 1989 City North charette emphasized, "if Los Angeles is to compete favorably with Vancouver and San Francisco as a market for real estate development by Hong Kong and Singapore dollars, for investment from Chinese-Asian money, it must bolster that part of its city which represents its strong Chinese heritage. . . ."[56]

But this concept of packaging City North, including Union Station, for sale to the Chinese diaspora ignores the competing interest of Japanese capital in establishing a strong link between Little Tokyo and the station. Little Tokyo's Main-Street-like function for Los Angeles's Japanese-American community has been eclipsed by its new role as a luxury hotel and shopping precinct for Japanese businessmen. Now, however, its developers (in the words of the *Downtown News*) "are making a bold play to capture the tourist windfall expected from the Convention Center expansion." Over a million square feet of hotel, retail, and residential construction is under way near First and Alameda (extending Little Tokyo to the edge of the Los Angeles River), and developers are pushing for a mixed-use, high-rise rezoning of the industrial corridor east of Alameda. Union Station, revived by Metro Rail as downtown's transit hub, is hungrily envisioned as an integral part of Little Tokyo's expanded sphere of influence.

As different forces contend for the future of Union Station, another major eruption of development may be ready to occur on the CBD's southern flank. Since *Silverbook* days, most observers have believed that the CRA's ultimate goal is to extend the corridor of high-rise redevelopment along Figueroa to the Jefferson or Exposition Street edges of the University of Southern California campus. With utter conviction in its inevitability, one landowner (an auto dealer) has spent twenty years patiently assembling most of the long, low-rise stretch between Jefferson and Adams for conversion into office and hotel-block developments. USC, on the other hand, has been preoccupied since the Watts rebellion with fortifying its borders (an impressive Maginot Line of shopping centers and parking lots) and promoting the gentrification of its Hoover Street fringe. Few doubt, however, that the university is nurturing a far more ambitious vision, linking its housing strategy to the commercial development of Figueroa under joint auspices with the CRA. The 1988 appointment of Gerald Trimble, high-powered former redevelopment director for Pasadena and San Diego, as USC's development director has fueled endless speculation about the university's game plan as well as stimulated local councilmember Robert Farrell to agitate for a link—à la Molina's West Bank and Alatorre's Union Station cash cows—between commercial and community development in the south downtown—USC nexus.

◼ Perestroika . . . or End Game?

In summary, the West Bank countergame, together with the emerging moves on the north, east, and south faces of downtown, is beginning to disorganize the Community Redevelopment Agency's central business district game plan. The casino is in chaos, the developers are seen shooting craps with politicians in every alley. Existential questions are raised: Can downtown grow in every compass direction at once? Who will supply the demand for one, two, three, or many downtowns?

For the CRA, the problem is even more complicated, since it must confront these centrifugal tendencies while simultaneously surmounting the 1977 Bernardi cap and renewing its mandate to orchestrate downtown's expansion. Moreover, Mayor Bradley's position as the agency's patron has been made more delicate by a highly publicized ethics scandal as well as by charges of benign neglect from his own Black political base.[57] An atmosphere of quiet crisis has served to concentrate minds in the CRA's Spring Street headquarters.

The "solution" being hammered out from above necessarily proposed both a political realignment and a new design for downtown. In 1989, the CRA survived a close call when its opponents on the city council almost achieved a majority for a takeover of the agency.[58] In the aftermath, Mayor Bradley urged a sweeping concordant between the CRA and its most trenchant community critics. In return for supporting a huge increase of the CBD's tax-increment capacity to $5 billion, the mayor has offered to split the addition evenly between CBD redevelopment and citywide housing needs. He also dramatically co-opted two of the CRA's leading housing critics into his administration (one as his housing adviser, the other as a CRA commissioner). Simultaneously city hall instituted new Boston-style housing linkage fees, taxing high-rise development to support affordable home construction. Unsurprisingly, the former united front of CRA foes—community groups, public-interest lawyers, progressive planners, and so forth—has disintegrated.[59]

The mayor has appointed a Downtown Strategic Plan Advisory Committee to wrestle with the challenge of Central City West in the framework of a new, twenty-year master plan for downtown. Chaired by two veterans of the *Silverbook* task force, CRA commissioners Frank Kuwahara and Edwin Steidle, the committee is dominated by a two-thirds majority of developers and corporate lawyers, including such familiar suspects as Ira Yellin, Chris Stewart (former secretary of the CCA), and the irrepressible Art Snyder. Although the CRA's authority ends at the Harbor Freeway, the committee has been specifically encouraged to visualize the CBD's future in the "broadest context"—that is, to work out some reconciliation of developer interests on both sides of the freeway (taking into account USC, Little Tokyo, Central City North, and possibly Hollywood as well). In the meantime, the mayor and the CRA are readying a proposal to drastically expand the CRA's domain downtown: taking in City North, the USC area, part of the West Bank, and perhaps the area in transition east of Alameda. If adopted, the expanded project areas would allow the agency to deal with two problems at once: reconciliation of growth poles and the linkage of community and commercial redevelopment.

The CRA has encouraged the view that these various initiatives are the beginning of an authentic downtown perestroika that will eventually transform redevelopment to please everybody, from Japanese developers to the homeless on Skid Row. Despite the "encouragement," however, a hard core of doubt remains. Indeed, in the view of many insiders, the end game has already begun, as downtown plays against the clock—perhaps time bomb— of two insurmountable contradictions: overbuilding and the coming traffic apocalypse.

The smart money on both sides of the Harbor Freeway has ceased to believe in the downtown—Pacific Rim perpetual motion machine, and, like Ray Watt, are racing to bring their projects in and stuff them with high-class tenants before the market crashes. Even before the official arrival of recession in summer 1990, the torrent of incoming Manhattan law firms and Japanese banks had slowed to a trickle. In Japan itself, where convulsed stock markets registered the overaccumulation of fictional capital, high interest rates were beckoning capital to stay home. The 1980s fantasy of an infinite supply of offshore capital to sustain Southern California's real estate boom seems increasingly like a psychedelic aberration.

If the trophy-class downtown office market still purred sweetly at the end of 1990, it was only because existing downtown tenants (like First Interstate and Unocal) have been vigorously "trading up." As they have bailed out of their old offices (usually circa 1960s–70s structures like the First Interstate Tower), vacancies have soared in the corporate schlock, or "class two" market. New development, in other words, is devaluing old, slowing job creation, and potentially undermining the CRA's putative tax base as well.[60]

But, as happens in all business cycles, production drastically overshoots demand in the final, fervid phase of the boom. In a situation where even redevelopment's *eminence grise,* CRA commission president Jim Wood, is admitting that downtown is overdeveloped and the Japanese are acting nervous,[61] science-fiction-like quantities of office space are scheduled for delivery over the next decade. In the flush conditions of the 1980s, the downtown market absorbed about 1.4 million square feet of new space per year. With more than 12 million square feet already approved and in the construction pipeline and with the financial-services expansion ending, supply should easily meet demand through to the millennium. Yet a further 20–30 million square feet are on drawing boards, chasing investors and mortgage bankers around the city. (Altogether, councilmember Marvin Braude estimates sixty-four new projects creating 37 million square feet of office space.)[62] With Southern California diving into deeper recession, who will occupy this embarrassment of space? (And why should tax dollars subsidize its construction?) Even in Los Angeles, speculators cannot go on endlessly building space for other speculators.

But a downtown depression may be the lesser of potential evils. Worse still is the specter of hyper-gridlock paralyzing downtown and a large part of Los Angeles County. The traffic nightmare of the 1990s—regardless of an economic slowdown—will be the simple addition of current planning exemptions and special cases. For example, two recently approved megaprojects— the Watt City Center and, directly across the Harbor Freeway, the Metropolis— will each add *fifteen thousand* trips per day to overloaded downtown streets. Total new development will generate an additional 420,000 trips per day, making "the existing Harbor Freeway [according to councilmember Braude] a parking lot and paralyzing the movement of traffic in the downtown area."[63] Lest Metro Rail and downtown "village living" be immediately wheeled in as a deus ex machina, it is sobering to observe that a recent survey discovered that only a tiny fraction of downtown office commuters (just 5.4 percent) have both the means and the desire to live in Bunker Hill or South Park. Certainly the nightmare of perpetual gridlock will persuade a larger percentage of commuters to reluctantly abandon Pasadena or Studio City,[64] but these same horrors may also persuade Mitsui and CitiCorp to look afresh at Wilshire Boulevard, Long Beach, or Orange County's Golden Triangle. They may even convince shaken Los Angeles voters to reexamine the premises of the city's pharaonic and socially irresponsible redevelopment strategy.[65]

1. Reyner Banham, Los Angeles: *The Architecture of Four Ecologies* (London: Penguin, 1971), p. 201.
2. See Central City Association, *Downtown 2000* (Los Angeles, 1985).
3. Cf. Scott Bottles, *Los Angeles and the Automobile: The Making of the Modern City* (Los Angeles: Univ. of California Press, 1987) and Robert Fogelson, *The Fragmented Metropolis: Los Angeles 1850–1930* (Cambridge, Mass.: Harvard Univ. Press, 1967).
4. For downtown interests' zealous but ultimately unsuccessful crusade to use zoning against centrifugal development, see Marc Weiss, "The Los Angeles Realty Board and Zoning," chap. 4 in *The Rise of the Community Builders* (New York: Columbia Univ. Press, 1987).
5. Especially for the role of the *Times*, see Robert Gottlieb and Irene Wolt, *Thinking Big* (New York: G. P. Putnam's Sons, 1977), pp. 152–55, 306–17). Big public projects have been repeatedly used to revive or recycle real estate values in declining sectors of downtown.

Thus the construction of the Civic Center in the 1930s bolstered the value of *Times* properties in the older, circa-1900 core area, which had been in decline after the westward migration of the downtown center in the early 1920s.
6. Bottles, chaps. 4 and 5 of *Los Angeles and the Automobile;* Central Business District Association, *A Quarter Century of Activities: 1924–1949.* (Los Angeles: Univ. of California, 1950); Mike Davis, "Tunnel Busters: The Strange Story of the Hollywood Subway," unpublished, 1988; and Steven Mikesell, "The Los Angeles River Bridges," *Southern California Quarterly* (Winter 1988).
7. See Sy Adler, "Why BART But No LART? The Political Economy of Rail Rapid Transit Planning in the Los Angeles and San Francisco Metropolitan Areas, 1945–57," *Planning Perspectives* 2 (1987).
8. See David Brodsly, *L.A. Freeway* (Berkeley: Univ. of California Press, 1981), p. 96.
9. Rudolfo Acuna, *A Community Under Siege: A Chronicle of Chicanos East of the Los Angeles River,*

1945–75 (Los Angeles: Chicano Studies Center, Univ. of California, 1980).
10. Frank Wilkinson, "And Now the Bill Comes Due," *Frontier* (October 1965).
11. In 1956, Los Angeles had one of the largest skid rows in the nation, with fifteen thousand residents "in everything from abandoned buildings to packing crates in alleys and from 306 hotels to eleven flophouses." See Aubrey Haines, "Skid Row, Los Angeles," *Frontier* (September 1956).
12. See "Civic Center Plan" in Municipal League of Los Angeles, *Bulletin* 2 (March 1925), p. 13.
13. Cf. William Babcock, *Regrading the Bunker Hill Area* (Los Angeles: 1931) and Pat Adler, *The Bunker Hill Story* (Glendale, Calif.: 1965).
14. Cited in William Pugsley, *Bunker Hill: The Last of the Lofty Mansions* (Corona del Mar, Calif., 1977), p. 27.
15. See Gene Marine, "Bunker Hill: Pep Pill for Downtown Los Angeles," *Frontier* (August 1959).

16. Cf. John Brohman, "Urban Restructuring in Downtown Los Angeles" (M.A. thesis, School of Architecture and Urban Planning, UCLA, 1983) and Joel Friedman, "The Political Economy of Urban Renewal: Changes in Land Ownership in Bunker Hill" (M.A. thesis, School of Architecture and Urban Planning, UCLA, 1978).

17. *Centropolis 1—Economic Survey*, December 1960; *Centropolis 2—General Development Plan*, January 1962; *Centropolis 3—Transportation Study*, January 1963; and *Centropolis 4—Master Plan*, November 1964. The Central City Committee, appointed by Mayor Norris Poulson in 1958, was chaired by Walter Braunschweiger.

18. *Los Angeles Times*, 4 November 1965 and 24 December 1972.

19. By 1967, the Wilshire corridor had seventy financial headquarters versus forty-seven in the CBD. Only oil companies maintained their high headquarters concentration downtown. (See Abraham Falick, "Transport Planning in Los Angeles: A Geo-Economic Analysis" [Ph.D. thesis, Department of Geography, UCLA, 1970, pp. 172–75].) Eugene Grisby and William Andrews, moreover, claim that the CBD lost forty thousand jobs between 1961 and 1967. (See "Mass Rapid Transportation as a Means of Changing Access to Employment Opportunities for Low Income People" [paper for the fifteenth Annual Meeting, Transportation Research Forum, San Francisco, October 1974].)

20. Gottlieb and Wolt, *Thinking Big*, p. 431. They argue, moreover, that the shadowy "Committee of 25," organized by Asa Call and Neil Petree with the support of the Chandlers, was the ultimate invisible government behind the CCCP and other epiphenomenal forms of elite organization (pp. 457–58).

21. See Robert Meyers, "The Downtown Plan Faces Open Rebellion," *Los Angeles* (December 1975), p. 85.

22. Certainly the study played lip service to upgrading Broadway and Seventh Street retail as well as preserving Spring Street, but the greatest area of opportunity defined by the *Silverbook* was expansion southward, along a Figueroa axis, into the South Park area.

23. The proposed circulation system corresponded entirely to the envisioned Figueroa corridor of the southward-moving office and apartment construction, completely ignoring the needs of tens of thousands of existing workers in the garment center—a bias reproduced in every subsequent phase of downtown transportation planning.

24. Although all the different proposed "action areas" of the *Silverbook* were combined into one overall plan and project area, Bunker Hill remained legally and administratively separate under its original 1959 plan.

25. Councilman Donald Lorenzen, who had briefly left the chambers to chat with an aide, later claimed that his vote had been faked by another member to support the plan. He subsequently endorsed the Bernardi suit. See Meyers, "The Downtown Plan Faces Open Rebellion," p. 82.

26. The downtown leadership brazenly proposed to destroy the old library (now recognized as downtown's most distinguished architectural landmark) in order to create a development greenfield while simultaneously using the new facility to roll back Latino "intrusions" in the vicinity of the May Company and Broadway department stores. A study commissioned by Meyer and Helfeld in 1976 brilliantly rebuked the myth of Broadway blight. See Charles Kober Associates, *Broadway/Central Library: Impact Analysis* (Los Angeles, 1976).

27. See J. Gregory Payne and Scott Ratzan, *Tom Bradley: The Impossible Dream* (Santa Monica, Calif.: Roundtable Publishing, 1986), pp. 142–43, 149–50.

28. See Dick Turpin in the *Los Angeles Times*, 21 September 1986—confirmed by the *National Real Estate Investor* (December 1986), p. 102; the higher estimate is from Howard Sadlowski in the *Los Angeles Times*, 17 June 1984.

29. Stephen Weiner of Bear Stearns quoted in the *National Real Estate Investor* (December 1986), p. 132.

30. See Davis, "Tunnel Busters," pp. 34–38. In the summer of 1990, rumors began to fly that the CRA was considering a monorail system to link nodes of development downtown.

31. The Southern California Rapid Transit District is proposing to impose $75 million in special taxes on the ninety-eight hundred commercial property owners who stand to profit most from proximity to eleven Metro Rail Phase II stations. In an ominous precedent for the plan, however, MCA Inc., which owns Universal City (an unincorporated enclave) in Cahuenga Pass between Hollywood and Burbank, seems to have found a technical loophole to avoid assessment, although the entertainment conglomerate is planning massive new development next to its Metro Rail station. (See *Los Angeles Business Journal*, 15 January 1990.)

32. SCRTD, *Los Angeles Rail Rapid Transit Project SEIS/SEIR*, draft (November 1987), Table 3–21, p. 3–2–13.

33. In my view, Los Angeles's emerging transportation infrastructure will restructure land uses (and social groups) without necessarily alleviating gridlock. Thus Metro Rail will be a powerful link between development nodes (strengthening their sales value to offshore capital), whereas Light Rail (downtown to Long Beach) will allow downtown's low-wage workers to commute from a more dispersed labor-shed (opening up new development space in the CBD's periphery). It is unclear, however, whether any of this mass transit development will actually reduce freeway usage by downtown office workers and professionals commuting from the valleys and the Westside.

34. On the internationalization of downtown redevelopment and the new political alliances created in its wake, see Mike Davis, "*Chinatown,* Part Two? The 'Internationalization' of Downtown Los Angeles," *New Left Review* 164 (July/August1987).

35. There has been a double restructuring of power on the West Coast. On the one hand, San Francisco has been supplanted as a financial capital by Los Angeles. On the other hand, Los Angeles capital has increasingly been overshadowed by the arrival of the big Tokyo and New York banks, whose local headquarters are downtown. Booster hyperbole about the ascendancy of Los Angeles typically focuses on the first of these phenomena and ignores the second.

36. As Edward Soja has pointed out, the Los Angeles case is a unique combination of industrial decline (unionized auto, tire, and steel plants) and revival (military aerospace *and* new sweatshop manufacturers). In local impact, however, the loss of high-wage branch-plant jobs has had a devastating and long-term impact on Chicano and Black communities uncompensated by the addition of new high-tech jobs in the Valley or minimum-wage garment-making jobs downtown. See Soja, "L.A.'s the Place: Economic Restructuring and the Internationalization of the Los Angeles Region," in *Postmodern Geographies* (London: Verso, 1989).

37. Compare Brohman, "Urban Restructuring in Downtown Los Angeles," p. 111; and Friedman, "The Political Economy of Urban Renewal," p. 261.

38. My anonymous informant (interviewed the fall of 1989 for the *L.A. Weekly*) was referring to give-aways and discounts, on one hand, and to "positive externalities" (public investments raising private equities) on the other. The total present value of post-1975 private investment in downtown is probably around $8 billion.

39. Interviewed for the *L.A. Weekly* in the fall of 1989. A survey of other public agencies revealed a similar ignorance of the economic impact of redevelopment.

40. See Glendale Redevelopment Agency's myriad brag-sheets and press releases. Glendale, just a few miles north of downtown L.A., is also planning to dramatically "upscale" its Galleria mall to "Rodeo Drive standards"—another move that will steal thunder (and customers) from CRA-backed retail development downtown.

41. Again, CBD chief Spivak (in the interview noted in footnote 39) confessed that the CRA "had never considered or studied the question of 'back-office' investment as an opportunity in its own right."

42. *Downtown News,* 16 November 1987.

43. See Dick Turpin, "Downtown Expansion to Take Southerly Direction," *Los Angeles Times,* 9 February 1986.

44. Developers fought like tigers to rezone South Park for offices. Ultimately an Urban Institute Panel had to be brought in to adjudicate whether, in light of land values, it was still possible to develop a residential community in the area. See *Urban Land,* September 1987, pp. 13–17; also *Los Angeles Business Journal,* 19 October 1987.

45. An internal CRA memo secured by the *L.A. Weekly* indicates that the agency wants to spend a further $372 million on developing South Park. See Ron Curran, "The Agency at a Crossroads," *L.A. Weekly,* 2–8 March 1990. Curran has been the only journalist in Los Angeles to doggedly follow the CRA's footsteps over the last five years, and his many articles in the *Weekly* are essential reading for anyone interested in downtown L.A. or the politics of redevelopment.

46. *Los Angeles Times,* 25 June 1989. See also, ibid., 10 January 1988.

47. Just as Glendale has waylaid back-office jobs, so too is Long Beach preparing to hijack downtown's convention trade. With nearly as much convention space as downtown and a new oceanfront cityscape under construction on the site of the former "Pike" (once the West Coast's Coney Island), as well as a potential Disneyland II next to the Queen Mary, Long Beach (like Anaheim in Orange County) is geared up for competition.

48. Quoted in Leon Whiteson, *Los Angeles Times,* 22 March 1990.

49. Cf. *Miracle on Broadway—Annual Report 1989; Downtown News,* 10 February 1990; *Los Angeles Business Journal,* 6 November 1989; *Los Angeles Times,* 10 and 27 February, 9 April, and 22 September 1989.

50. Cf. *Los Angeles Times,* 16 October 1989; and *Downtown News,* 16 October 1989.

51. See CRA, "Memorandum: Historic Core Three Year Work Program," 21 December 1988.

52. I have been fascinated to learn that even the CRA study team assigned to evaluate the draft specific plan (for in-house purposes only) regarded the housing element as a "crock . . . not proposing to do anything at all." *L.A. Times* architecture critic Sam Hall Kaplan has repeatedly questioned the adequacy of its housing provision as well as condemned its "segregation of uses . . . and office tower ghetto in the southeastern portion of the community, and the isolation elsewhere of schools, housing and streets."

53. "In 1979 a parcel of land was sold to Unocal for $11 a square foot. Towards the end of 1988, an adjacent parcel was sold to Unocal for $270 a square foot. And just last spring, Hillman Properties reportedly purchased the entire contiguous site for $370 a square foot." (*Los Angeles Business Journal*, 29 January 1990). As land prices rise on the West Bank, it nonetheless retains the important comparative advantage, vis a vis the CBD, of being "parking rich"—that is, of having more generous on-site parking allowances—an increasingly important variable for developers and their tenants in Los Angeles.

54. Councilmember Gloria Molina illustrates the classic dilemma of an inner-city politician negotiating with international capital without the clout of an activist community movement backing her up. Although a tireless advocate of rehousing for her low-income community, she has chosen to accept developer ground rules (and campaign contributions) as a strategy for generating at least a modicum of decent replacement units. Friendly critics have suggested that she would have saved more housing—or at least wrestled a better deal—by mobilizing the largely Central American community of the West Bank in opposition to the CCWA's redevelopment strategy. For an interesting profile of Molina (who many believe will become L.A.'s first Latina mayor), see Ron Curran, "Gloria Molina—A Perennial Outsider Comes to Power and Now Plans to Run for Mayor," *L.A. Weekly,* 13–19 October 1989.

55. For Union Station redevelopment in the context of the restructuring of railroad land holdings, see Mike Davis, "The Los Angeles River: Lost and Found," *L.A. Weekly,* 1–7 September 1989.

56. Los Angeles Design Action Planning Team, *A Plan for City North,* 5 December 1989.

57. On "Bradleygate," see Mike Davis, "Heavyweight Contenders," *Interview,* August 1989.

58. The vote took place along a pork barrel divide. Historically, council attitudes toward the CRA have been shaped less by ideology than by whether or not the councilmember has a significant CRA project in his or her district. Even Ruth Galanter, the recent "environmentalist" addition to the council from Venice Beach, has had a change of heart about the agency after working with them to renovate the aged Crenshaw Shopping Center.

59. The mayor meanwhile has tried to mollify the county board of supervisors—Bernardi's major ally in the original suit—by deregulating development rights for county properties downtown and increasing their share of the tax flow from Hollywood redevelopment. This leaves only Bernardi and Valley homeowners' groups as intransigent opponents of lifting the cap.

60. See Morris Newman, "Old Buildings Square Off Against New in Los Angeles Office Battle," *Los Angeles Business Journal,* 23 October 1989; also ibid., 29 January 1990.

61. See interview in *Los Angeles Business Journal,* 16 October 1989. The *Downtown News* (22 January 1990) reported the growing dissatisfaction of Japanese owners with the advice they had been receiving from asset managers and brokers about the quality of the downtown market.

62. See Chip Jacobs, "Braude, Saying Downtown Growth 'Out of Control'. . . ," *Los Angeles Business Journal,* 9 October 1989.

63. Ibid.

64. Is it conceivable that some downtown visionaries are actually counting on gridlock to make their Manhattanized urban villages work? As CRA chairman Jim Wood explained in an interview last year, "We *planned* for there to be lots of traffic downtown; we *wanted* traffic because that would make Metro Rail work."

65. For a preface to a "Green" counterplan for downtown, see Mike Davis, "Deconstructing Downtown," *L.A. Weekly,* 1–7 December 1989, as well as Davis, "The Los Angeles River: Lost and Found," previously cited.

Two Institutions for the Arts

Diane Ghirardo

I. Crossover Dreams

At a conference at the University of California, Irvine, in October 1989, Peter Eisenman firmly announced, "Never believe what architects tell you about their work."[1] Despite this cautionary remark, Eisenman's alter egos and other

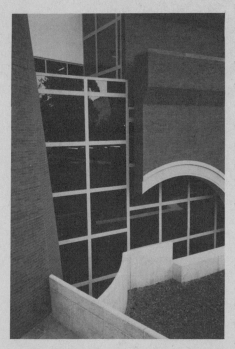

students of his work have elaborated in considerable detail the design strategies that he adopted for the Wexner Center for the Visual Arts for the Ohio State University in Columbus, Ohio: the surveyor's grids for the state of Ohio, the city of Columbus, and the university; FAA flight paths into Columbus; and the university football stadium, among others.[2] In perusing these indicators, I am reminded of a map published in the original *Domus* in 1933, which purported to chart examples of modern architecture in Rome. Concocted by the Milanese staff of *Domus,* the guide could only have frustrated the eager tourist, for the map was printed with north and south reversed. Such a map reveals next to nothing about the subject, but a great deal about those who assembled it. So, too, with the plethora of grids Eisenman has laid out for the Wexner: it reveals much about the crafty cartographer, but gives only marginal information about the genesis of the building.

Eisenman has long employed a compositional strategy—for which he is greatly indebted to Italian architect Giuseppe Terragni—in which cubes are

rotated, pulled apart, gridded, and transformed, and mathematical relationships are elaborated and calibrated in highly structured, regulated ways.[3]
Terragni, too, sited his Casa del Fascio in Como, Italy, with reference to the
city's ancient Roman grid, but Eisenman's nimble manipulations of multifari-
ous, highly abstracted grids are light years away from Terragni's elegantly
straightforward ones.[4]

   After working with such tools for several house designs, Eisenman
"broke ground" with the plane of the earth in House Eleven in a program
elaborated by Kurt Forster, now director of the Getty Center in Santa Monica,
California. Later, in the competitions for Cannaregio in Italy and the International Architectural Exhibition (IBA) in Berlin, again following cues from
Forster, Eisenman excavated the various grids belonging to the sites' complicated urban histories for his own buildings.[5] Most of Eisenman's subsequent
projects have either fabricated or located grids of some sort to serve as the

abstract field upon
which to work out
his compositional
strategies; or, as
Michael Graves
wryly noted at the
Wexner inaugural
symposium, to play
out the games that
Eisenman invents
and controls, with
rules known only to
him. As in that old
con, the shell game, Eisenman directs attention to completely specious references while proceeding to manipulate the game at will.

   But the Wexner Center does not depend upon the web of obfuscations
spun around it, and quite unexpectedly, it is a fine building. Much credit goes
to Eisenman's partner, Richard Trott, for the careful construction and high-
quality detailing, work for which he is well known in Ohio and which belies

the standard complaints about the inevitability of shoddy workmanship. Eisenman knows he could not have chosen a better partner, for the team is also building the Columbus convention center and two other projects.

Resisting the temptation to produce a freestanding monument was both daring and wise and is the source of much of the Wexner's strength. Most of the building consists of a three-block slice between two older buildings, at once joining them and nearly doubling the floor area. It therefore appears deceptively small, even though it extends three stories in places and exceeds 100,000 square feet of floor area. Most of the spaces are underground, which works well for the film theater, studios, and gallery, but is not particularly felicitous for the Fine Arts Library. Here natural light was sacrificed in order to preserve the integrity of the sandstone plinths for landscaping above—a questionable choice at best.

The central arcade and passageway of scaffolding mark the spine along which the various functions are deployed. Although a second axis complicates it, this straightforward scheme is deliberately blurred both within and without, for Eisenman/Trott defy conventional expectations at every turn, blocking vistas and introducing multiple complications such as dead ends and dangling columns. For example, they add perceptual puzzles with the shadows and reflections of the scaffolding on the gridded curtain walls of translucent and tinted glazing, not to mention locational puzzles for the visitor who struggles to tease an order out of the complex spatial organization. But it is not incomprehensible: diversity of spaces and materials ensures that one finally has enough clues to grasp and remember the building.

Having recognized the quality of the Wexner project, I want to register three qualifications. The first concerns that element of the Wexner that stubbornly resists the artifice of the grids: the reconstructed armory, the link between city and campus. The brick shells arose from the fabricated foundations of the old ROTC (Reserve Officers' Training Corps) and armory building, a strange structure to resurrect for any reason. Its forbidding, fortresslike brick towers explicitly resuscitate a highly problematic era in the life of American universities, when uniformed officer candidates marched about on the campuses and even carried arms. The original armory dated from 1898 and, as with armories on many other land grant colleges, accommodated the national guard, the state's strike force against its own citizens: striking workers in the nineteenth and twentieth centuries, civil rights marchers in the 1950s, antiwar demonstrators in the 1960s and 1970s. For Ohio, this building immediately summons memories of the slaughter of unarmed university students by the Ohio National Guard at Kent State University in May 1970.

American cities initiated massive armory construction campaigns during the 1930s, when the fear of a revolution by the poor and unemployed prompted stern precautionary measures by frightened authorities. ROTC facilities on college campuses became common in the 1950s during the McCarthy red-baiting and hysteria over communism, serving as symbols of government might placed precisely where the far right has long believed that communism and leftism are bred: the university. Government incursions onto college campuses—including covert operations to ferret out "dangerous" sorts who supported such things as low-income public housing in the 1950s and opposed the war in Vietnam in the 1960s and 1970s—were conducted from ROTC offices on campuses that became local beachheads of state authority. Perhaps it is no coincidence that uniformed and armed students parade once again on university campuses, so that the Wexner is of a piece with larger reactionary politics. This is not, then, an innocent gesture.

The exhumation of this troubling symbol brings me to my second qualification. Much is made in Derridean deconstruction and in Eisenman's version of it of uncovering the hidden, of revealing the "repressed," hence the conflation of multiple grids in the Wexner and, of course, the armory.[6] Here, the site's *real* political history is repressed in favor of a decorative shell, perhaps the most compelling and powerful feature of the whole project. With its delicate craftsmanship and playful slices of tower, arch, and wall, in its Disneylandish caricature of the earlier structure, it effectively realizes the gloomy prognosis of Walter Benjamin about the aestheticization of politics.[7] The fetishized structures are wittingly emptied of their history and rendered nothing more than cheerfully manipulable images that direct attention only to formal games. As Benjamin noted, such architecture, whatever other claims are made for it, serves as nothing more than elegant distraction.

Eisenman has used Derrida's theory on deconstruction much as he now appears to be using Gianni Vattimo's "weak thought": to legitimize the endless formal games with an intellectual gloss, and to foil criticism.[8] When all reality is only textuality, when everything is a free play of signifiers, and when the architect's agenda consists of revealing the repressed, undermining, disclosing, summoning forth the fragmentation and alienation of today's society, all possible criticism is swallowed up in a black hole. Like total dogmatism, total relativism renders any discussion impossible. It is also a straitjacket for the architecture itself, which brings me to my third point.

In more recent projects, such as at Carnegie Mellon, Eisenman has liberated the grid from its Cartesian limbo and adopted formal motifs clearly derived from Aldo Rossi. It is instructive to place the Wexner against the work of the two architects to whom Eisenman owes most, Giuseppe Terragni and Aldo Rossi.[9] Perhaps it is unfair to measure the Wexner against their work, but the degree of hyperbole surrounding its inauguration demands some such comparison. The inaugural symposium—orchestrated by Eisenman himself—was a thinly disguised tribute to Eisenman, and the potpourri of avant-garde art the Wexner claims to shelter turns out to be the product of mainstream glitterati whose work would never be subjected to *de facto* or *ex post facto* censorship because their art is so profoundly inoffensive.[10]

Terragni indeed struggled with grids, cubes, and transformations, but those manipulations neither remain concealed nor are overwhelmingly present in the built work; they are discovered rather than forced upon the viewer. In a project such as the Casa del Fascio in Como, these formal moves share center stage with sensitively handled transparent, opaque, translucent, and reflective surfaces playing off one another, and with infusions of multiple light qualities—all of which are impossible to photograph or grasp in one image. Each material is handled with great subtlety, and the building is finally open-ended in its many possibilities. By contrast, the Wexner is flat and very nearly two-dimensional; its grids impose upon one another and at times verge on cacophony. It seems that this is Eisenman's intention, and in line with suggestions from Vattimo, he seeks a "weak image," which cannot be photographed or grasped in one view. In fact, the Casa del Fascio is far more elusive, far more difficult to capture on film, even if its exterior elevations apparently lend themselves to the "strong image" that Eisenman now opposes. And surprisingly, although Eisenman's theories would appear to offer uncommon possibilities for rich spatial invention, he has not exploited them with the Wexner.

Eisenman's gridded passageway also does not measure up to similar passageways in Aldo Rossi's work. In the arcades at the Gallaratese, the Broni school, and the Modena cemetery, Rossi, too, relied upon repetitive elements along one, two, or three sides of a passageway, but because of the materials and the dimensions and spacing of the elements, they extend with a measured, almost timeless dignity, an elegant and majestic backdrop to the promenade, and they articulate with elegant subtlety different kinds of passageways. Contrast this with Eisenman's scaffolding, which drives through the site with the relentless monotony of a picket fence. Without the roofs, parapets, or even vines of Rossi's arcades, the Wexner grid offers no prospect of transformation by different angles or degrees of light, no visual variety or delight. It is as if Eisenman's vision is that of the X ray, which registers only skeleton and the faintest trace of muscle, tissue, and flesh. And yet those elements he neglects may be the most necessary components of a design.

The difference between the Wexner and works by Terragni and Rossi lies in the absolutely controlled, if apparently arbitrary, surprises that the Wexner offers, surprises that skirt dangerously close to one-liners. The other two architects do not rely upon such complicated artifice to entice the viewer, but instead allow their buildings to yield their treasures, many of which are unanticipated, slowly and over time. With his highly diagrammatic structures (some interiors seem not unlike a dentist's waiting room), Eisenman apparently deliberately seeks out the "depthlessness" that some commentators believe is characteristic of postmodernism. Unfortunately, he has succeeded. But he has failed in another objective: he claims to advocate an alienating architecture, but this building is profoundly ingratiating and has been warmly received by a wide range of precisely those people Eisenman sees as complacent and deceived by contemporary consumer culture. That it is a fine building is testimony to the resilience of materials and construction to the artifice of theory.

■ II. Invisible Acropolis

Is it possible for architecture to distinguish itself from the institutional aims and philosophies of the patron, those which are its virtual *raison d'être?* More important, should it? In Los Angeles, The Getty Trust's institutional impera- tives are cloaked in the gauzy trappings of impeccable and unquestioned cultural and economic verities, so that it constantly engages in an elaborate game of transparency and opacity, apparent openness and adroit conceal- ment. Faced with the task of designing The Getty Trust's new center for its seven operating programs, architect Richard Meier has produced a project that exposes the modalities of this game with unerring—if too literal—clarity.

   With an endowment of several billion dollars, the proceeds of which must be spent for "the diffusion of artistic and general knowledge," The J. Paul Getty Trust (known as The Trust or The Getty to intimates, just as the tycoon Donald Trump is known as "The Donald") rapidly became the top player in the international art game during the 1980s. Beyond its striking ability to pay unheard-of sums for works of art (an estimated $57 million doled out for Vincent van Gogh's *Irises* in March 1990), The Trust has also moved aggressively into grant-making to institutions, individuals, and publica- tions; into document, archive, and book collecting; and into art education and art information: in short, into nearly every area of connoisseurship and aca- demic pedagogy associated with "the arts."[11] The first of several conflicting tendencies with which The Getty is riven emerges here, for despite embrac- ing the arts, the Trust focuses on classical and postclassical western Euro- pean art up to 1900; everything else is largely ignored.[12]

   Until Meier's twenty-four-acre cultural complex is completed in 1995, The Trust conducts its far-flung activities from skyscraper towers—built with Mellon money—in Century City. Here, on the former back lots of the old Twen- tieth Century Fox Studios (the preferred destination of white flight from down- town Los Angeles following the Watts rebellion in 1965), the fiction of an all-white society is fashioned by investment companies, brokerage houses, law firms, insurance companies, and mortgage bankers, an ironic variation on the old Hollywood fictions once cranked out in celluloid on the same site. As

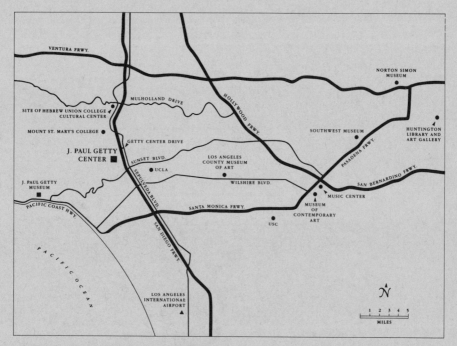

Map of Los Angeles provided by The Getty Trust. Among the related institutions whose vectors apparently do not intersect with those of The Getty on this schematic map are Loyola-Marymount University, The Natural History Museum, Southern California Institute of Architecture (SCI-Arc), the Afro-American Museum, and the Santa Monica Museum. Perhaps the most notable feature of the map is the large white section in the lower-right corner: traversed by no highways and marked by no cultural institutions recognized by The Getty, this largely poor and minority area includes Watts, Lynwood, and other mostly Black neighborhoods. (J. Paul Getty Trust)

the corporate art behemoth par excellence, The Trust, with a board of trustees drawn largely from that same hard world of corporate deal-making, has managed to make itself virtually indistinguishable from its more explicitly corporate neighbors. The move to a hilltop site in the Santa Monica mountains constitutes a variation on the theme manifested in Century City: the fantasy of a world apart from the real world, one that is dedicated to the "higher" things of life—the arts—and one that remains uncontaminated by the mundane preoccupations of the crowded city at its feet. Not surprisingly, these two informing motifs—the diffusion of artistic and general knowledge and a dedication to the "higher" things of life—come into open conflict with

View of the preliminary site model of The J. Paul Getty Center looking north. The museum sits to the right, and behind it are the facilities for The Trust and five of the operating programs. To the far left is The Getty Center, a building that has changed dramatically in subsequent design elaborations to a circular form. (Jack Ross)

Preliminary site model looking south, with the parking facilities and tram stop at the bottom, the tramway leading to the plaza on axis with the museum rotunda. The Getty Center is at the top right. The automated tram winds up the hill away from the bustle of the San Diego Freeway on the lower left. (Tom Bonner)

Aerial view of the preliminary site model of The Getty Center. Counterclockwise from the reflecting pool: the museum; The Trust administrative offices and facilities for the Conservation Institute, Education in Arts Center, and Art History Information Program; an auditorium; dining facilities; and at the bottom center, The Getty Center for the History of Art and the Humanities. (Tom Bonner)

one another, but the differences are more apparent than real, since in the end both converge on the most basic assumptions and goals.

Despite a kind of administrative structure, personnel, and board of trustees—not to mention income—that originated overwhelmingly in the boardrooms of corporate America, The Getty harbors a very different image of itself. A schematic map of Los Angeles produced by The Trust offers a telling indication of the Getty worldview: for just as late-medieval cartographers identified cities solely by their religious structures and monuments, so Los Angeles is imaged by The Getty as consisting of a few universities, colleges, and arts institutions. Nowhere does this anachronistic view emerge with greater clarity than in the choice of the site itself: a secluded spot high atop the Santa Monica Mountains overlooking, but decidedly remote from, Los Angeles. The Trust categorically dismissed sites that would have immersed it in the city. The other Getty operating programs have been housed temporarily in a variety of places: the Conservation Institute in a Marina del Rey warehouse, the museum in a fake Pompeiian villa overlooking Malibu, the library in another warehouse, and the Art History Information Program (AHIP) and The Getty Center for the History of Art and the Humanities (not to be confused with the new Getty Center complex, the subject of this essay) in a corporate office building above the First Federal Bank in Santa Monica. Enmeshed as it is in the city's fabric, The Trust is unable to seal off its international array of scholars and visitors from the vexing problems besetting Los Angeles's poor and homeless, who are visible everywhere, living at bus stops and in doorways near Getty offices. Even though the scholarly work remains remote from these surroundings, the scholars themselves cannot escape whenever they enter, leave, or even look out from the windows of their offices. It is precisely this that the site on the hilltop will allow The Trust to mediate. The parking facility at the foot of the hills—mandated by anxious neighbors in an effort to preserve their pristine privacy—and the automated tram that will control public access to the summit, drive home its exclusivity and remoteness. There will be no homeless on Getty Center Drive to mar the idyllic landscape.

But The Getty's mission to engage in "the diffusion of art" summons contradictory objectives. At least one-third of Meier's architectural project is devoted to the museum for collections of pre-twentieth-century western European paintings, drawings, sculpture, illuminated manuscripts, furniture, decorative arts, and photography (no living photographers are represented). These collections will be made available to the public, along with the associated cafés and gift shops that are part of the standard package for today's museums. Of The Trust's seven operating programs, only the museum is public in nature: the others are decidedly private.

Charged with articulating the dual impulses of public and private, Meier made several key moves. The buildings line up on two axes displaced by approximately 22.5 degrees, with the public building and the museum along one axis and the nonpublic buildings straddling the other. Following the ascent via tram, visitors will disembark to face the museum's rotunda. The Trust and other programs are set slightly back to the left, and the research facilities, archives, and library of The Getty Center sink one level below grade to the right. Meier emphasizes the public goals of the museum by distributing the galleries and related spaces in a series of pavilions extending out from the rotunda: space is provided for temporary exhibitions in rotated cubes and for permanent ones in the axially aligned pavilions. Likewise, traffic patterns through the museum allow—but do not require—movement inside and outside and between different levels.

The relative openness and spaciousness of the museum contrast with the tightly circular footprint of The Center, the art-think tank where the visiting scholars, library, and archives are sequestered. Placement on the site and the circular form of the building plan articulate the private, withdrawn character of the activities within. The private buildings, to be clad in sandblasted stainless-steel panels, will flank stone-clad museum buildings with skylights and a few modest openings for fenestration. The exterior therefore delicately balances a serene timelessness and an austere modernity.

The interiors promise to be quite a different story. The ideal modernist gallery is a white cube bereft of any cues that would interfere with the art. Although since the late eighteenth century, the museum in general has isolated its objects from the rest of the world in a hushed atmosphere more traditionally associated with religious sanctuaries, The Getty plans to recover an even earlier model.[13] Current museum director John Walsh seems to want to re-create aristocratic interiors—with regal wainscotting and flocked wall-paper—in which to display the artworks, reminding the cultural literati of the elite origins of these objects.

Such a gesture is by no means out of character. In its collection, display, and study of art, The Getty epitomizes the history of bourgeois art within its institutional confines: the passage from an exclusive diversion of the idle aristocracy to its bourgeois appropriation and mass dissemination.[14] The presupposition of the necessity of an economic surplus that would free the individual from a daily struggle for existence gave art its aristocratic status and made it desirable as a measure of status to collect, commission, and display. Precisely the uselessness of art and of the aesthetic appreciation associated with it (the idle luxury of the rich in contrast with the bourgeois world of production) came to constitute one of the most compelling emblems of high status. With the museum, The Getty must avoid being impaled on the horns of a dilemma, for if its mission to disseminate western European culture is successful, if the art is truly popularized beyond its "legitimate" receivers, then the efficacy of those artifacts as opiates for the elite is challenged.[15] It must, therefore, strike the delicate balance between making art and culture available to more than just "the few," and on the other hand, elevating (and thereby imposing exclusivity on) the level of discussion about that art and culture. So, the public function must artfully integrate the traditional museum as a temple to art with its more recent incarnation as a cultural shopping center, with designer originals on the walls and cheaper knockoffs in the gift shop.

In contemporary society, individuals and institutions are assessed, above all else, according to their capacity to spend and consume; in this category, The Getty wins the prize. The Trust manages to accomplish the imperatives of a cultural and economic aristocracy by ratifying an impeccable taste structure, rarefying it out of reach of the masses, and finally, manipulating more economic capital than almost anyone else can muster. With a staggering fortune at its disposal, The Getty confines its collections, academic activities, and publications to matters long blessed by elites of Europe and America as the acme of classical and postclassical western civilization. The great collections were assembled, in the past as now, by greed, robbery, and enormous expenditures and became accessible to a wide public only within the last two centuries.[16] The dominant groups of this dominant culture have fashioned the artistic and cultural production of a tiny fraction of the world into an unquestioned and unquestionable standard of quality against which everything else must be measured. Those who purchase, study, or display those artifacts claim the arbitrary authority to exclude or devalue other artifacts, or even to reappropriate those previously scorned (such as the work of postimpressionists like Vincent van Gogh). These fundamental premises of The Trust—and most other such institutions in America and Western Europe—make it a very problematic institution indeed.

Culture here is not presented as a terrain contested by classes, ethnic groups, gender, or nations, but as already determined, absolute, pure. In this sense, The Getty calls to mind Disneyland's fantasy re-creations of idealized worlds of the past: Main Street, U.S.A., for example, scrubbed clean of poverty, homelessness, class, race, or ethnic struggle, and even of labor and industrial production. So, too, the art enshrined in institutions such as The Getty is effortlessly remote from a world of cares. The negative reference point against which this aesthetic culture defines itself is that which is called popular, middlebrow, or lowbrow. Instead of positing art and culture as the living products of collectivities, of struggles, it is here simply presented as a bourgeois fetish wherein the less meaningful the object of artistic attention (such as irises), the more valuable the work, and the greater the emphasis on formal qualities as the measure of the art to the exclusion of other possibilities. Although The Getty Trust is not responsible for formulating these attitudes toward a certain class of artifacts, it is responsible for promulgating them: one could have wished for an engaged institution rather than a detached one, one which problematized the notion of culture or art rather than enshrined it. Given the hegemony of these goals, it is considered barbaric to ask how such art enriches or improves. But it is one thing to study and appreciate artifacts of the past, and quite another to fetishize them.

In the end, despite moves that subtly attenuate the tension between conflicting impulses, the weight of the institution proves too much, even for Meier. The art to be studied and exhibited here, while ostensibly available to the masses, is clearly destined for what is held to be an especially gifted minority whose aesthetic sense or scholarly acumen distinguishes it from the rest of the world—which, by implication, is how things ought to be. By its very definition, the museum in general neutralizes and decontextualizes artifacts, thereby institutionally perpetuating a single dominant attitude and a specific aesthetic, and privileging form and the detached gaze of the aesthete over everything else. The architecture that makes this possible cannot but be complicit in the enterprise as a whole. It appears that Meier's project for The Getty will enhance this privileged status of the western European work of art. Although from many sight lines, The Getty Center complex will be invisible, it remains an acropolis, a bastion for white, western European culture transplanted to the shores of the Pacific.

1. "Postmodernism and Beyond: Architecture as the Critical Art of Contemporary Culture," symposium at the University of California, Irvine, 26–28 October 1989.
2. See the November 1989 issue of *Progressive Architecture* dedicated to the Wexner; *A + U*'s January 1990 issue dedicated to the Wexner; and the book, *Wexner Center for the Visual Arts, The Ohio State University* (New York: Rizzoli, 1989).
3. For at least eighteen years, various publishers have been announcing Eisenman's book on Terragni. At this writing, it has still not appeared.
4. Terragni explains the relationship of the old Roman city grid to the siting of the Casa del Fascio in *Quadrante 35/36* (1936), in a special issue dedicated to this building.
5. Forster is also the mind behind Daniel Libeskind's winning scheme in the recent competition for the Jewish Museum in Berlin.
6. Among the avalanche of publications on deconstruction that have appeared in the last three years, see Andreas Papadakis, Catherine Cooke, and Andrew Benjamin, *Deconstruction, Omnibus Volume* (London: Rizzoli, 1990).
7. Walter Benjamin, "The Work of Art in the Age of Mechanical Reproduction," in *Illuminations*, ed. Hannah Arendt (New York: Schocken, 1968), pp. 242–3.
8. Only one book by Vattimo has been translated into English: *The End of Modernity*, trans. Jon R. Snyder (Baltimore: Johns Hopkins Univ. Press, 1988). Vattimo's *Il pensiero debole* (Milan: Feltrinelli, 1983) and *La società trasparente* (Milan: Garzanti, 1989) are two of his most important recent works.
9. In the 1970s, Eisenman was instrumental in bringing Rossi to America and seeing to the English translation of his two books: *The Architecture of the City*, trans. Diane Ghirardo and Joan Ochman (Cambridge, Mass.: MIT Press, 1982) and *Scientific Autobiography*, trans. Lawrence Venutti (Cambridge, Mass.: MIT Press, 1981).
10. Among the luminaries who graced the opening of the Wexner were Colleen Dewhurst, Laurie Anderson, Trisha Brown, Philip Glass, the Kronos Quartet, the gospel group J. D. Steel Singers and the Simultaneous Revival Choir, and Barbara Walters. The symposium included current *architectural* luminaries Philip Johnson, Kurt Forster, Harry Cobb, Michael Graves, Charles Gwathmey, Richard Meier, and Stanley Tigerman.

11. Most of the details of The Trust's activities derive from annual reports, pamphlets, and quarterly bulletins. Although the price of the Van Gogh painting remains secret, the last known price was $57 million.

12. Getty staffers have called my attention to the activities of The Getty Center, one of The Trust's operating programs, which has made forays into the twentieth-century arts. The bulk of its activities remain pre-1900.

13. For an extended discussion of spaces for the display of art, see Brian O'Doherty, *Inside the White Cube: The Ideology of the Gallery Space* (San Francisco and Santa Monica: The Lapis Press, 1986).

14. Joseph Rykwert, "The Cult of the Museum from the Treasure House to the Temple," *Museos Estelares, A & V, Monografias de Arquitectura y Vivienda* 18 (1989); Helmut Seling, "The Genesis of the Museum," *Architectural Review* 141 (February 1967), pp. 103–14.

15. Pierre Bourdieu has undertaken an extensive and exhaustive sociological analysis of these and other matters in *Distinction: A Social Critique of the Judgment of Taste* (Cambridge, Mass.: Harvard Univ. Press, 1984).

16. I owe this formulation to Rykwert, "The Cult of the Museum," p. 81.

Low Cost Housing
in Twentieth-Century Rome

Ferruccio Trabalzi

The appearance of a city derives not from a single intervention, but from many that intersect one another over time. Some are so deeply embedded in the past that they would seem to have disappeared. It is the task of the historian to unearth them and to identify the signs of their persistence into the present. This essay traces the underlying motifs of the development of low-income housing in Rome since 1870 and the relation of the architectural profession to this kind of housing. In particular, I privilege the perspective from below, that is, the poor, casting light on superstructures of the city and those micro-elements that emerge only as picturesque details in the urban architectural panorama. The key examples I present are not directly connected to one another but represent important moments in the history of the building of modern Rome.

The 120 years since Rome became the capital of Italy can be divided into four distinct periods of low-income housing construction.[1] The first period dates back to the late nineteenth century and the decision to transfer the capital of the new Italian state to Rome—a decision with consequences that rippled throughout the peninsula. The second embraces the twenty years of fascism, during which the government's often ambiguous politics of low-income housing alternated between benevolent paternalism and resolute apartheid. The years immediately following World War II were characterized by an architecture sensitive to the needs of the poor but riven by internal contradictions and dwarfed by the explosion of illegal building outside the framework of the "master plans" for the city. The result was the shapeless, disfigured city we know today. The final period dates from the 1970s, the years of popular rebellion.

In tracing the development of low-income housing in Rome, I examine three projects: the fascist-planned Primavalle *borgata* built in 1937 for the low-income population;[2] a neorealist experiment, the Tiburtino quarter of

1949; and finally, a district called the Magliana, for which the original plan dates from the 1920s but which came to fruition only at the hands of private developers in the 1970s. My concern is not just for the buildings, but for the quality and modalities of life in these settlements, insofar as the ideals of architecture are so often contradicted by circumstances and contingencies that rob the architecture of its intended meaning.

■ I

I. Living in the city offers countless possibilities for fascinating mental journeys simply because of the constant movement to and fro—from anywhere to nowhere—that is typical of major metropolises. But in reality, few people in Rome are able to "live in the city": its endless periphery in fact calls into question the myth of the metropolis as privileged site of mobility and as comprising all possible experiences. In effect, Rome has seen both movement from the country into the city and of residents forced to recede from the historic center to the endless peripheral suburbs that lack nothing but the city itself. Here, in the limitless periphery, one lives Rome's solitude, its individuality, its homogeneity. Here, ORDER plays its cards and reveals its face in endless housing blocks lacking social services—dormitories whose sameness impedes the possibility of any truly collective social life. Here, one discovers the face of domination as it manifests itself in a "free" society. Here, freedom terminates in the right to beautify one's own apartment and to live the illusion of serving one's own interests by doing so, while in fact one struggles to participate in a culture largely determined by elite interests.

Identity in this context is understood as *consumer identity*, such that the center of Rome—not to mention countless other Italian cities—has been transformed into one giant shopping center, and former residents and their descendants have been cast into the shapeless outer periphery. Much research has been undertaken to discover who, exactly, lives on the outskirts of the historic center; but an analysis of social composition is difficult because the dichotomy between bourgeoisie and working class has been blurred beyond distinction by the effects of mass consumerism. We know that three-quarters of the city's people live in these peripheral zones, and therefore, they are not a marginal population but rather the essence of the city itself: that (polity) which "counts" politically. If the folkloristic Rome of tradition still exists in the minds of Italian politicians, in the pages of foreigners' diaries and magazines as they search for exotic treats, or in the pages of tourist brochures that still image the city of *la dolce vita,* in reality, it is difficult to find that Rome today. A rupture exists between center and periphery that has polarized the city. It expresses the politics of a ruling class that has for half a century monopolized the development of Rome, inserting itself into a discourse already under way during the twenty-year period of fascist rule, and that has produced the idiosyncrasies of today. This rupture has widened under left-wing governments, which, on the one hand, liberated Rome from the embarrassment of shanty villages, but on the other, created the vast, crowded periphery that congeals around and strangles the center.

2. Although we typically conceive of cities as spatiotemporal unities of asphalt, glass, and concrete, the city is arguably far more appropriately defined as an entity composed of the diversity of experiences of living in and using it. Precisely the desire to be part of a city leads us to reflect upon the character of the places where we live, not in terms of routines and the abstractions this fosters, but rather in terms of the need for dense inhabitations and frequent interactions with others whereby we participate in fashioning the city of lived experience, "making the city" or *fabbricare la città.* With this we return to the origins of urban growth, the political and economic imperatives that shaped individual cities, their urban forms, and in turn, the political groups and ideologies that constitute the city's shifting configurations. For some time, things have been changing in Rome in response to the long dominant imperative for development at all costs: a new political agenda of regulation and limitation has been drawn up, paralleled by the growth of an environmental culture dedicated to preserving the city landscape. This essay touches upon the history of Rome's twentieth-century growth as it was managed by those who governed the city on behalf of private interests rather than for public good.

3. The Master Plan of 1931 already indicated some of the features that would determine the city's development. Among those features, I especially want to point out the demolitions conducted in the historic center between 1924 and 1940 that led to the Rome of a thousand squatter camps. When it was decided to tear down the borgate and these squatter camps during the 1960s, they had already inscribed themselves as directional axes for the future urban growth of the city for two reasons: on the one hand, they grew up on the flanks of the ancient Roman roads; on the other hand, they annexed themselves to the official borgate that had been hastily constructed to house those displaced from the city center as well as the thousands of immigrants who arrived every day from the countryside. I cannot undertake here an exhaustive account of modern Rome's history; I merely want to explore from the bottom up, so to speak, the itinerary of the ideas that have underlain the development of low-income housing in the twentieth century.

■ II

I. With Italian unification in 1870, and with the decision to transfer the capital to the new state of Rome, new ideas began to circulate after centuries of stagnation under papal authority. Rome lacked everything appropriate to its new role as capital. Between 1871 and 1887, Rome saw an unprecedented building boom, with an uninterrupted flow of construction activity throughout its walled enclosure. Northern Italian and foreign investors and developers transacted deals with the aristocracy of Rome to sell their villas, inside and ultimately outside the Aurelian walls, which up to that point had marked the boundary between city and countryside. Anyone who could manage to gather a bit of money became a developer overnight.

With its new concentration of government and foreign ministries and state bureaucracies, Rome was a magnet for chronically impoverished rural families who saw in it new sources of employment.[3] The mass immigration of unskilled laborers from the countryside contrasted with the flood of professionals, clerical workers, and petty bureaucrats coming from northern Italy. The missing element in Rome, in sharp contrast to other European capitals,

Typical early twentieth-century low-income apartment house, via G. Branca, Testaccio, Q. Pirani, architect, 1918. Because no typology had yet been developed for such housing, designers adapted upper-class housing types. Later low-cost housing is far less decorated.

Courtyard of low-income unit on via G. Branca, Testaccio.

was a concentration of the industrial proletariat. Only workers in the service sector enjoyed a strong group identity, and from this group operating through cooperatives came the first moves toward the construction of moderate income housing. A financial crisis in 1887 arrested building activity, but not the steady flow of new residents, at the rate of eighteen thousand to twenty thousand per year up until 1900. Building activity slowly picked up again, but remained well below the level of demand until it virtually ceased with the onset of World War I. Christian Democrat administrations responded sluggishly to the demand for housing, especially for the lowest income groups.

Among the typical low-income housing projects built immediately prior to and following World War I was the Testaccio quarter, the second largest of all of the housing projects completed by the government between 1903 and 1930.[4] With fewer than eighteen hundred apartments, however, it barely made a dent in the housing needs of Rome's new residents. Designed in two groups, one by Giulio Magni and the other by Quadrio Pirani, the buildings evidenced the indecision over building typology for mass housing. In the absence of a fixed type, the designers reverted to the example of upper-class housing, outfitting the building blocks with broad arched entrances over rusticated bases, egg and dart moldings, elaborate baroque windows, decorative string courses, and so forth.

2. With the advent of fascism, the housing market recovered and speculation picked up more feverishly than ever; at the same time, a rhetoric of a return to the grandeur of Augustan and imperial Rome guided planning decisions within the old walls. The national agricultural crisis of 1923 to 1927 urged ever greater numbers of people to move to Rome, and with apartments and space at a premium, they erected so-called spontaneous borgate.[5] Rome's urban fringes began to take on the appearance of modern shantytowns, with shacks built using the debris left by the rest of the city. The lingering relationship between Rome and its countryside was now forever ruptured.

The situation dramatically worsened with the displacement of thousands of people from within Rome as a result of the *sventramenti* or demolitions—in Italian, literally, "disemboweling"—that were undertaken in order to unearth the ruins of ancient Rome from the fifteen hundred years of building that had entombed them. Fascism's political liturgy had already exhumed the classical ideal as a bridge between contemporary Italians and ancient Romans. Thus that which had grown atop ancient ruins—called national monuments after 1870—was to be torn down. To be sure, this demolition had been under way well before fascism, but under Mussolini, it became the top priority in Rome. It is easy to recognize a free transposition by regime intellectuals of the concept of noble simplicity and that of serene grandeur that Winkelmann in 1755 identified as the essence of the classical ideal of Greek beauty.[6] Here it was linked to Roman monumentality in order to adapt it to the age of mass politics. The *Duce* himself remarked:

In five years, Rome will appear beautiful to everyone in the world; vast, ordered, and powerful as it was under Augustus. You will liberate the trunk of the great oak from everything that encumbers it. You will open up the areas around the theater of Marcellus, the Pantheon, and the Campidoglio; everything that was created during the centuries of decadence must disappear. In five years one must be able to see the Pantheon from Piazza Colonna. You will also free the majestic temples of Christian Rome from their parasitical constructions. The millennial monuments of our history must stand isolated and gigantic.[7]

At this point, urban planners could unite ethics and aesthetics, and archaeologists could rewrite history to emphasize results while ignoring explanation. One result of this was to promote the city of Rome as a stage set and, in so doing, sacrifice the integrity and coherence of the living city in favor of the dead city of regime parades: architecture here is used for imperial prestige.

The inhabitants of the historic center, who had always been integrated into the urban fabric, suddenly learned that they were in the way and ended up joining the ranks of the thousands of homeless in shacks at the city's edge. To these groups were suddenly added yet more families, rendered homeless by the end of rent control in 1930.[8] Between 1924 and 1930, following the demolitions orchestrated by archaeologist Corrado Ricci and architect Marcello Piacentini, fifty-five hundred inhabitable flats disappeared.[9]

The various attempts to house the homeless following World War I were governed by the demagogy that accompanied the end of hostilities and the rise of fascism. The government slogans were "sunlight" and "clean air": only on the outskirts of the dense city could these be found in abundance, and the political power in Rome deemed such locations necessary for the lower classes. During the period of the major demolitions, the government began building urban hotels—something of a paradox, given their peripheral location—in the Garbatella working-class district and then quickly wherever shantytowns had sprung up. Although they offered a new architectural typology, these hotels were signs of a major failure, since the absence of permanent housing immediately upset their original purpose: the families who moved in ended up permanent rather than temporary residents. In the end, the hotels had to be transformed into real apartments. The public dormitories built in the other new zones constructed under fascism continued in operation until the late 1970s.[10]

3. Thus Rome's housing stock suffered exogenous pressures by virtue of the removal of the lower classes from the historic center, and endogenous pressures with the arrival of rural Italians from the countryside. The so-called

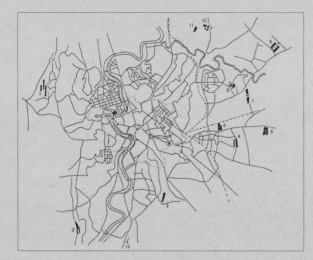

Plan of Rome with the borgate
of the fascist era:

1 Primavalle
2 Trullo
3 Tor Marancio
4 Gordiani
5 Quarticciolo
6 Prenestino
7 S. Maria del Soccorso
8 Pietralata
9 S. Basilio
10 Tufello
11 Val Melaina
12 Acilia

villaggi abissini (a late-thirties term for shantytowns) were intolerable eye-
sores to the new fascist state and were also seen as potential sites of political
unrest. Pressure mounted for the government to do something: the answer
turned out to be the official *borgate rapidissime,* quickly built suburban enclaves. Not incidentally, once the unsightly shacks disappeared, the land
closest to the city became free for speculation and for the construction of
housing for the middle and upper classes.

    The guiding ideas for low-income housing had two fundamental prin-
ciples: one was to avoid settlements typically seen as lower-class within the
walls of Rome; the other was to prevent the lower classes from coming into
sufficient contact with one another to perceive themselves as a class and
thereby risk the formation of political groups.

    With the establishment of the borgate, the tendency toward class segre-
gation accelerated. The planning criteria adopted for their construction have
traditionally been disparaged by historians; indeed, they have largely been
ignored except for an occasional mention, and they have been seen as more
successful for maintaining order than as workable urban plans.[11] In fact, this
represents a simplistic analysis of the fascist borgate in Rome: for although
there is much to criticize, many features have proven far superior to the postwar additions.

The Master Plan of 1931 set the limits of urban growth. All twelve of the fascist borgate ignored the 1931 plan, thus setting the pattern for private developers to do likewise.[12] In the planning of the borgate, the government tended to place them both far from the historic center and far from each other, isolating them in easily controlled ghettos (many of the citizens transferred to the borgate were anarchists, communists, and others deemed dangerous by the regime). The architects and planners then eagerly undertook the technical realization of the borgate without ever questioning the actual living conditions that they were supposed to be providing.

The delicate connection between Romans and their city, which virtually depended upon residence, was fully ruptured in the borgate. The small merchant or artisan displaced to a borgata found himself several kilometers from the nearest transportation depot; the same was true for the women who performed domestic work for the upper classes: the buses they needed for transportation to work were far away, ran infrequently, and were unreliable. The trip to work became long and uncomfortable and soon led to the loss of jobs, to long hours away from home and family, and to increasing tension, which in turn often erupted in violence. As always, such eruptions simply reinforced the belief that these people needed to be controlled: it is not surprising that many of the borgate—including the focus here, Primavalle—were situated close to military forts or police barracks. What came to be the predominant characteristics of the borgate were ironically cast as features of popular folklore—cultural expressions of the lower classes—by neorealist filmmakers of the postwar era. Only later were the degradations of the borgate denounced by intellectuals, chief among them Pier Paolo Pasolini, who lost his life in a borgata of Nuova Ostia.

4. The fascist borgate have similar historical constellations, but the story of Primavalle is in many ways emblematic. Like the other borgate, it was situated far from the historic center of the city, and since it was not included in the master plan, for nearly twenty-five years it was officially treated as if it did not exist from the point of view of services such as transportation and education.[13]

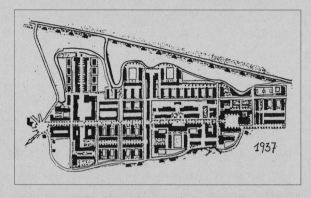

Giorgio Guidi, plan of Primavalle, first version, 1937. (Istituto Autonomo delle Case Popolari, Rome)

Giorgio Guidi, plan of Primavalle, final version, 1937. (Istituto Autonomo delle Case Popolari, Rome)

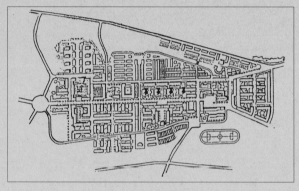

The site chosen was a thirty-seven-hectare [one hectare=2.471 acres] high plateau in the countryside to the north of the city. In the early 1930s, a few shacks and a public dormitory were erected in the middle of open fields. Architect Giorgio Guidi's project of 1937 for an urban core, which was to house between seven and eight thousand people, was articulated along a central southeast-northwest axis, a disposition that conditioned the building typology and solar orientation. The buildings parallel to the axis were single, two-story blocks, with entrance stairs on the street in various arrangements, while the orthogonal buildings used single-loaded covered galleries, or *ballatoio*, usually three to four stories high. Guidi's plan provided for southern exposure and ample light on the street elevations even in the middle of winter. Aside from its soundness from a planning point of view, this provision would help offset the total absence of a heating system.

Public dormitory, Primavalle, 1930. The dormitory remained in use until the early 1970s as a refuge for those in the worst state of poverty. Every day at 7:30 am inhabitants had to leave and could not return until evening. With no place else to go, they wandered around Primavalle with their belongings, much as the homeless do today in American cities.

Piazza Clemente IX, southern terminus of via Federico Borromeo, Primavalle. The two buildings visible are the only ones completed according to Guidi's plan (although the one to the left had additional stories added). The fountain—originally surrounded by several travertine benches, trees, and two drinking fountains—served as a public center.

Wing of porticoes and housing on Piazza Capecelatro, Primavalle. Residents undertook to renovate the porticoes and the housing on their own, despite the fact that the building is still publicly owned.

Though it boasted an intelligent urban plan, the original design underwent numerous variations, and in the end, only six blocks were completed
according to Guidi's plan, along with parts of the two *piazzas*. The rest was
improvised according to the needs of the moment.[14] The plan also included
the incorporation of the preexisting elementary school and the church, for
many years the only social amenities available in Primavalle. The public
spaces that Guidi's plan provided for—new church, Casa del Fascio, police
station, post office, new school, gymnasium, cinema, market, and athletic
field—either were built much later or were never built at all.

An assessment of Guidi's plan can be made only on the basis of the
blocks constructed between 1937 and 1940, and indeed, they are the only
ones with a minimum of dignity and livability in a subsequently chaotic suburban fabric. In contrast with later apartment houses in the district, the buildings are usually only two or three stories high and never exceed four stories;
along the main axis (via Federico Borromeo), each building meets the street
differently, with considerable variety from unit to unit. Guidi took up the modern movement's search for an *existenz-minimum* for low-income housing,
along with other objectives such as green space and adequate insulation, but
without succumbing to the visual monotony that tended to afflict low-income
housing projects inspired by the modern movement: one thinks of Giuseppe
Pagano's design for Milano Verde, or the Filzi apartment district in Milan by
Albini, Camus, and Palanti, but also of many in the United States, like Lathrop
Homes in Chicago or Parkside in Detroit.[15] Although not immune to the lean
modern movement aesthetics, Guidi still held onto old-fashioned notions of
buildings as framers of spaces, of streets that terminate at significant public
buildings (even modest ones), of visually pleasing variety in mass, orientation, and elevation: in short, streets and spaces as events, even in such an
impoverished setting.

Primavalle's main street terminates at each end with a piazza, one
square and one round, each dominated by a church. Each of the piazzas is
framed by arcuated porticoes, although not all of those in Piazza Clemente IX
were completed as designed. The variations in building placement and elevation make the street far more visually appealing than most critics have been

Third block of Primavalle; detail of external corridor type with adjacent front and rear buildings. The open space between buildings contains vegetation, playgrounds, and laundry lines.

Low-income units from the 1930s in Primavalle with still-vacant land abutting the housing.

Entrance to buildings in fourth block, Primavalle.

Via Pietro Bembo, Primavalle; four-story public housing unit, with later private higher-density building surrounding it.

The edge of Piazza Clemente IX that was not completed according to Guidi's plan. This street is a dead end, awash with cars and difficult to traverse on foot or in a car.

Public housing in Primavalle, 1970s version; notably more dense and with higher (eight stories) buildings than found in the earlier projects.

willing to admit. Within the adjacent blocks, interior courtyards—with vegetation, playgrounds, and areas for hanging clothes—as well as varied building types make for pleasant oases in the otherwise densely inhabited quarter. In all of Primavalle, only these areas are closed to automobiles, a source of much of their appeal.

Guidi's project also suffered from revealing shortcomings. The most glaring concerned links to the city: in effect, the plan presumed the presence of roads that simply did not exist. The closest bus stops, between two and three kilometers away, were not connected to Primavalle by roads, and on top of that, it was a steep climb up and then down the valley to arrive at the borgata. The city, not recognizing Primavalle officially, was uninterested in building roads to it.

The apartment units were invariably small—one or two rooms with kitchen and bath—but were still more spacious than contemporary low-cost housing projects. The most important technical shortcoming, common to most Italian low-cost housing at the time and also later, concerns precisely this notion of a habitable cell where size is not established by an analysis of the family size of future residents but rather by an arbitrary decision to give them one or two rooms.[16] That is, the concept of existenz-minimum is not based on the amount of space necessary for each resident, but rather on the minimum number of rooms necessary to constitute an apartment. Poorer families, then more than now, tended to be quite large, so it is easy to imagine the difficulties residents of the borgata faced.[17] Some recount tales of eighteen people living in two rooms.

Collecting the lower classes and suspected subversives into these ghettos also facilitated another fascist practice, that of surrounding the area and closing it off whenever foreign dignitaries were in Rome. The residents were sealed in until the events were over and the visitors gone, and the smooth waters of diplomatic protocol were never ruffled by any visible resistance to fascism.

Between 1948 and 1958, various plans were set up to assist Primavalle, with the result of completely distorting the volumetric program, beginning with the construction of apartment blocks of five or more stories, without the gardens, courts, laundry lines, and porticoes that enriched the earlier units. The final blow came in the 1960s with the construction of more and taller buildings at an accelerated pace, filling in the natural slope along the western edge of the borgata, now the most debased area of the quarter.

In other respects, little changed in the lives of the inhabitants after the fall of fascism. Only in the 1960s did the city move to introduce basic services—two schools, one post office, a medical clinic—but by this time the original urban plan was long overwhelmed by the surrounding growth. Illegal building and wild real estate speculation, with corrupt owners joining forces with indifferent city officials, gave a much enlarged Primavalle its current image: an anonymous and, in parts, squalid agglomeration of cement. Primavalle has two hundred thousand residents, but not a single cinema— the only one built burned down in the 1970s and remains as it was the day after the fire on Piazza Clemente IX—much less more sophisticated cultural apparatus.

Since Guidi's plan, street planning and building codes have not figured in Primavalle's growth, with the result that everyone has a car and no place to park. Postwar democracy broadened the community's demographic base, but under the Christian Democratic government, tutelage of the land simply amounted to a wild free-for-all of development. Professionals, small business owners, employees of the state, and students have joined the earlier residents in a fashion unimaginable by the architects of fascist apartheid. But the image of Primavalle as a dangerous haven of political radicalism and crime persists, fueled by the uprisings of the 1970s and by drug traffic, neither of which is exclusive to Primavalle or any of the other borgate.

Primavalle's history is the common story of other official borgate that grew in the wake of demolitions designed to provide the fascists with grand streets for parades, the archaeologists with monuments, and the former residents with suburban ghettos.

1. By the end of the war, Rome was a bureaucratic city surrounded by shanty-towns and legal ghettos. In the adjacent Agro Romano, individual families began to build permanent nuclei of houses and apartment blocks, indifferent to planning considerations. In sum, these haphazard enterprises brought illegal building to a staggeringly high level in the ensuing years. By contrast with equatorial countries and even with its own earlier history, Rome's illegal building during the 1950s and 1960s consisted of solid brick structures fashioned according to the owner's taste, usually one story high but later being modified to add a second or even third floor. These illegal structures became in time permanent additions to Rome's patrimony.[18]

In the meantime, autonomous political movements (such as the Comitati popolari) began to develop outside of traditional political alignments. These movements gave voice to the protests of thousands of forgotten residents of Rome's urban periphery. The movements managed to have political input, in part because of a series of local but extremely important actions. Reverse strikes date from this period, wherein the unemployed in the borgate organized themselves to build the infrastructures long denied by the city itself, such as roads (Primavalle), water lines, and bus routes (Casilina and Tiburtino). Rome became a laboratory for political protest movements with the willingness of ever larger numbers of people to descend into the streets and publicly expose their struggles and problems as well as the contradictions in the behavior of the city's administrations. Public protests were seen by the left as an avant-garde of class consciousness, while the populist wing of rightist parties saw them either as troublesome disruptions or as reservoirs of possible votes. In this explosive situation, Italian architects sought an identity of their own in the new social conditions, a search rendered more difficult by the twenty-year alliance with fascism, in which both neoclassical architecture and rationalist modernism struggled to become the regime's representative architecture.[19]

Some measure of political engagement was a necessity, and reflection on the immediate past permitted architects and critics to attempt a preliminary evaluation. Unfortunately, these reflections centered on questions of style or form rather than content or political relations, and whole bodies of research initiated during the 1930s were abandoned by postwar architects.

The architects' encounter with the masses was another specific aspect of this historical moment. Newly elevated by the antifascist resistance and postwar struggles, the masses came to be seen as the new repositories of "truth," in a tendency generally described as *neorealist* as the term is applied to cinema and literature. This reading soon revealed its limits in that it did not lead to the fabrication of a unified strategy, but rather to highly individualistic proposals that exposed the tensions within the movement itself.[20] The 1945 Congress for Reconstruction (Convegno nazionale per la ricostruzione edilizia) organized by Ernesto Rogers and others issued a general condemnation of speculation and a proposal to valorize Italy's historic urban centers and develop new alternative cities that would take shape outside of and untouched by traditional political games.[21] These well-meaning proposals remained utopian and academic ideas that proved incapable of confronting the stubborn realities of political life. Even the adherence to popular ideals was conducted with the bad conscience so typical of opportunistic intellectuals.

2. Let us turn to a concrete example: the Tiburtino quarter of 1949. The project was built in response to the INA-Casa Statute (Istituto nazionale assicurazioni, or National Insurance Service). This series of laws provided for increased construction of low-income housing and for increases in lower-class employment opportunities, but it was transformed into a public instrument actually under private control and therefore a useful tool for blackmailing the working class.

The principal designers of the Tiburtino project, Lodovico Quaroni and Mario Ridolfi, were members of APAO (an association founded by Bruno Zevi that recognized the ambiguous and instrumental goals of the INA-Casa project and refused to participate in any of its building schemes).[22] However, Quaroni and Ridolfi belonged to a faction that contested the majority view in the APAO and, perhaps for fear of being marginalized and isolated, elected to participate in the Tiburtino project.

The total area set aside for the Tiburtino project was relatively small—

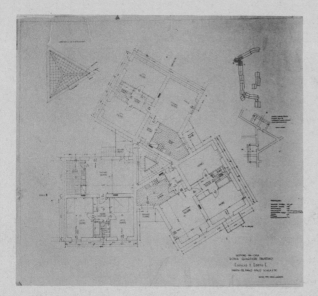

INA-Casa district in Tiburtino, Rome, 1949. Architects L. Quaroni, M. Fiorentino, F. Gorio, P. Lugli, M. Ridolfi, and students C. Aymonino, C. Chiarini, M. Lanza, S. Lenci, C. Melograni, G. Menichetti. Typical building plan.
(Archivo Quaroni)

General plan of the Tiburtino district as planned by the Quaroni-Ridolfi group.
(Archivo Quaroni)

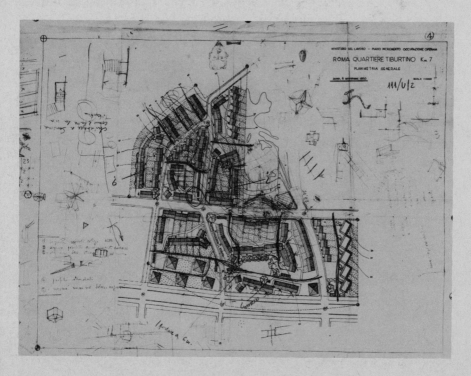

8.8 hectares—and was to contain 770 housing units distinguished by diverse typologies ranging from attached two-story townhouses to five-story apartment blocks and seven- to eight-story apartment towers, with the street functioning as the unifying element for the various buildings. The architects' project could be seen as an intervention nominally on behalf of the masses as opposed to bourgeois arrogance because the group elected to use traditional building materials such as brick, stucco, iron railings, and pitched roofs, all of which were to act as provocative appeals for a humanization of the residential fabric in opposition to the rationalist monumentality of the 1930s, still visible on the urban fringes of northern European cities such as Stockholm, Göteborg, and Helsinki, and of Rome's periphery of the 1970s, in such areas as Tor bella Monica, Cinecittà, San Basilio, and Spinaceto.

Although this putatively provocative project has been used as an exemplary case study for subsequent generations of architects, it is not a particularly felicitous example. The city's failure to comply with its own regulations, and the contractors who failed to respect the standards laid out in the design, produced a zone perched uneasily between city and country, with none of the positive qualities of either and nothing distinguishing of its own. Tiburtino passed from a small-scale, quasi-agrarian district to an urban fortress in short order. The assault of private speculation quickly encircled and swallowed it, and the quality of life followed the same trajectory as that of life in the prewar fascist borgate. From the outset, the inhabitants had to struggle for minimal city services, starting with transportation links to the city and potential employment for residents. In other words, postwar governments were no better prepared to outfit new housing districts with the bare necessities than the fascists had been.

Beyond being an emblematic monument of an architecture from high conceded to lower classes—and above all, an aesthetic that represented the designers' intellectual needs but that was quickly repudiated (for example, Ridolfi never set foot in the Tiburtino again), the quarter remains, living on in the daily experiences of those constrained to live there. The poor materials have deteriorated, and the areas left unbuilt by the city have turned into the proverbial garbage dumps. The projects exhibit a poor understanding of how

General view of buildings in the
Tiburtino district.
(Gabriele Morrione)

General view of buildings in the
Tiburtino district.
 (Gabriele Morrione)

Rustic-looking housing in the
Tiburtino district.
(Gabriele Morrione)

the people who lived there would really want to live; the preoccupation of the architect remained at the intellectual level and never arrived at a political or sociological analysis.

Of course, the design itself cannot be blamed for all of the serious shortcomings of the Tiburtino, even though it was retrograde in many ways. As in the case of Guidi's design at Primavalle, here, too, in the Tiburtino, the contingencies and various interests at play weighed far more heavily than the philosophy behind the design ideas. That is, the developers, or *palazzinari,* saw to it that their interests prevailed in an atmosphere lacking the political will to plan for the future. This little hot-house experiment was going up at the same time as an enormous speculative fever was under way in Rome, including the immediate surroundings of the INA-Casa project at Tiburtino. In order to design at all, the architect had to do so within the realm of two basic compromises:

a. The architect accepts the responsibility openly and consciously to be the handmaiden of a coercive, dominant power that uses architectural projects of all scales and however different in style for its own purposes. Clearly it is difficult to avoid this, but as Giorgio Tonieri says, it is one thing to collaborate with the hope of wringing some new improvements out of it, and quite another to refuse to participate at all, which produces effects that are certainly no better, and possibly even worse.

b. The second compromise involves the relationship between the public realm and the private realm. If city authorities fail to oversee the development of urban land so that the public realm tempers the activities of the private one, then there is no hope for any kind of regulation of development, and when the architect raises no objections, the lacunae quickly become obvious, and here, in the Tiburtino, they are given body. A more hopeful scenario would see the public realm intervene at the level of experimentation and in order to resolve particular problems, and then to serve as a counterpoint and a brake on the fever of private speculation, right down to the level of the individual lot, in effect preventing the intense development of apartment towers. Public power manipulated along these lines would offer not just words, but an example against which private building would have to be measured. In the

Tiburtino, the entire project was submerged by the palazzinari, so it was almost worse than doing nothing at all.

IV

I. Let us turn to the Magliana project, slowly, because the crush of traffic brings most movement in this part of Rome to a dead halt several times a day. The painful story of one of the most unfortunate sections of the city would be largely unknown were it not for the resistance and the vocal public struggles of its residents, which, along with a judicial inquiry, brought to light a long history of abuses aided and abetted by Rome's city officials and a large group of urban planners, architects, and palazzinari.

The speculation between 1965 and 1971 on these thirty-seven hectares of land in the southwest section of the city along the banks of the Tiber brought to fruition a scheme that dated back to 1925 when the idea was to extend Rome to the sea.[23] At that time, the rail link from the Ostiense Station to the beach at Ostia was built, and the highway to the sea was opened in 1928. Along this axis, two of the official borgate for those displaced by the demolitions in the historic center were built, Trullo and Acilia.

In the wake of the 1937 decision to set up the Universal Exposition of 1942 in Rome (E'42, now known as EUR), it seemed as if Rome's destiny was to expand to the Mediterranean. EUR president Vittorio Cini proposed a building plan in 1937, one that Mussolini subsequently authorized.[24] This plan established as lands to be expropriated those lying outside the boundaries of the 1931 master plan; the EUR agency thus received enormous decision-making power, as the direction of development would be determined by a special commission and without the hindrance of dealing with detailed plans for the urban growth of the rest of the city. In other words, EUR's directors were not bound to specific declared uses of the lands. Speculative fever set in on the lands around the EUR project immediately, including the Magliana, which was initially discarded by the EUR project because its location was considered unsuitable (four meters below the level of the Tiber, Magliana was plagued by fog and humidity, not to mention at risk from flooding).

The possibilities for speculation were confirmed again after the war, testimony to the fundamental continuity in the administration of the city of Rome through different regimes: the secretary of the EUR agency from 1951 to 1973, Virgilio Testa, for example, had occupied the same position in the Roman city administration from 1935 to 1943. Between 1954 and 1956, the city drew up detailed development plans, although the area still lay outside the boundaries of the master plan. The need of INA-Casa to build one of its quarters was used as a justification for proceeding in this fashion. In 1958, construction began but was soon interrupted with no official explanation. This "error" of the INA-Casa not only cost the public dearly, but also left sixty thousand people without housing. This inauspicious beginning should have led to a more judicious land use, but nonetheless, in 1960, the lands—still property of Count Tournon, a descendant of the French prefect who drew up the first urban plan in Rome in the early nineteenth century—were split up into lots, and the city approved building permits for a limited number and size of buildings on the condition that the builders undertook to raise the ground plane to eliminate the four-meter drop along the banks of the Tiber. Once they had received their approvals, work began immediately, but not, however, on landfill. This was the first and most crucial abuse, for the first two floors of each apartment building sank below the water level. The second abuse was to build extra floors above the water level (the city had approved two floors above the level of the Tiber after the hypothetical landfill). Although the abuses took place in the open, the city elected not to intervene and, in fact, continued to approve building permits. In 1967, the idea of raising the ground level was definitely abandoned, and Statute 862, which mandated fines for failure to respect size limits, was never applied. This allowed developers free reign to earn some $20 million above their original estimates. By 1975, the entire thirty-seven hectares was built up to the point that the density swelled to three thousand inhabitants per hectare, including the floors below the level of the Tiber. The city had at one point negotiated with the builders to make these two floors garages and storerooms, but they became apartments anyway. In fact, the Magliana is just one of many postwar housing quarters that lacks garages.

A wall of buildings and a sea of cars in via dell'Impruneta, Magliana quarter.

Viale Vicopisano, morning market. Temporary markets must be held here because no central market was planned and, contrary to custom, few shops were placed on the ground floors.

Via Magliana in Toscana, space between apartment buildings.

If the story of the Magliana ended here in the distorted optic of Rome's history, it would not be all that abnormal, for Magliana's lack of customary services is no different from the other quarters we have looked at: these amenities are conspicuously missing in all of the speculative districts. The absence of parking areas or garages leaves the quarter's own streets and the city's thoroughfares choked with cars and practically impassable. The area also has a noticeably higher incidence of hospitalizations for illnesses common to humid climates: the water table has been polluted, and the sewer system was inadequate within a year after the first structures were erected. Still, all of this is more or less typical for Rome.

But the Magliana has an anomaly in its history: Near the end of April 1962, the city rented one thousand apartments from palazzinari to give to those who had been living in the shanties that the city was determined to eradicate. Rents for private tenants in the district—generally unskilled or semiskilled laborers—ranged between 40 and 50 percent of their net income. The former shantytown dwellers, however, received significant assistance from the city to pay their rents, and this proved to be the breaking point for Magliana's residents. A popular rights group, the *fronte populare,* was set up to undertake the struggle, with the immediate objective of reducing rents and cleaning up the quarter. At the end of June, more than a thousand residents refused to pay 50 percent of their rents. They won their battle and set an example for the rest of the city, ultimately forcing the city administration to come out into the open with a political program for requisitioning unoccupied apartments to assign to families without housing. This ushered in the era of rent control or *equo canone,* of unions for the assignment of low-income housing, and of evictions only in cases of just cause.

So began the season of apparent hope and promise in post-economic-miracle Rome. Like the other quarters explored here, the Magliana falls deeper and deeper into decay, exhausting the inhabitants' energies, while Rome's development remains largely in the hands of those who have made a gift of the city to private interests since the postwar period.

In the long and painful process of its growth during the twentieth century, Rome has suffered from the neglect and indifference of its politicians as well as its architects. It staggers under a chaotic burden of traffic and chokes under a suffocating blanket of smog, and the only proposals issuing from the architects are to unearth the buried sections of the Roman forum again. Meanwhile building continues, services lag, and the countryside is plundered for new, often illegal housing. The attention of architects has not been on the city, nor have they developed the political will to combat abuses. Architecture with a capital *A* leads not out of the problems but more deeply into them.

1. Several publications treat the urban transformation in Rome since 1870: G. Accasto, R. Nicolini, V. Fraticelli, "Roma città e piani," *Urbanistica*, nos. 27, 28–9 (1959); G. Berlinguer and P. Della Seta, *Borgate di Roma* (Rome: Editori Riuniti, 1960); A. Calza-Bini, Il fascismo per le case del popolo: l'opera dell' Istituto *per le Case Popolari in Roma nel primo quadriennio d'amministrazione fascista* (Rome: IAFCP, 1927); P. Della Seta and R. Della Seta, *I suoli di Roma* (Rome: Editori Riuniti, 1988); F. Ferrarotti, *Roma da capitale a periferia* (Rome-Bari: Laterza, 1979); V. Fraticelli, *La Casa popolare a Roma* (Rome: Kappa, 1984); I. Insolera, *Roma moderna. Un secolo di storia urbanistica 1870–1970* (Turin: Einandi, 1978); L. Maroi, *Un ventennio di attività edilizia a Roma 1909–1929* (Rome, 1929). For a general history of the politics of building in twentieth-century Italy, see L. Bortolotti, *Storia della politica edilizia in Italia* (Rome: Editori Riuniti, 1978).

2. The term *borgata* (plural, *borgate*) was first used, according to Italo Insolera, in 1924 when the hamlet of Acilia was built, south of Rome in a malarial zone, to house the former inhabitants of the forums of Trajan and Caesar and the future via del Mare. The term is a disparaging reference to a section of the city too small to be called a quarter or a district—neither part of the countryside nor part of the city. Cited in Berlinguer and Della Seta, *Borgate di Roma*, p. 152.

3. As much information as is available on immigration and unemployment can be found in Istituto Centrale di Statistica del Regno d'Italia, *Annuario statistico italiano, 1922–1943* (Rome, annual) and in the same agency's *Compendio statistico, 1930–1941* (Rome, 1942); and *Sommario di statistiche storiche italiane, 1881–1955* (Rome, 1958).

4. Fraticelli, *La casa popolare*, pp. 13–48, on Testaccio and other pre–World War I housing; also Insolera, *Roma moderna*, p. 67.

5. Maroi, *Un ventennio*, p. 9; Istituto Centrale di Statistica del Regno d'Italia, *Annuario statistico italiano, 1935* (Rome, 1936), p. 12; Gustavo Giovannoni, *Vecchie città ed edilizia nuova* (Turin: Unione typografica-editrice torinese, 1931), p. 68; G. Zucca, "Delenda Baracca," *Capitoleum* (January 1931).

6. George Mosse, *The Nationalization of the Masses* (New York: H. Fertig, 1954), especially p. 51ff.

7. Benito Mussolini, discourse of 31 December 1925, cited in D. D'Apice-Mazzetti, *Roma la città contro l'uomo* (Rome, 1970); Spiro Kostof, *The Third Rome* (Berkeley, California: Univ. Art Museum, 1973).

8. 30 May 1930, RDL 3 June 1928, n. 1165.

9. For a full account of these maneuvers, see Paolo Sica, *Storia dell'urbanistica. Il Novecento* (Rome-Bari: Laterza, 1985), pp. 399–413.

10. Accasto et al., "Roma città," pp. 391–93. There have been numerous studies of life in the official and spontaneous borgate in Rome; among the most important are F. Crespi, "Aspetti del rapporto tra strutture urbanistiche e relazioni sociali in una borgata alla periferia di Roma," *Rivista di sociologia* 13 (1967), pp. 621–74; Franco Ferrarotti, *Vite di baraccati* (Naples: Liguori, 1974); Franco Martinelli, *Roma Nuova: Borgate spontanee e insediamenti pubblici* (Milan: Franco Angeli, 1988). The Martinelli book has a complete bibliography.

11. Piero Ostilio Rossi, "Dove non c'è piu la città: nascita e sviluppo della Borgata di Primavalle," *Parametro* 7 (March 1976), pp. 38–47.

12. The twelve borgate of fascist Rome are Primavalle, Trullo, Tor Marancio, Gordiani, Quarticciolo, Prenestino, S. Maria del Soccorso, Pietralata, S. Basilio, Tufello, Val Melaina, and Acilia.

13. Rossi, "Dove non c'è piu la città," p. 44.

14. See Giorgio Guidi, *Piano Urbanistico della Borgata Residenziale di Primavalle*, in its detailed version at the Istituto Autonomo delle Case Popolari, Rome.

15. See Cesare de Seta, *Giuseppe Pagano: Architettura e città durante il fascismo* (Rome-Bari: Laterza, 1976).

16. See Giuseppe Samonà, *La Casa Popolare* (Venice-Padua: Marsilio, 1973; reprint of 1935 edition).

17. Rossi, "Dove non c'è piu la città," p. 46.

18. In the 1950 census, shanties, refuges, and hovels were home for some 105,000 people—and surely even this was a conservative estimate. Aldo Tozzetti, *La casa e non solo* (Rome: Editori Riuniti, 1989). For additional information about housing in the immediate postwar period, see Manfredo Tafuri, *A History of Italian Architecture 1944–1985* (Cambridge, Mass.: MIT Press, 1989).

19. See especially the section in Tafuri, *A History of Italian Architecture*, pp. 3–33.

20. Irene Guttry, *Guida di Roma Moderna* (Rome: Daedalo, 1976), pp. 26–7.

21. Tafuri, *A History of Italian Architecture*, pp. 3–32.

22. Pippo Ciorra, *Lodovico Quaroni 1911–1987. Opere e progetti* (Milan: Electa, 1989), pp. 92–99; Tafuri, *A History of Italian Architecture*, pp. 15–19.

23. The most comprehensive account of the Magliana story is the volume edited by Il Comitato di quartiere (the District Committee), *La Magliana. Vita e lotta di un quartiere proletario* (Milan: Feltrinelli, 1977). I need hardly add that this kind of exploitation and abuse has not characterized building in upper-class districts.

24. *La Magliana. Vita e lotta*, pp. 21–42; for further general information on EUR, see Italo Insolera and Luigi Di Majo, *L'Eur e Roma dagli anni Trenta al Duemila* (Rome-Bari: Laterza, 1986).

■ Uneven Development:

Public Art in New York City

Rosalyn Deutsche

The true issue is not to make beautiful cities or well-managed cities, it is to make a work of life. The rest is a by-product. But, making a work of life is the privilege of historical action. How and through what struggles, in the course of what class action and what political battle could urban historical action be reborn? This is the question toward which we are inevitably carried by our inquiry into the meaning of the city.

—Raymond Ledrut, "Speech and the Silence of the City"

■ Beauty and Utility: Weapons of Redevelopment

By now it is clear to most observers that the visibility of masses of homeless people obstructs belief in positive images of New York, constituting a crisis in the city's official representation. Dominant responses to the crisis assume two principal, often complementary, forms: they treat homelessness as an individual social problem isolated from the realm of urban politics or, as Peter Marcuse contends, "attempt to neutralize the outrage homelessness produces in those who see it."[1] Because substantial efforts to deal with homelessness itself would require at least a partial renunciation of its immediate causes— the commodification of housing, existing patterns of employment, the social service policies of today's austerity state—those committed to preserving the status quo try, instead, through strategies of isolation and neutralization, to cope with the legitimation problems that homelessness raises.

Exemplary of the "social problem" approach is a widely circulated report issued in June 1987 by the Commission on the Year 2000. Obedient to its governmental mandate to forecast New York City's future, the panel defined New York as "ascendant," sustaining this image by pointing to the city's "revitalized" economy and neighborhoods. Conspicuous poverty and patent stagnation in other neighborhoods compelled the commission, nonetheless, to remark on the unequal character of this rise: "We see that the benefits of prosperity have passed over hundreds of thousands of New Yorkers."[2] But the group's recommendations—prescribing the same pro-business and privatizing policies that are largely responsible for homelessness in the first place—failed to translate this manifest imbalance into a recognition that uneven economic and geographical development is a structural, rather than incidental, feature of New York's present expansion. The panelists' own expansive picture required, then, a certain contraction of their field of vision. Within its borders, social inequities appear as random disparities and disappear as linked phenomena. An optical illusion fragments the urban condition: "growth" —believed to occur in different locations at varying paces of cumulative development, but ultimately to unfold its advantages to all—emerges as a remedy for urban decay, obscuring a more integrated reality that is also inscribed across the city's surface. For in the late capitalist city, growth, far from a uniform process, is driven by the hierarchical differentiation of social groups and territories. Residential components of prosperity—gentrification and luxury housing—are not distinct from, but in fact depend upon, residential facets of poverty—disinvestment, eviction, displacement, homelessness. Together, they make up only one aspect of the city's comprehensive redevelopment, itself part of more extensive social, economic, and spatial changes, all marked by uneven development. Consequently, redevelopment proceeds, not as an embracing benefit, but according to social *relations* of ascendancy, that is, of domination. Consensus-oriented statements such as *New York Ascendant* disavow these relations, impressionistically offering proof of growth side-by-side with proof of decline; both pieces of evidence acquire the appearance of discrete entities. But today there is no document of New York's ascendancy that is not *at the same time* a document of homelessness. Whether such documents are municipal reports, landmark buildings, or what we call public spaces, they exhibit an ambiguity as to their meaning.

Faced with the instability pervading New York's urban images, the second major response to homelessness—the neutralization of its effects on viewers—attempts to restore to the city a surface calm that belies underlying contradictions. To legitimate the city, this response delegitimates the homeless. In the spring of 1988, Mayor Ed Koch demonstrated the neutralizing approach while speaking, fittingly, before a group of image makers, the American Institute of Architects, convened in New York to discuss, even more appropriately, "Art in Architecture." Answering a question about Grand Central Terminal—landmark building and public place—Koch, too, underscored the dual signification of New York's urban spaces by directing his listeners' attention to the presence of the homeless who now reside in the city's train stations.

These homeless people, you can tell who they are. They're sitting on the floor, occasionally defecating, urinating, talking to themselves—many, not all, but many—or panhandling. We thought it would be reasonable for the authorities to say, "You can't stay here unless you're here for transportation." Reasonable, rational people would come to that conclusion, right? Not the Court of Appeals.[3]

The mayor was denigrating the state court's reversal of an antiloitering law under which police would have been empowered to remove the homeless from some of the public areas they currently inhabit. But even had police action succeeded in evicting the homeless, it is doubtful that it could have subdued the fundamental social forces threatening the station's aspect as an enduring symbol of New York's beauty and efficiency. Deprived of repressive powers, however, Koch could protect the space only by ideological means, proclaiming its transparency, in the eyes of reasonable people, to an objective function—transportation.

To assert in the language of common sense that an urban space refers unequivocally to intrinsic uses is to claim that the city itself speaks. Such a statement makes it seem that individual locations within the city and the spatial organization of the city as a whole contain an inherent meaning determined by the imperative to fulfill needs that are presupposed to be natural, simply practical. Instrumental function is the only meaning signified by the built environment. What this essentialist view systematically obstructs—an obstruction that is actually its principal function—is the perception that the organization and shaping of the city as well as the attribution of meaning to space are social processes. Spatial forms are social structures. Seen through the lens of function, however, spatial order appears instead to be controlled by natural, mechanical, or organic laws. It is recognized as social only in the sense that it meets the purportedly unified needs of aggregated individuals. Severed from its social production, space is thus fetishized as a physical entity and undergoes, through inversion, a transformation. Represented as an independent object, it appears to exercise control over the very people who produce and use it. The impression of objectivity is real to the extent that the city is alienated from the social life of its inhabitants. The functionalization of the city, which presents space as politically neutral, merely utilitarian, is, then, filled with politics. For the notion that the city speaks for itself conceals the identity of those who speak through the city.

This effacement has two interrelated functions. In the service of those groups whose interests dominate decisions about the organization of space, it holds that the exigencies of human social life provide a single meaning that necessitates proper uses of the city—proper places for its residents. The prevailing goals of the existing spatial structure are regarded as, by definition, beneficial to all. Correlatively, the ideology of function obscures the conflictual manner in which cities are actually defined and used, repudiating the very existence of those groups who counter dominant uses of space. For these reasons, critical evaluations of the relations of domination materialized in space depend on the recognition that the production and use of the city are conflictual processes. As the urban critic Raymond Ledrut observes, "The city is not an object produced by a group in order to be bought or even used by others. *The city is an environment formed by the interaction and the integration of different practices.* It is maybe in this way that the city is truly the city."[4]

Ledrut's definition of the city as the product of social practice, negating its hypostatization as a physical entity, strongly opposes the technocratic definition of the city as the product of experts. The city, Ledrut insists, is not a spatial framework external to its users, but is produced by them. These competing definitions are themselves a stake of political struggle. Deceptively simple, Ledrut's formulation has far-reaching implications. Not only does it explicitly acknowledge the participation of diverse social groups in the production of the environment, it argues against an environment imposed from above by state institutions or private interests, one that is dictated by the necessities of control and profit but legitimized by concepts of efficiency or beauty. Delineating the city as a social form rather than a collection and organization of neutral physical objects implicitly affirms the right of presently excluded groups to have access to the city—to make decisions about the spaces they use, to be attached to the places they live, to refuse marginalization. It describes a concrete social reality suppressed by dominant urban spaces, sketches the terms of resistance to those spaces, and envisions the liberation of the environment in what Henri Lefebvre calls a "space of differences."[5] In place of the image of the "well-managed city," it proposes the construction of a "work of life," suggesting that such a vital work is extinguished by a discourse that separates people endowed with "eternal" needs from an environment supposedly built to meet them. It restores the subject to the city. The struggle to establish the validity of Ledrut's definition of the city is, then, irrevocably fused to other controversies about the city's form and use. "The definition of urban meaning," Manuel Castells maintains, describing the inscription of political battles in space,

will be a process of conflict, domination, and resistance of domination, directly linked to the dynamics of social struggle and not to the reproductive spatial expression of a unified culture. Furthermore, cities and space being fundamental to the organization of social life, the conflict over the assignment of certain goals to certain spatial forms will be one of the fundamental mechanisms of domination and counter-domination in the social structure.[6]

Koch's assignment of a directing purpose—transportation—to Grand Central Terminal in order to prevail over what he portrayed as a parasitic function—shelter for homeless people—encapsulates this means of domination. First, it sequesters a single place from broader spatial organization. But the real efficacy of the functionalization of the city as a weapon of power in struggles over the use of urban space rests on its ability to deny the reality that such struggles are productive of spatial organization in the first place. Yet the presence in public places of the homeless—the very group that Koch invoked—represents the most acute symptom of a massive and disputed transformation in the uses of the broader city. Far from a natural or mechanical adjustment, this reorganization is determined in all its facets by prevailing power relations. It includes a transformation of New York into a center for international corporations and business services with attendant changes in the nature of employment. The shift of manufacturing jobs elsewhere, frequently overseas, is accompanied by a loss of traditional blue-collar jobs and the rise of poverty-level wages in low-echelon service sector or new manufacturing jobs. Even mass media analyses now routinely note this change as a cause of homelessness, although they view it as a technological inevitability. Since, under capitalism, land and housing are commodities to be exploited for profit, the marginalization of large numbers of workers engenders a loss of housing for the poor as New York devotes more space to profit-maximizing real estate development—high-rent office towers, luxury condominiums, corporate headquarters—that also provides the physical conditions to meet the needs of the new economy.

Today's homeless, therefore, are refugees from evictions, secondary and exclusionary displacement—the conversion of their neighborhoods into areas they can no longer afford.[7] More broadly, they are products of wage and property relations and of governmental policies allocating spatial resources to the uses of big business and real estate while withdrawing them from social services such as public housing. And the homeless are produced by technical decisions made by state and municipal planning agencies about land uses, decisions that increasingly reinforce an economically and racially segregated spatial structure by directing low-income groups toward the city's periphery. To elucidate the specific historical, rather than mythical, reasons for the presence of today's homeless, they should, more accurately, be called "the evicted." Koch's attempt, exemplified in his address to the architects' convention, to extract New York's urban space from the very social relations that create it further marginalizes the poor. Having first been expelled from their apartments and neighborhoods, they are now denied, by means of what the French situationists termed "a blackmail of utility,"[8] a right to the city at all.

Exhortations to the authority of objective use are considered in situationist pronouncements to be one of two mechanisms shielding the capitalist conquest of the urban environment from challenge. The other is aesthetics, characterized, along with urban planning, as "a rather neglected branch of criminology."[9] This appraisal retains its pertinence in New York today, where, in unison, notions of beauty and utility furnish the ideological alibi for redevelopment. Under its protection, the conditions of everyday life for hundreds of thousands of residents are destroyed. The reciprocity between discourses of beauty and utility is evidenced by the fact that Koch's question and answer session at the architects' meeting, where he made his remarks about utility, replaced, at the last minute, a prepared speech the mayor was to deliver on the subject not of the well-managed city but of the beautiful one. The substitution does not indicate a reversal of priorities. Both urban images are equally instrumental for the redevelopment process. In the name of needs and corresponding functions, Koch engaged in narrow problem-solving about the uses of public spaces. But his espousal of the city that speaks for itself permits a remarkable silence to prevail about the incompatibility of true functionality and a social system in which production "is accomplished not for the fulfillment of needs in general, but for the fulfillment of one particular need: profit."[10] Indeed, as Baudrillard warns, "any system of productivist growth (capitalist, but not exclusively) can only produce and reproduce men—even in their deepest determinations: in their liberty, in their needs, in their very unconscious—as productive forces."[11] Within such a system, if a person "eats, drinks, lives somewhere, reproduces himself, it is because the system requires his self-production in order to reproduce itself: it needs men."[12] In bourgeois society, when people such as today's evicted are redundant in the economy—or needed to cheapen labor costs—they are converted from residents of the city into predators on the "fundamental" needs of New Yorkers. No longer required as productive forces, the evicted themselves have no requirements.

The stunning reversals enacted in the name of utility—invoking for the purpose of demonstrating natural needs the very group whose existence testifies to the social mediation of needs—occur also in the name of beauty. The mayor's prepared speech on the topic of government's relation to aesthetics celebrated the city's preservation of historical landmarks, architectural heterogeneity, and neighborhood context, mobilizing a protectionist discourse of permanence and continuity under whose aegis patterns of development progressively threaten historical action, diversity, and entire communities with elimination. Such inversions are possible because, presupposed to lie outside of sociomaterial conditions, commitments to beauty and utility present themselves as incontrovertible evidence of public accountability. Thus, as further proof of the advantages of New York's "ascendancy," Koch's planned speech stressed the current administration's interest in the aesthetics of the city—its revitalization of the municipal art commission, programs of flexible zoning regulations, planning controls, design review panels, and public art. "Once again," the speech asserted, "public art has become a priority."[13]

It is not difficult to understand why an increase in public art commissions attends New York's "ascendancy." As a practice within the built environment, public art participates in the production of meanings, uses, and forms for the city. In this capacity, it can help secure consent to redevelopment and to the restructuring that make up the historical form of late capitalist urbanization. But like other institutions that mediate perceptions of the city's economic and political operations—architecture, urban planning, urban design—it can also question and resist those operations, revealing the suppressed contradictions within urban processes. Since these contradictions stamp the image of the city with a basic instability, public art can be, in Althusserian terms, a "site" as well as a "stake" of urban struggle.

It is also not unexpected that, along with demonstrations of the new city's beauty and utility, intensified talk of "the public" should accompany the accelerating privatization and bureaucratization of land-use decisions in New York. Wholesale appropriations of land by private interests, massive state interventions that deterritorialize huge numbers of residents, and inequitable distribution of spatial resources by government agencies insulated from public control: these acts governing the shape of New York's landscape require a legitimating front. Citing "the public," whether this word is attached to art, space, or any number of other objects, ideas, and practices, is one means of providing the uneven development of New York with democratic legitimacy.

Discourse about "the public" is frequently cast as a commitment made by the principal actors in the real estate market—developers, financial institutions, landlords, corporations, politicians—to rescue, for New Yorkers, a significant quantity of "public space" from the ravages of "overdevelopment." Routinely, for instance, public areas, paid for with public funds, furnish private redevelopment projects with the amenities necessary to maximize profits.[14] In other cases, city regulations require corporations, in exchange for increased density allowances, to build privately owned atriums or plazas. The resulting locations are designated "public" spaces. These phenomena mirror each other as facets of the privatization of public space. They represent individual answers to the problems faced by municipal governments confronted with the need to facilitate capital accumulation and still maintain responsiveness to residents' demands for participation in decisions about the uses of the city. Private public space is most frequently acclaimed as an innovative partnership between the public and private sectors—falsely supposed to be distinct spheres. Such an alliance, we are told, if extended to the entire configuration of the city, would benefit all New York residents. Yet the provision of space for "the public" testifies, under present circumstances, to the wholesale withdrawal of space from social control. Clearly, the local state can meet with only limited and precarious success in harmonizing its goals of meeting capital's demands and maintaining democratic legitimacy, since the two goals are, objectively, in conflict. Not surprisingly, therefore, New York's new public spaces, materializations of attempts at reconciliation, are the objects of contests over uses and, moreover, are hardly designed for accessibility to all. Rather, they permit, through a multitude of legal, physical, or symbolic means, access by certain social groups for selected purposes while excluding others.

When disputes do arise that threaten to expose the political implications of such exclusions, an ideology of "the public" justifies particular exclusions as natural. Because "the public" is conceived either as a unity or, what amounts to the same thing, as a field composed of essential divisions, dilemmas plaguing the use of public spaces can be attributed to the inevitable disruptions attendant on the need to harmonize the "natural" differences and diverse interests characteristic of any society. Heightened diversity is viewed, even further, as a distinctive feature of modern urban life, whose problems, in turn, are understood to result from the inevitable technological evolution of human society. Neutralizing concepts of diversity form part of the urban ideology and are wielded to defeat genuine diversity. "The public," employed as an imprecise and embracing rubric, substitutes for analysis of specific spatial contests, ascribing discord to quasi-natural origins. Exclusions enacted to homogenize public space by expelling specific differences are dismissed as deeds necessary to restore social harmony. This perspective disavows the social relations of domination that such deeds make possible.

Exclusions and homogenization, operations undertaken in the name of "the public," distinguish what German filmmaker Alexander Kluge has called the "pseudo–public sphere." With Oskar Negt, Kluge has theorized various permutations in the bourgeois public sphere and, especially, its transformation in the interests of profit-maximization. The pseudo–, or, as variously labeled, the representative, classical, or traditional, public sphere, conventionally deemed to be a spatial and temporal arena where citizens participate in political dialogue and decision-making, is, according to Negt and Kluge, an arena that in practice represses debate. This repression, a hallmark of the bourgeois public sphere, results from its origins in the false demarcation drawn in bourgeois society between the private and public realms. Because economic gain, protected from public accountability by its seclusion within the private domain, actually depends on conditions that are publicly provided, the bourgeois public sphere developed as a means by which private interests seek to control public activity. But since capitalism requires the preservation of the illusion that a well-defined boundary divides the public and private realms, the contradictions that gave birth to the public sphere are perpetuated and "reconciled" in its operations. Conflicts between groups are obfuscated by transmuting differential interests into an abstract equality supposedly based on universal reason and by privatizing whole realms of social experience. Homogenization of divergent concerns can, however, only be effected through exclusions: "A representative public sphere," Kluge argues, "is representative insofar as it involves exclusions." It "only represents parts of reality, selectively and according to certain value systems. . . ."[15] Negt and Kluge describe how, increasingly, the pseudo-public sphere has yielded to a public sphere that is privately owned, determined by profit motives, and characterized by the transformation of the conditions of all aspects of everyday life into objects of production. Within this public sphere, "the public" is defined as a mass of consumers and spectators.[16] Against the pseudo- and private public spheres, grounded in relations of exclusion and private property, Negt and Kluge conceptualize the construction of an oppositional public sphere—an arena of political consciousness and articulation of social experience that would challenge these relations.

Recently, artists and critics have sought to initiate such a challenge within art practice by constructing what has been termed a cultural public sphere. The ideas that art cannot assume the preexistence of a public but must help produce one and that the public sphere is more a social form than a physical space nullify, to a considerable extent, accepted divisions between public and nonpublic art. Potentially, any exhibition venue is a public sphere and, conversely, the location of artworks outside privately owned galleries, in parks and plazas or, simply, outdoors, hardly guarantees that they will address a public. But while, in these ways, the concept of a public sphere shatters the category of public art, it also raises unique questions for art that has been conventionally so categorized and, especially, for work commissioned to occupy New York's public spaces. Given the proliferation of pseudo- and private public spaces, how can public art counter the functions of its "public" sites in constructing the dominant city? We can at least begin to answer this question by discarding the simplifications that pervade mainstream aesthetic discourse about "the public." Rather than a real category, the definition of "the public," like the definition of the city, is an ideological artifact, a contested and fragmented terrain. "'The public,'" as Craig Owens observes, "is a discursive formation susceptible to appropriation by the most diverse—indeed, opposed—ideological interests."[17] But crucial as this perception is, significant challenges to dominant interests will continue to elude us unless this basic understanding prompts inquiries into the precise identity of those interests and the concrete mechanisms of their power. Unless we seriously respond to Owens's subsequent query—"who is to define, manipulate and profit from 'the public'" today?[18]—critical interventions will remain inchoate and directionless. Paramount among the issues confronting all urban practices is the present appropriation of public space and of the city itself for use by the forces of redevelopment. Public art shares this plight. Although its current predicament is not without historical precedent—most notably in late nineteenth-century civic beautification and municipal art movements—the complexities of the present conjuncture necessitate a new framework for analyzing the social functions of public art.

■ Public Art and Its Uses

Most existing aesthetic approaches can neither account for current conditions of public art production nor suggest terms for an alternative, possibly transformative, practice. Even when they comprehend the problems of the public sphere or entail sophisticated materialist critiques of aesthetic perception, they are generally formulated with an inadequate knowledge of urban politics. Needless to say, traditional art-historical paradigms cannot explicate the social functions of public art—past or present—since they remain committed to idealist assumptions that work to obscure those functions. Maintaining that art is defined by an independent aesthetic essence, prevailing doctrines hold that, while art inevitably "reflects" social reality, its purpose is, by definition, the transcendence of spatiotemporal contingencies in the universal, timeless work of art. Conventional social art history provides no genuine alternative. Frequently attracted to the study of public art because of what they perceive to be its inherently social character, social art historians, in keeping with the discipline's empiricist biases, confine themselves to describing either the iconography or the historical "context" of individual works. Hostile to forms of analysis that penetrate surface phenomena, they restrict meaning to the work's overt subject matter and relegate social conditions to the status of a backdrop. They thus preserve the idealist separation of art—its ontological status intact—from social environments with which art merely "interacts." In addition, art history mystifies the social environment just as it does the work of art. With few exceptions, all tendencies within art history are informed by notions of the city as a transhistorical form, an inevitable product of technological evolution, or an arena for the unfolding of exacerbated individualism.[19]

More significantly, the present role of public art in urban politics also calls into question ideas informing some critical perspectives on public art. Beginning in the late 1960s, contemporary art and criticism questioned idealist tenets of artistic autonomy by exploring art's social functions. In part, the critique was initiated by shifting attention away from the "inside" of the artwork—supposed in mainstream doctrine to contain fixed, inherent meanings—and focusing, instead, on the work's context—its framing conditions. Site-specificity, a technique in which context was incorporated into the work itself, originally developed to counteract the construction of ideological art objects, purportedly defined by independent essences, and to reveal art's determination by its institutional frame. Over the years, in what is now a familiar history, site-specificity underwent many permutations. Most fruitfully, context was extended to encompass the individual site's symbolic, social, and political meanings as well as the discursive and historical circumstances within which artwork, spectator, and site are situated. Insofar as this expansion stressed the social relations structuring the artwork and site, exclusive concern with the physical site often signaled an academic fetishization of context at the aesthetic level. Critical site-specific art, as opposed to its academic progeny, continued, however, not only to incorporate context as a critique of the artwork, but also to attempt to intervene, through the artwork, in its site. The reciprocity between artwork and site altered the identity of each, blurring distinctions between them and preparing the ground for the enhanced participation of art in wider cultural and social practice. For public art, the alteration, rather than affirmation, of the site required that the urban space occupied by a work be understood, just as art and art institutions had been, as socially constructed spaces.

The most radical promise embodied in the public art that attempted to defetishize both art and urban space was the potential for artists and critics to articulate their aesthetic opposition to the spaces of art's reception with other elements of social resistance to the organization of the city. Such a step does not mean that art must relinquish its specificity as a political practice—as some realist or "activist" positions imply—but, rather, entails the recognition that art's identity is always modified by its encounter with its sites. It is, for example, insufficient to support site-specificity by simply stating that Richard Serra's *Tilted Arc* intervenes in the city in order to redefine space as the site of sculpture;[20] the significance of the work's intervention also depends on the way in which art itself is redefined in the process. Without addressing the stakes of urban redefinition, *Tilted Arc* exhibits a combination of specificity and generalization that is symptomatic of the split it maintains between critical aesthetic issues and critical urban problems. On the one hand, it is undoubtedly wedded concretely to its site: it establishes its difference from surrounding architecture, engages and reorients spatial patterns, invites viewers into the space of the work, and traces the path of human vision across the Federal Plaza. Perhaps, as Douglas Crimp argues, positing *Tilted Arc* as an example of radicalized site-specificity, it metaphorically ruptures the spatial expression of state power by destroying the plaza's coherence.[21] It might also, as Crimp less speculatively suggests, reveal the condition of alienation in bourgeois society. These are the most provocative claims made for *Tilted Arc* as a practice that addresses the material conditions of art's existence, and although they identify a radical potential for public art, they tend, as an interpretation of Serra's work, toward exaggeration. For in its own way *Tilted Arc* still floats above its urban site. The lingering abstraction of the sculpture from its space emerges most lucidly in the attitude the work and its supporters adopt toward urgent questions about the uses of public space.

Indeed, "use" was elevated to a central position in the debates about public art generated by the hearings convened in 1985 to decide whether Serra's sculpture should be removed from its site. The proper use of the site became a banner under which crusades against the work were conducted; supporters countered with alternative uses. *Tilted Arc*'s most astute defenders problematized the assumptions about utility that justified attacks on the sculpture, challenging, as does the work itself, simplistic notions of natural or populist uses. Yet, in proposing aesthetic uses for the space, isolated from its social function in specific circumstances, supporters substituted one ideological conception of use for another, perpetuating, as did the work's detractors, a belief in essential—noncontingent—uses of space. Moreover, the notion that *Tilted Arc* bestows on the Federal Plaza an aesthetic use that is simply available to all users ignores questions recently posed in a number of disciplines about differences among users and, further, about users as *producers*—themselves not unitary—of the environment. Phenomenological readings, placing subjective experience of space outside the sociomaterial conditions of the city, fail to see that the primary object of their study is already ideological. "The situation of man confronting the city involves other things than schemas of perceptive behavior. It introduces ideology."[22] Precisely because the ideology of spatial use was, in fact, never introduced, discussions about the work, despite the prominence they accorded to questions of use, remained aloof from critical public issues about the uses of space in New York today: oppositions between social groups about spatial uses, the social division of the city, and the question of which residents are forcibly excluded from using the city. These issues occupy the heart of urban politics. They were also the hidden agenda of assaults from certain quarters against *Tilted Arc*, which, represented as an impediment to the beneficial uses of public space, became a foil for public art that celebrates the dominant uses of space. Yet these questions remained unexcavated during the hearings, because, confined within the boundaries of critical aesthetics, discussions failed to perceive the function of public art in contemporary urbanism—the social processes producing the city's tangible form. While they frequently entailed complicated materialist critiques of art's production and of aesthetic perception, they obstructed an interrogation of the conditions of production of New York's urban space.

Opening the question requires that we dislodge public art from its ghettoization within the parameters of aesthetic discourse, even critical aesthetic discourse, and resituate it, at least partially, within critical urban discourse. More precisely, such a shift in perspective erodes the borders between the two fields, disclosing the existence of crucial interfaces between art and urbanism in the subject of public art. The need for criticism to conceptualize this meeting ground is especially pressing now, since neoconservative forces are appropriating that task in order to promote a type of public art that complies with the demands of redevelopment. "In fact," to quote just one journalist who has established the "new criterion" for public art, "public art needs to be seen as a function not of art, but of urbanism. It needs to be thought of in relation to, rather than insulated from the numerous other functions, activities and imperatives that condition the fabric of city life."[23] The problem we face, then, is not so much the absence of a consideration of the city in current discourse about public art; it is rather the fact that this discourse perpetuates mythologized notions about the city. Typically, it claims to oppose cultural elitism while remaining committed to artistic quality, a claim that corresponds to broader assertions that the redeveloped city provides quality public space. Consistent with these allegations, journalists promote a type of public art that is fully incorporated into the apparatus of redevelopment. My desire to approach contemporary public art as an urban practice is, then, an abstraction for heuristic purposes, but one that is motivated by the imperative, first, to respond to concrete events changing the function of public art and, second, to contribute to an alternative. An oppositional practice, however, must possess an adequate knowledge of the dominant constructions within which it works. In the case of public art, it depends, therefore, on a critical perception of the city's metamorphosis and of the role public art is playing within it.

When Mayor Koch's speechwriters for his talk before the American Institute of Architects stated that "once again, public art has become a priority," they were drawing attention not only to an increase in the number of public commissions, but also to enhanced support for a qualitatively different kind of public art. And even though their reference to art was contained within a speech on aesthetics—the beautiful city—it could equally have supported the mayor's later remarks about utility—the well-managed city. In fact, the new public art illustrates the marriage of the two images in the redevelopment process.

What distinguishes the "new" public art in the eyes of its proponents, and, further, what renders it more socially accountable than the old, is precisely its "usefulness." "What is the new public art?" asked an art journalist in one of the earliest articles reporting on the new phenomenon:

Definitions differ from artist to artist, but they are held together by a single thread: It is art plus function, *whether the function is to provide a place to sit for lunch, to provide water drainage, to mark an important historical date, or to enhance and direct a viewer's perceptions.*[24]

From this indiscriminate list of functions it is difficult to ascertain precisely how the new public sculpture differs from previous types. Nineteenth-century war memorials, after all, commemorate important events, and *Tilted Arc,* against which the new art opposes itself, directs a viewer's perception. Yet advocates do specify, albeit confusedly, a quality that distinguishes the work of new public artists:

All share a dedication to extra-aesthetic concerns. Use—not as in criticality but as in seating and tables, shade and sunlight—is a primary issue.[25]

We are putting function back into art again.[26]

This architectural art has a functional basis. Unlike most traditionally modern works of painting and sculpture, which modern artists were careful to define as "useless" in comparison to other objects of daily life, recent architectural art is often very much like a wall, a column, a floor, a door or a fence.[27]

Scott Burton—whose work, primarily pieces of furniture designed for public places, epitomizes the phenomenon—repeatedly declared that "utility" is the principal yardstick for measuring the value of public art.[28]

The new art, then, is promoted as useful in the reductive sense of fulfilling "essential" human and social needs. Just as Koch designated Grand Central Terminal a place for travel, this art designates places in the city for people to sit, to stand, to play, to eat, to read, even to dream. Building on this foundation, the new art claims to unify successively a whole sequence of divided spheres, offering itself in the end as a model of integration. Initially setting up a polarization between the concerns of art and those of utility, it then transcends the division by making works that are both artworks and usable objects. Further, it claims to reconcile art, through its usefulness, with society and with the public benefit. Use, we are told, ensures relevance.

As an artist working toward the social good, he [the public sculptor] produces works that are used by the populace, that inhabit its plazas, that are part of its plans for urban design and economic redevelopment—works that rapidly leave the environment of art to enter the realm of artifacts.[29]

Just as function is limited to utilitarianism, social activity is constricted to narrow problem-solving, so that the provision of "useful" objects automatically collapses into a social good. "The social questions interest me more than the art ones," said Scott Burton, describing his furnishings for the Equitable Assurance Building, whose function in raising real estate values remains thoroughly unexamined. "I hope that people will love to eat their lunch there."[30] And, he continued, "Communal and social values are now more important. What office workers do in their lunch hour is more important than my pushing the limits of my self-expression."[31]

The conflation of utility with social benefit has a distinctly moralistic cast: "All my work is a rebuke to the art world,"[32] Burton stated. Critics agree: "[Scott Burton] challenges the art community with neglect of its social responsibility. . . . Carefully calculated for use, often in public spaces, Burton's furniture clearly has a social function."[33] All of these purported acts of unification, predicated as they are on prior separations, conceal underlying processes of dissociation. Each element of the formula—art, use, society—first isolated from the others, has individually undergone a splitting operation in which it is rationalized and objectified. Art possesses an aesthetic essence; utilitarian objects serve universal needs; society is a functional ensemble. They surmount specific histories, geographies, values, relations to subjects and social groups, to be reconstituted as abstract categories. Individually and as a whole, they are severed from social relations, fetishized as external objects. This is the real social function of the new public art: to reify as natural the conditions of the late capitalist city into which it hopes to integrate us.

The supreme act of unification with which the new public art is credited, however, is its interdisciplinary cooperation with other professions shaping the physical environment.

The new public art invariably requires the artist to collaborate with a diverse group of people, including architects, landscape architects, other artists and engineers. So far, most of the public artists have had few problems adjusting to the collaborative process; indeed, many have embraced it with enthusiasm.[34]

"Few might have guessed that these collaborations would so seriously affect the art, design and planning professions in such a short time,"[35] writes one critic with surprise. Yet, given the fact that the new public art rallies all the notions that currently inform the planning of redevelopment, it is hardly surprising, if not in fact completely predictable, that such work should be fully integrated into the process of designing New York's redeveloped spaces. Presented as beautiful, useful, public, and expertly produced, it advertises these environments as images of New York's ascendancy. Indeed, the rise of collaborative public art accompanied the acceleration of urban redevelopment almost from its inception. In 1981, John Beardsley concluded his survey of "community-sponsored" art projects, *Art in Public Places,* by identifying a recent shift in artistic attitudes. "A new kind of partnership is emerging between contemporary artists and the nation's communities," he explained in a chapter entitled "New Directions: Expanding Views of Art in Public Places,"

with the result that artists are increasingly involved in significant development efforts. In part, this is a consequence of new initiatives within cities. As an element of major building programs in the last decade and a half, some have sought the participation of artists in developing innovative solutions to public design problems.[36]

Since their emergence in the late 1970s, public art collaborations have grown to such an extent that they now dominate accounts of public art. "This is a season," writes Michael Brenson,

that is bringing the issue of artistic collaboration to a head. Over the past few years a great deal of hope has been invested in the partnership between sculptors and architects, and between sculptors and the community. There is a widespread feeling that this is the future for public sculpture and perhaps for sculpture in general.[37]

The consistent invocation of "the community" in passages such as these typifies the terminological abuses pervading discussions of public art and endowing the new type with an aura of social accountability. That Beardsley's book consistently describes government-funded art as "community-sponsored" is especially ironic, since the "new initiatives within cities" and "major building programs" he mentions as the impetus for collaborations frequently comprise state interventions in the environment, interventions that destroy minority and working-class communities and disperse their residents. "Community" conjures up images of neighborhoods bound together by relations of mutual interest, respect, and kinship; "community-sponsored" connotes local control and citizen participation in decision-making. But it is community, as both territory and social form, that redevelopment destroys. Redevelopment converts the city into a terrain organized to fulfill capital's need to exploit space for profit; if anything, clashes, rather than confluence, between communities and state-imposed initiatives are more likely to characterize urban life today.

Inaccuracies of language, demonstrating indifference to the issues of urban politics, resemble other distortions pervading discourse about public art collaborations, distortions that confuse the issues of aesthetic politics as well. Like the appropriation of urban discourse, these misrepresentations try to invest the recent marriage of art and urban planning with a social justification, using the vocabulary of radical art practice. The new public art is deemed to be anti-individualist, contextualist, and site-specific. Collaborative artists frequently display a lack of concern with private self-expression and, thereby, an opposition to the autonomy and privilege of art. As part of urban design teams, they also reject notions of public art as "decoration," because, as they contend, they are not merely placing objects in urban spaces but creating the spaces themselves. If writers such as Beardsley single out "new initiatives within cities" as one factor contributing to the growth of public art collaborations, they see the second crucial factor to be developments within contemporary art itself.

In part, it [the shift to public art partnerships] follows as well from the increasingly interdisciplinary character of contemporary art. . . . There is a

pronounced shift in these projects from the isolated object to the artwork
integrated with its environment and from the solitary creator to the artist as
a member of a professional team.[38]

Of course the new public art is born of recent tendencies within urbanism and art practice. To say so tells us very little. Genuine explanation hinges on understanding the nature of each of these developments and of their interaction. The new art's promoters misunderstand both sources of the new public art. The difference between their version of site-specificity and its original meaning is obvious and needs only to be summarized here.

Commitment to developing an art that neither diverts attention from nor merely decorates the spaces of its display originated from the imperative to challenge the neutrality of those spaces. Contextualist art intervened in its spatial context by making the concealed social organization and ideological content of that space visible. The new public art, in contrast, moves "beyond decoration" into the field of spatial design in order to create, rather than question, its space, to conceal its constitutive social relations. It moves from a notion of art that is "in" but independent of its spaces to one that views art as integrated with its spaces and users but in which all three are independent of urban politics. It simply combines twin fetishisms and is thus instrumental for redevelopment. One critic, delineating "a right way and a wrong way to insert art in public places," wrote regarding a collaborative art project in New York that exemplified the "right way" that it

represents the gentrification of site art—it's been successfully, even brilliantly, tamed, its sting removed. You can sometimes miss the good old days when artists were fierce individualists wrestling the wilderness to its knees, like Dan'l Boone with the bear; the "otherness" of art out on the American desert touched some mythic nerve. But times have changed. The two traditions—the gentrified and the wild—can't be mixed.[39]

The statement constructs false dualisms that conceal genuine differences. What has been eliminated from the new "site-specific" art is not "individualism," as opposed to teamwork, but political radicalism in favor of collaboration with the forces of power. The real measure of just how depoliticized this art has become—and how political it actually is—under the guise of being "environmentally sensitive" is the author's assumption that gentrification is a positive metaphor. As anyone genuinely sensitive to New York's social landscape realizes, however, the prior symbolization of gentrification as the domestication of wild frontiers profoundly misapprehends the nature of the phenomenon. Gentrification only appears to result from the heroic conquest of hostile environments by individual "pioneers"; in truth, as Neil Smith writes,

it is apparent that where the "urban pioneers" venture, the banks, real-estate companies, the state or other collective economic actors have generally gone before. In this context it may be more appropriate to view the James Rouse Company not as the John Wayne but as the Wells Fargo of gentrification.[40]

The depiction of gentrification—a process that replaces poor, usually minority, residents of frequently well-established neighborhoods with white middle-class residents—as a beneficial activity taming uncivilized terrains is not only naive about economics, it is an ethnocentric and racist conceit as well. The use of this conceit in art criticism epitomizes the arrogance inherent in aesthetic practices claiming to respond to urban environments while lacking any commitment to comprehend them.

Instead, absorbing dominant ideology about the city, proponents of the new public art respond to urban questions by constructing images of well-managed and beautiful cities. Theirs is a technocratic vision. Insofar as it discerns a real problem—the loss of people's attachment to the city—it reacts by offering solutions that can only perpetuate alienation: a belief that needs and pleasures can be gratified by expertly produced, "humanized" environments. The incapacity to appreciate that the city is a social rather than technical form renders this perspective helpless to explain a situation in which the same system that produces, for the purposes of profit and control, a city dissociated from its users, today, for the same reasons literally detaches people from their living space through eviction and displacement. Under these

circumstances, the technocratic view is left with limited options: encouragement of these actions, disavowal, or dismissal of homelessness as an example of how the system fails rather than, more accurately, how it currently
works. Society's "failure" can produce a resigned abandonment of the most
troubling facts of city life, resulting in attitudes supporting the use of the city
for economic growth even while proposing degrees of regulation. One urban
designer, dedicated to institutionalizing urban design as a technical specialty
and arm of public policy, freely acknowledges, for instance, that gentrification
and historic preservation displace "earlier settlers" in city neighborhoods. He
suggests measures to "mitigate the adverse effects of social change in historic districts. However," he succinctly concludes,

*the dynamics of real estate in a private market always mean that someone
profits at someone else's expense. On balance, the preservation and restoration of old neighborhoods has to be considered valuable for the economic
health of a city, even if there is hardship for individuals.*[41]

Believing that the dominant forces producing today's city represent the collectivity and, despite references to "social change," that such forces are
immutable, interdisciplinary urban design teams—including public artists—
fashion the mental and physical representations of New York's ascendancy.
To do so, they must suppress the connection between redeveloped spaces
and New York's homelessness.

■ The Social Uses of Space

Public artists seeking to reveal the contradictions underlying images of well-
managed or beautiful cities also explore relations between art and urbanism.
Their interdisciplinary ventures differ, however, from the new collaborative
and useful ones. Instead of extending the idealist conception of art to the
surrounding city, they combine materialist analyses of art as a social product
with materialist analyses of the social production of space. As a contribution
to this work, urban studies has much to offer, since it analyzes the concrete
mechanisms by which power relations are perpetuated in spatial forms and

identifies the precise terms of spatial domination and resistance. Over the last twenty years, the "social production of space" has become the object of an impressive body of literature generated by urbanists in many fields—geography, sociology, urban planning, political economy. Critical spatial theories share a key theme with critical aesthetic thought, and the two have unfolded along a similar trajectory. Initially, each inquiry questioned the paradigm dominating its respective discipline. Just as materialist art practice challenged formalist dogma, critical urban studies questioned mainstream idealist perspectives on urban space.[42] "The dominant paradigm," as sociologist Marc Gottdiener summarizes it,

loosely identified as urban ecology, explains settlement space as being produced by an adjustment process involving large numbers of relatively equal actors whose interaction is guided by some self-regulating invisible hand. This "organic" growth process—propelled by technological innovation and demographic expansion—assumes a spatial morphology which, according to ecologists, mirrors that of lower life forms within biological kingdoms. Consequently, the social organization of space is accepted by mainstreamers as inevitable, whatever its patterns of internal differentiation.[43]

The ecological perspective views forms of metropolitan social life in terms of the adaptation of human populations to environments in which certain processes tend to remain constant and invariable. Employing biologistic analogies, it attributes patterns of urban growth to "laws" of competition, dominance, succession, and invasion, and thus explains the form of the city as a product of seminatural processes. Even when the ecological legacy of environmental determinism has been complicated or discarded altogether, many tendencies within urban studies continue to view space as an objective entity against which already existing subjectivities are measured and therefore to marginalize the wider social system as cause of urban spatial form. But just as critical art practice in the late 1960s and 1970s sought to defetishize the ideological art object, critical urban studies did the same with the ideological spatial object—the city as an ecological form. The two inquiries investigated the ways in which social relations produce, respectively, art and the city.

Having insisted, however, on the relationship between society and art, on the one hand, or space, on the other, both critiques rejected the notion that this relationship is one of simple reflection or interaction. If formalism reentered aesthetic discourse in the notion that art inevitably mirrors society, so idealism returned to spatial discourse in the formulation that space simply reflects social relations. But "two things can only interact or reflect each other if they are defined in the first place as separate," observes urban geographer Neil Smith.

Even having taken the first step of realization, then, we are not automatically freed from the burden of our conceptual inheritance; regardless of our intentions, it is difficult to start from an implicitly dualistic conception of space and society and to conclude by demonstrating their unity.[44]

Indeed, by means of such separations, not only are space and art endowed with identities as discrete entities, but social life appears to be *unsituated,* to exist apart from its material forms. Space and art can be rescued from further mystification only by being grasped as socially produced categories in the first instance, as arenas where social relations are reproduced, and as, themselves, social relations.

Framing my remarks about kindred developments in two distinct fields is a belief that they share a common purpose. Both attempt to reveal the depoliticizing effects of the hegemonic perspectives they criticize and, conversely, share an imperative to politicize the production of space and art. These comparable goals do not merely present an interesting academic parallel. Nor, as in the standard conception of interdisciplinary endeavors, do they simply enrich each other. Rather, they converge in the production of a new object—public art as a spatial activity. Understanding the fusion of urban space with prevailing social relations reveals the extent to which the predominant tendency within public art to design the landscape of redevelopment fully implicates art in spatial politics.

Such a statement only makes sense, however, in light of a theory of spatial organization as a terrain of political struggle. Urban theories, far from monolithic, are characterized by debates that are much too complex to receive justice within the scope of this essay.[45] Still, it is necessary to outline, however briefly, why space is on the political agenda as it has never been before. Henri Lefebvre, originator of the phrase "the production of space," attributes the significance of space, in part, to changes in the organization of production and accumulation under late capitalism. New spatial arrangements assure capitalism's very survival. Because, according to Lefebvre, production is no longer isolated in independent units within space but, instead, takes place across vast spatial networks, "the production of things in space" gives way to "the production of space."[46] Due to this growth and to revolutions in telecommunications and information technology, "the planning of the modern economy tends to become spatial planning."[47] The implications of this fundamental premise are clear. Individual cities cannot be defined apart from the spatial totality—the relations of spaces to one another within and between various geographic levels: global, regional, urban. The spatial restructuring of New York—a process at the urban level—can be comprehended only within the global context: the internationalization of capital, new international division of labor, and new international urban hierarchy.[48] Cities such as New York, occupying the upper ranks of the hierarchy, function within the division of labor as centers for decision-making and administrative control of finance capital and global corporations. Productive activities and, now, low-level clerical jobs are exported, permitting savings on labor costs along with enhanced flexibility and control. But the corporate center itself materializes not only because of global restructuring but also through a restructuring within the city. Concentrations of luxury housing, office buildings, and high-status entertainment and recreational facilities serve the new work force and destroy physical conditions of survival for blue-collar workers. This restructuring is paradoxical, entailing as it does simultaneous processes of deindustrialization and reindustrialization, decentralization and recentralization, internationalization and peripheralization. Crucial to grasping the character of New York, however, is the key insight that within the finance and service center, as on the global level, individual spaces have no intrinsic substance: their character and condition can be explained only in relation to other city spaces.

Specific spatial relations within the city correspond, in part, to the circumstances of accumulation under late capitalism. Today the accumulation process occurs not by absolute expansion but through the internal differentiation of space. It is, then, a process of uneven development. The idea that uneven spatial development is "the hallmark of the geography of capitalism"[49] combines insights of geography with a long and embattled tradition within Marxist political economy. Theorists of uneven development explain capital accumulation as a contradictory process taking place through a transfer of values within a hierarchically unified world system. "In this whole system," writes Ernest Mandel,

development and underdevelopment reciprocally determine each other, for while the quest for surplus-profits constitutes the prime motive power behind the mechanisms of growth, surplus-profit can only be achieved at the expense of less productive countries, regions and branches of production. Hence development takes place only in juxtaposition with underdevelopment; it perpetuates the latter and itself develops thanks to this perpetuation.[50]

While urban geographers and sociologists routinely include uneven development among the features distinguishing the production of late capitalist space, Neil Smith has extensively analyzed it as a structural process governing spatial patterns at all scales. Smith's work is essential to a comprehension of the spatial restructuring of New York since it explains phenomena such as gentrification and redevelopment as manifestations of the broad, yet specific, underlying process of uneven development affecting land use in the city.

Smith theorizes two factors responsible for uneven development at the urban scale. Following David Harvey, he applies to explanations of urban space theories maintaining that overaccumulation crises prompt capital, in an attempt to counteract falling rates of profit, to switch its investment from crisis-ridden spheres of the economy into the built environment. Gentrification and redevelopment represent this attempt. But uneven development in the city operates not only in response to such broad economic cycles but also because of corresponding conditions within metropolitan land markets. According to Smith, the profitability of investment in the built environment depends on the creation of what he calls a "rent gap."[51] The rent gap describes the difference between the present value of land and its potential value. The devalorization of real estate, through blockbusting, redlining, and abandonment of buildings, creates a situation in which investment by real estate and finance capital for "higher" land uses can produce a profitable return. In Smith's analysis, redevelopment results from both the uneven development of capital in general and of urban land in particular. Whether or not one agrees that the creation of a rent gap is sufficient to produce redevelopment, Smith's thesis discloses the concealed relation between processes such as gentrification and those of abandonment. The decline of neighborhoods, rather than being corrected by gentrification, is its precondition. Smith's theorization of uneven urban development offers, as well, a key to understanding the construction of the image of the redeveloped city. The identity of redeveloped spaces as symbols of beneficial and uniform growth requires that declining spaces be constituted as separate categories. Growth as redifferentiation is disavowed. Consequently, the repressed "other" of spaces of ascendancy has a concrete identity in deteriorating areas and the immiseration of city residents.

Uncovering the economic determinations of spatial redifferentiation in New York does not, however, illuminate the operations of space as a determining weight on social life or as ideology. For urbanists such as Lefebvre, however, advanced capitalism creates a distinctive and multivalent space that reproduces *all* social relations. "It is not only supported by social relations, but it also is producing and produced by social relations."[52] Capitalist space, which Lefebvre, among others, calls abstract space, serves many functions. It is, at once, a means of production, an object of consumption, and a property relation. Abstract space is also a vehicle for state domination, subordination, and surveillance. According to Lefebvre, it possesses a distinctive combination of three features. Abstract space is homogeneous or uniform so that it can be used, manipulated, controlled, and exchanged. Within the homogeneous whole, which spreads over vast areas, it is fragmented into interchangeable parts, so that, as a commodity, it can be bought and sold. Abstract space is, further, hierarchically ordered, divided into centers and peripheries, upper- and lower-status spaces, spaces of the governing and governed. All three features require that space be objectified and universalized, submitted to an abstract measure. But above all else, numerous contradictions haunt this space. As a global productive force, space is universalized, but it is also, as Lefebvre describes it, "pulverized" by relations of private property that demand its fragmentation into units. This conflict expresses a broader contradiction in the asymmetrical development of the forces of production— geographical space in this case—and the social relations of production— here the economic ownership and control of space. The universalization-pulverization contradiction embodies still another conflict—that between homogenized space serving as a tool of state domination and the fragmentation of space required by economic relations. Abstract space can serve as a space of control because it is generalized from specificity and diversity, from its relation to social subjects and their uses of space. But while abstract space homogenizes differences, it causes them at the same time to assert themselves. This contradiction emerges as cities—which Lefebvre defines as arenas for the encounter between differences—are homogenized, by means of exclusion, into centers of wealth, decision-making, and power. "The dominant space, that of the spaces of richness and power, is forced to fashion the dominated spaces, that of the periphery."[53] The relegation of groups of people and particular uses of space to enclosed areas outside the center produces an "explosion of spaces." Thus, through homogenization, a multitude of differences become available to perception as abstract space imposes itself on the space of everyday life. This process embodies a further contradiction, that between the production of space for profit and control—abstract space—and for social reproduction—the space of everyday life, which is both created by and yet escapes the generalizations of exchange. Abstract space represents, then, the *unstable* subordination of integrated social space by a centralized space of power. Because space is essential to daily life, the space of domination is resisted by what Lefebvre terms the "appropriation" of space for individual and social purposes. It follows that society's essential spatial conflict entails the appropriation of space from its alienation in capitalist spatial organization. This reparative goal is what Lefebvre refers to as "the right of the city,"[54] and it includes the struggle of the marginalized to occupy and control space.

Lefebvre's intricate formulations about the preeminence of space in social conflicts have provoked extensive criticism, including charges of "spatial fetishism," "vagueness," and "reproductionism." Largely untranslated from the French, they originally became familiar to English-speaking readers in Manuel Castells's *The Urban Question,* where the author opposed Lefebvre in a debate on the theory of space.[55] Although Castells himself has subsequently returned to many of Lefebvre's ideas, which have also been advanced by numerous English-speaking urbanists, Lefebvre's emphasis on social reproduction rather than production has made him vulnerable to criticism from those who continue to privilege production as the primary locus of political activity. Surely Lefebvre's rejection of reformist measures to ameliorate urban problems and his refusal to propound doctrinaire solutions frustrate those who are searching for a single explanatory factor or new system. Yet the rejection of such systems and of predictable solutions is one of Lefebvre's principal strengths. Meaning, for him, is not fixed in economic structures, but is continuously created in the practice of everyday life. Moreover, his analysis of the spatial exercise of power as a construction and conquest of difference, although it is thoroughly grounded in Marxist thought, rejects economism and opens up possibilities for advancing analysis of spatial politics into realms of feminist and anticolonialist discourse, into considerations of space as representations of difference. Certainly, more successfully than anyone of whom I am aware, Lefebvre has specified the operations of space as ideology and built the foundation for cultural critiques of spatial design as a tool of social control. For Lefebvre, space is broadly ideological because it reproduces existing social relations. Through the auspices of coherent spatial order, efforts are made to control the contradictions inherent in abstract space. "One of the most crying paradoxes of abstract space," Lefebvre observes,

is that it can be simultaneously the birthplace of contradictions, the milieu in which they are worked out and which they tear up, and finally, the instrument which allows their suppression and the substitution of an apparent coherence. All of which confers on space a function previously assumed by ideology.[56]

Professions such as urban planning and design—and now, public art— assume the job of imposing such coherence, order, and rationality on space.

They can be regarded as disciplinary technologies in Foucault's sense insofar as they attempt to pattern space so that docile and useful bodies are created by and deployed within it. In performing these tasks, such technologies also take on the contradictory functions of the state. Called upon to preserve space for the fulfillment of social needs, they must also facilitate the development of an abstract space of exchange and engineer the space of domination. Consequently, urban practitioners who view planning as a technical problem and politics as a foreign substance to be eliminated from spatial structures mask spatial politics.

The contours of New York's redevelopment cannot be conceptually manipulated to fit exactly within the mold of Lefebvre's depiction of late capitalist space. Yet the concept of abstract space, together with that of uneven development, specifies the terms, distilled from concrete events, of urban spatial struggle. Materialist analyses of space enable us to evaluate the consequences of cultural practices, such as the new public art, engaged in that struggle on the side of real estate and state domination. They also indicate the points where public art can enter the arena of urban politics in order to resist that domination, perhaps facilitating the expression of social groups excluded by the current organization of the city. Participation in urban design and planning enmeshes public art, unwittingly or not, in spatial politics. But public art can also appropriate the city, organized to repress contradictions, as a vehicle for illuminating them. It can transform itself into a spatial praxis, which Edward Soja has clarified as "the active and informed attempt by spatially conscious social actors to reconstitute the embracing spatiality of social life."[57] Against aesthetic movements that design the spaces of redevelopment, interventionist aesthetic practice might—as it does with other spaces—redesign these sites. For if official public art creates the redeveloped city, art as spatial praxis approaches this city in the cautious manner of the cultural critic described by Walter Benjamin. Confronted with "cultural treasures"—"documents of civilization"—Benjamin's critic unveils the barbarism underlying their creation by brushing their history "against the grain."[58] Likewise, we can brush New York's spatial documents of ascendancy against the grain, revealing them to be, at the same time, documents of homelessness. First, however, they must be admitted to have a history.

■ The Soul of Battery Park City

"In Battery Park there was nothing built—it was landfill—so it was not as if there was a history to the place. This was a construction site."[59] The sentiment that New York's waterfront development lies not only on the edge of the city but outside history is widespread. Here it is voiced by a public artist who recently cooperated as part of an urban design team creating a "site-specific installation"[60] called South Cove, a park located in a residential area of Battery Park City in lower Manhattan. South Cove is just one of several collaborative "artworks" sponsored by the Fine Arts Committee of the Battery Park City Authority, the state agency overseeing what has become "the largest and most expensive real estate venture ever undertaken in New York City."[61] The elaborate art program, corresponding in its ambitiousness to the scope of the real estate program, "will be," most critics agree, "New York's most important showcase for public art."[62] As a massive state intervention in New York redevelopment and, concurrently, exemplar of the governmental priority now accorded public art, Battery Park City elicits virtually unanimous accolades from public officials, real estate and business groups, city planners, art and architecture critics alike. The apotheosis, individually, of urban redevelopment and of the new public art, it also seals their union. Dominant aesthetic and urban discourses dissemble the nature of the alliance. A typically hyperbolic example of the role the art world plays is John Russell's response, in 1983, to the unveiling of designs for a major Battery Park City art collaboration—the public plaza of the World Financial Center, the project's commercial core. Interpreting for his readers the interaction between art and urbanism embodied in this event, Russell set the stage by defining Battery Park City's essence to be, in the first instance, aesthetic—the encounter between land and water.

Battery Park City is just across the water from the Statue of Liberty, as everyone knows, and it therefore occupies a particularly sensitive position. In every great city by the sea there comes a moment at which land meets with moving water. If the city is doing a good job, whether accidentally or by grand design, we feel at that moment that great cities and the sea are predestined partners. Their interaction can turn whole cities into works of art.[63]

Having intimated that maritime cities are shaped by transcendent forces, Russell invents romantic precedents for Battery Park City, first in a lineage of seaside cities—St. Petersburg, Constantinople, Venice—and, then, in the "great" painting, music, and literature they inspired. Yet Battery Park City's topographical configuration—land meeting water—conditions the meanings attributed to the area far less than do elusive presuppositions, drawn from art history, about the nature of another encounter—that between art and the city. The discipline's habitually accepted links—the city as a work of art and as the inspiration for works of art—lend support to Russell's later implication that Battery Park City's "natural" potential to become an aesthetic object generates reciprocal possibilities for revitalizing art as well. Discharging its task of effecting the city's metamorphosis, art, too, will be transformed.

What they [the Battery Park City Fine Arts Committee] did was to redefine the respective roles of architect, artist and landscape designer in the planning of large-scale building projects. Instead of being assigned pre-existing spaces in which to present works of art, the artists are to function from the outset as co-designers of the spaces.[64]

Characterizing the "new notion of public art," Russell slips into another ready-made formulation about art and the city—the artwork in the city or the discourse about public art. Here, he celebrates public art that is immersed in, rather than aloof from, metropolitan life: "The general thrust of the plan was away from the hectoring monumentality of 'public sculpture' and toward a kind of art that gets down off the pedestal and works with everyday life as an equal partner."[65] Yet his identification of Battery Park City as a work of art in aestheticist terms has already released the author from the responsibility to understand the city's social processes and their effect on everyday life. The purported metamorphosis of Battery Park City and, by extension, all New York, into a work of art conceals the city's real metamorphosis. If, then, the new art proudly relinquishes its status as aesthetic object isolated from "life," it is only in order to confer that mystifying status on Battery Park City itself.

Similar mystifications pervade descriptions of all facets of Battery Park City. Surpassing even the usual promotional enthusiasm with which the mass media announce the progress of New York real estate developments, articles and speeches about the completion of Battery Park City treat it as a symbol of New York's ascension from "urban decay," "urban crisis," and "urban fiscal crisis." Battery Park City exemplifies multiple victories—of public policy, public space, urban design, city planning.

The phoenix-like rising of their [major corporations'] collective new home [Battery Park City] is demonstrating that predictions of lower Manhattan's demise were unduly hasty—like forecasts for other downtowns across the nation.[66]

For this is the real significance of Battery Park City—not the specific designs of its parks or its buildings, good though they are, but the message the large complex sends about the importance of the public realm.[67]

Battery Park City . . . is close to a miracle. . . . It is not perfect—but is far and away the finest urban grouping since Rockefeller Center and one of the better pieces of urban design of modern times.[68]

A major governmental success and an example of what government can do.[69]

In short, an "urban dream,"[70] and, in Governor Mario Cuomo's succinct assessment, "a soaring triumph."[71]

The project's physical foundation on a manufactured landfill generates still other optimistic tropes. Battery Park City is fresh, untrodden territory unencumbered by historical fetters and past failures, a glittering token of New York's ability to reverse deterioration, an emblem of hope. Ironically, the image granted to land that is *literally* produced figuratively severs the space from the social activities that constituted it. Such conceits unwittingly convert Battery Park City's imaginary landfill into a palpable incarnation, not of the city's triumph, but of a mental operation that fetishizes the city as a physical object. The landfill thus bespeaks the triumph of the technocratic city produced by powers that surpass people. From the project's inception, it was described as the creation by urban professionals of a "community." It provides, according to one planning critic, "the urban functions and amenities—shops, restaurants, schools, parks, rapid transit, utilities, public and recreational facilities—that make a real community."[72] "We see plan making and implementation," reads the master plan, "as interrelated parts of the same process: successful city building."[73] So attenuated are the bonds tying the landfill to its social foundations that, unsurprisingly, Battery Park City almost speaks for itself, stressing its origins in a technical achievement: "It is what it calls itself: a city. It begins by making its own land."[74]

Of course, Battery Park City does have a history. It did not spring full-blown from the sea or, as public relations accounts present it, from the imagination of "visionaries" such as Governor Nelson Rockefeller and Mayor John Lindsay, who bequeathed their "dreams" to Governor Cuomo and Mayor Koch. It emerged, instead, from a sequence of conflicts over the use of public land and especially over the social composition of city housing. Successive alterations in architecture and design occupy another historical dimension of the project. Intersecting these narratives, Battery Park City in its nearly complete present form occupies, synchronically, a key position in New York's historically constituted structure of spatial relations. Long overdue, an exhaustive critique of Battery Park City has yet to be undertaken. Here, I want to retrieve enough of the project's history to permit an understanding of the ways in which art and design intervened at a critical moment of the project's unfolding. Restoring the housing question to representations of Battery Park City is crucial, since it is the ramifications of this issue that Battery Park City's design collaborations conceal by deeming political questions to be outside the province of beauty and utility. The organization of housing provision embodies more vividly than any other factor the contradictions of contemporary urbanization. As the central expenditure of low-income families, housing most acutely reflects New York's social polarization, and its withdrawal from poor and minority residents most forcibly denies them a right to the city. To illuminate Battery Park City's role in the development and distribution of housing is, then, to apprehend the project as a graphic emblem, not of New York's triumph, but of its uneven development.

When, in May 1966, Governor Rockefeller first proposed Battery Park City as a "new living space for New York" and part of his overall program for lower Manhattan redevelopment, the plan included 14,000 apartments: 6,600 luxury, 6,000 middle-income, and 1,400 subsidized low-income units.[75] Mayor Lindsay also wanted to develop lower Manhattan, but solely for high-income residents. On April 16, 1969, Rockefeller and Lindsay presented a compromise plan allocating only 1,266 out of 19,000 units to the poor.[76] About 5,000 middle-income units were included, with the remaining apartments earmarked for luxury use. Charles J. Urstadt, then chairman of the Battery Park City Authority, speaking as the state's mouthpiece and anticipating protest against the small proportion of low-income housing, announced that the housing mix was "not immutable."[77] Indeed, the political tenor of the late 1960s was such that numerous liberal groups demanded greater proportions of low-income housing in Battery Park City in exchange for their support of Lindsay's reelection that year. Manhattan borough president Percy E. Sutton, calling the proposed development the "Riviera on the Hudson,"[78] stated that "it will use scarce public land resources and public powers to benefit mainly income groups and social classes fully capable of meeting their housing needs without public aid."[79] More radical elements—tenant groups in particular—also voiced their opposition. Yet Lindsay believed, as expressed in the 1969 Plan for New York City, that New York had to remain a "national center" in order to ensure the city's overall prosperity. "He saw preservation and enhancement of the central areas for the elite as crucial to the whole future of the city."[80] Placing low-income housing in Battery Park City was, in Lindsay's words, "equivalent to putting low-income housing in the middle of the East Side of Manhattan."[81] Nonetheless, Lindsay needed the support of liberal Democrats, and in August he reversed his stand, asking that two-thirds of Battery Park City's 15,000 apartments be built for low- and middle-income tenants.[82] At a City Planning Commission hearing, a Lindsay aide stated that the mayor believed that "the social benefits to be gained from having an economically integrated community in lower Manhattan far outweigh 'the financial burdens.'"[83] Two months later, the Board of Estimate approved the revised Battery Park City plan, although representatives of the East Side Tenants Council and City Wide Anti-Poverty Committee on Housing still protested the liberal decision, arguing that "the low-income New Yorker who most needs new housing was being forgotten by the Battery Park City planners."[84] Several months earlier, Jack Rand of the East Side Tenants Council had charged in a letter to *The New York Times* that the authority was discriminating between Manhattan and Brooklyn in the distribution of low-income housing.[85]

Under the legal arrangements for the approved plan, the city of New York, owner of the land, would lease it under the terms of a Master Lease to the Battery Park City Authority, which would control its development. The Master Lease went into effect in June 1970. The Authority planned to issue tax-exempt bonds to finance the project, with payment on the bonds to be made out of the revenues generated by development. The Authority also intended to select private developers to build all of Battery Park City's housing, but conditions in the construction and housing markets made developers unwilling to assume the risks involved without government support, and the city moved to provide it. In 1972, "a consensus developed that several provisions in the original Master Lease . . . would be cumbersome, time-consuming or overly costly in the execution of the physical construction of the project, or would impede the marketability of the completed facilities and the administrative operations of the Authority."[86] "Accordingly," the City Planning Commission and the Board of Estimate endorsed changes to "eliminate or modify the inevitable conditions."[87] These changes reduced the proportion of low-income housing to approximately 12 percent. Thirty percent of the units were to be luxury and 56 percent middle-income. But even the changed proportions do not indicate the full extent of the Authority's class-biased action. Officially designated limits for establishing low-, middle-, and luxury-income housing eligibility always require scrutiny, since housing costs increase, and income standards are constantly adjusted. By 1972, as sociologist Maynard T. Robison points out, "the cost of 'middle-income' housing was such that its residents would be quite well off."[88] Amendments that year to the Master Lease also eliminated the requirement that each of Battery Park City's residential buildings reflect the income mix of the entire project. This meant that low-income housing could be segregated. Between 1972, when the first Battery Park City bonds were issued, and 1979, a year before the first payment on the bonds came due, the proposed housing mix of Battery Park City remained stable, but little progress was made on implementing the project itself. Site development on the ninety-one-acre landfill continued, and various construction deals were worked out, only to collapse. Robison, who has extensively investigated the progress of Battery Park City from its inception until 1979, attributes the lack of activity to two interrelated factors. First, he believes, all the principal actors in the Battery Park City project—government officials, financial institutions, real estate developers—wanted to build it as a luxury district for corporate and real estate investment. But the site presented several obstacles impeding demand for expensive housing in the area: surrounded by unattractive and decaying terrain, it had no park, stores, restaurants, or entertainment and recreational facilities. The problem for the major groups involved in Battery Park City was, it seems, not whether the public sector should encourage the privatization of the city by subsidizing the rich and guaranteeing business profits, but "how to do so in the face of pressure to use public resources and the site to benefit groups other than the elite."[89]

By 1979, the turning point in Battery Park City's evolution, the answer had appeared in the form of the "fiscal" crisis. Sanctioned by orthodox explanations of the mid-1970s crisis in New York's public finance, the state ultimately transferred Battery Park City's spatial resources to the private sector. Leasing the land to private developers, the Authority sought to attract them through substantial tax abatements, exemptions, and financial incentives for the use of Battery Park City for office towers and luxury condominiums. The Authority also undertook the task of site-development for these projects by creating parks and other amenities to convert the area into an elite district as quickly as possible. In 1979, the immediate fiscal problem facing the Battery Park City Authority was the likelihood that, because it had not yet generated sufficient revenues, it would have to default on the first payment of principal—due November 1, 1980—of its outstanding bonds. City and state officials, developers, and urban planners concurred that Battery Park City's "failure" resulted from the project's overly ambitious conception and from New York's current fiscal troubles.[90] A "workout" plan, they believed, must be informed by knowledge of "the city's tough urban realities."[91] Thus, Battery Park City's situation assumed, just as the fiscal crisis itself did, an aura of inevitability that fostered acceptance of inequitable solutions.

Crises in public finance are not caused by inexorable economic laws, however, but by specific economic relations. Critics of conventional definitions of urban fiscal crisis stress varying alternative explanations, but, in general, position it within the broader economic crises of capitalist countries.[92] Local crisis is inseparable from larger crises of the public sector in which social services are cut back in order to aid business. Some economists analyze urban fiscal crisis as a reflection of the inability of municipal governments to raise revenues in a new era of capital mobility and flexible accumulation. Reacting to forces that are to a considerable extent outside their control, city governments adopt policies oriented toward attracting private investment. Peter Marcuse, emphasizing the ideological *uses* of "urban fiscal crisis" as a concept, points to two constituent factors.[93] The first is the problem inherent in capital accumulation, which, to counteract falling rates of profit, constantly seeks to cheapen labor costs and automatize production. To accomplish these goals, capital shifts locations. The state, however, must bear the social costs of capital mobility: infrastructure provision, facilities for the working population, the redundant work force left behind when businesses move elsewhere. Consequently, Marcuse identifies a real tendency to crisis within the economic and political systems, but he suggests that there is also a *fraudulent* crisis— one that justifies deliberate government policies transparently serving private interests. Both the real crises and the fraudulent one, however, should be perceived as processes in a particular social system, not the natural result of inevitable economic forces. In this sense, the dominant construction of the category "urban fiscal crisis" is ideological. It presents crises as natural and then uses that assumption to justify transferring resources to the private sector and withholding them from the services most needed by the poor. It thus perpetuates the conditions it purports to explain and vividly demonstrates the unequal weight of public and private interests in municipal finance policies.

In 1979 the ideology of crisis justified such inequitable measures in Battery Park City, measures declared to be the project's "last chance."[94] To rescue Battery Park City, a new legal framework, financial scheme, and master design plan were adopted in an attempt to "make something useful" out of the site.[95] Principally, the goal was to attract private financing. To do so, the new plan provided substantial tax abatements and other financial incentives and relocated Battery Park City's commercial zone, previously relegated to the landfill's southern end, to a central location. It eliminated all subsidized low-, moderate-, or middle-income housing.

To facilitate these changes, the new plan also included an altered legal arrangement, a version of a widespread mechanism by which government encourages the private sector and cushions it from direct public control. According to an agreement worked out between the Governor Hugh Carey and Koch administrations, the state used its power of condemnation to bring the Battery Park City land under the direct ownership of the state Urban Development Corporation. The city thus yielded much of its legal control over the project's course. Indeed, the purpose of this maneuver was "to free the project from the welter of city regulations."[96] But what, in this case, is meant by "the welter of city regulations"? The shift of legal ownership of Battery Park City from the city government to a state authority ensured, under the guise of antibureaucratic efficiency, that developers would be liberated, as far as possible, from constraints imposed by existing democratic procedures for regulating land-use and planning decisions in New York—community board reviews, public hearings, City Planning Commission approval. Authorities—public corporations empowered to issue bonds in order to undertake economic activity—are one of the few popularly accepted forms by which American government engages in economic ventures. As Annmarie Hauck Walsh concludes in her detailed study of government corporations, they are largely protected from public accountability. Justified by the claim that their quasi-independent status makes them less vulnerable to political influence, authorities are actually less accessible to government regulation, community interests, and local pressures. Removing Battery Park City from city ownership helped remove it from the demands to which municipal government is especially sensitive. "Hybrid creatures," in Walsh's words, authorities are "corporations without shareholders, political jurisdictions without voters or taxpayers."[97] Inquiries into the authority form of public business cannot be separated from questions about decision-making and resource allocation, since, organized and run according to business principles, authorities often undertake projects on the basis of financial viability rather than public service. Financing through the bond market—with its attendant imperatives to guarantee the security of bonds and, further, make them profitable on the secondary market—also affects the type of enterprises promoted by authorities. The significance of these criteria can be seen in the fact that in May 1980, following the adoption of the new Battery Park City Plan, a leading financial rating agency named Standard and Poor granted Battery Park City's new bonds the highest credit rating possible, assuring their successful sale.[98] Indeed, the new plan predicted financial results with such success that later in the same year, Olympia and York Properties was conditionally approved as developer of Battery Park City's entire commercial sector. Eventually, the commercial structures materialized, aided by tax advantages and low-interest loans, as the World Financial Center. By April 1982, Battery Park City had become New York's "newest prestige address."[99] "As a result of economic forces no one could have foreseen," *The New York Times* reported, "luxury-level housing for upper-middle income or higher-income people is at present the only kind that can be built."[100]

The Battery Park City scheme released physical planning and land-use decisions from "bureaucratic" entanglements only to submit them to the control of a technocracy amenable to redevelopment—New York's urban design professionals. Urban designers had, in fact, first been welcomed into New York City government as agents of public policy in the late 1960s, when Battery Park City was first proposed. Alexander Cooper Associates, an urban design firm that today engineers major redevelopment projects in New York and New Jersey, prepared the third component of the Battery Park City "workout"—its new master plan—complying with its mandate to make the project "more attractive for investment and responsive to current planning approaches."[101] The draft plan outlined the basic design that ultimately determined Battery Park City's final form. Both principals of the firm, Alexander Cooper and Stanton Eckstut, had been leaders of Mayor Lindsay's Urban Design Group. In 1971, Cooper served as executive director of the Urban Design Council, precursor of the Urban Design Group of which Cooper was, for a time, also director. It is a measure of the extent to which planning and aesthetic ideologies block comprehension of the urban social context that in 1969, during the height of agitation for low-income housing in Battery Park City, the mayor's Urban Design Council, along with the Municipal Art Society, had endorsed the strongly contested Battery Park City plan without referring to the housing controversy at all."[102]

More than ten years later, designers again marginalized housing as an issue in "successful city building" when they devised Battery Park City's master plan. Directing the appearance, use, and organization of Battery Park City land, the discourse about design and the actual spaces that planners produced also assumed the task of rewriting the site's history, not so much concealing social reality as transposing it into design. For if Battery Park City's plan became a medium for evacuating history as action and struggle, it did so by reinventing history as spectacle and tradition. Thus, in 1979, the moment when Battery Park City changed most definitively and New York entered its accelerated phase of restructuring, development proceeded under a master plan stressing principles of continuity, permanence, invariance. Just when decisions about land-use became increasingly privatized and withdrawn from public control, designers resurrected talk about public space in a form that represses its political implication. Just when Battery Park City was relegated to the needs of profit, ensuring not only that low-income housing needs would be unmet but also that more people would be made homeless through raised property values in the city, there was intensified emphasis on designed spaces that, we were told, would fulfill essential human needs. And coinciding with the construction of Battery Park City as the epitome of abstract space—hierarchical, homogeneous, fragmented—designers mobilized a discourse about diversity, history, and locational specificity. Early in the process, the Battery Park City Authority incorporated public art into the implementation of the master plan: in 1982, "as part of its commitment to good design," it established the Fine Arts Program "to engage artists in the planning and design of the community's open spaces."[103] Besides South Cove Park, collaborative ventures between artists, architects, and landscape architects now include the plaza of the World Financial Center, the South Gardens, and West Thames Street Park. Numerous other public works have been selected because they are considered to be "sensitive," even if not intrinsic, to their sites.

The 1979 master plan discarded the original futuristic plan for Battery Park City, which had been adopted, with Lindsay's support, in the late 1960s. Replacing the old arrangement, which accentuated Battery Park City's architectural disjunction from the rest of Manhattan, the Cooper-Eckstut design, labeled "A Realist's Battery Park City,"[104] aimed to integrate Battery Park City—physically, visually, functionally—with New York, making it an organic extension of adjacent neighborhoods in lower Manhattan and of the rest of the city. The layout extended—and slightly reoriented in the direction of the water—Manhattan's rectilinear grid, subdivided the land into smaller development parcels, and relocated the commercial area. Further, the plan emphasized the use of traditional architectural elements and street furniture for the waterfront esplanade and other public spaces, objects copied from past structures in old New York neighborhoods—Central Park, Gramercy Park, Madison Avenue, the Upper West Side—to confer on Battery Park City the status of tradition. "We wanted to make it look as though nothing was done," explained Eckstut.[105] In addition, the new plan created a system of conventional blocks to allow developers to take on small parcels, and it established flexible controls that do not prescribe final designs for individual buildings. All these features were intended to assure, within the framework of an accelerated redevelopment program, the diversity and sense of historical memory that mark a city incrementally produced over time. History, then, was to be simulated in a compressed time frame and diversity isolated in physical style and in the realm of historic "preservation." In city planning rhetoric, "history" has become so malleable that the notion that Battery Park City has no history can be arbitrarily exchanged for the notion that Battery Park City has always existed.

The Cooper-Eckstut plan, sanctioned by fiscal crisis ideology, stated unequivocally that "the mechanism for providing large numbers of subsidized middle- and moderate-income housing—as originally envisioned—does not now exist. . . . The State is not in a position to sponsor moderate-income housing, and there is no technique for meeting the needs of this income group."[106] Low-income housing received no mention, despite the designer's belief that a revised plan can "pursue a planning concept more in keeping with development realities . . . without sacrificing the amenities that make the project desirable."[107] When Governor Cuomo took office in 1983, however, he voiced concern about the fact that public land was being given over on a grand scale to luxury housing and commercial development. According to Meyer S. Frucher, president of the Battery Park City Authority, the governor told him to give the project "a soul." The "soul," which Cuomo has since designated as Battery Park City's "social purpose," materialized in 1986 in the form of the Housing New York Corporation, a state agency empowered to issue bonds backed by Battery Park City revenues in order to finance the provision of low- and moderate-income housing in New York City. The first phase of the plan, which contributes its funds to Mayor Koch's program to rehabilitate city-owned properties, consists of the renovation of 1,850 apartments in Harlem and the South Bronx, with one-third of the units reserved for the homeless. Battery Park City's "soul," a concept offered as proof of the benefits of public-private partnership, has also been loosely extended as a rubric under which all the project's "public" benefits—its art and open space—are categorized. No doubt the government agencies and officials most deeply implicated in Battery Park City would like to present the "soul" of the project as, indeed, its animating principle. Yet even without examining the details of the city's housing plan—what percentage of the units will actually serve the homeless, how they will be run and maintained, whether as part of cross-subsidy programs they will, primarily, encourage redevelopment—several realities frustrate this contention. First, it begs the question of whether low- and moderate-income housing should be provided by channeling public resources toward large-scale redevelopment. Since redevelopment, as part of broader restructuring, produces homelessness, no matter what palliatives are administered to mitigate and push out of sight its worst effects, we are being asked to believe that the housing crisis can be cured only by publicly encouraging its causes. Second, the assertion that the Battery Park City plan is a triumph for the public sector places the government squarely in support of the spatial relations the plan reinforces—luxury enclaves in the city center shielded from areas for the poor and minorities on the periphery. Public resources, it holds, should be directed toward the production of New York as a segregated city.

It is, of course, true, as one expert observed about Battery Park City's low- and moderate-income housing program, that "advocates of low-income housing will take housing wherever and however they can get it."[108] But this understanding should not obscure, due to resignation or a false sense of victory, the realization that what the Battery Park City program confirms is not the triumph of public policy but the manner in which New York's preeminent space of richness, power, and decision-making has been forced to fashion the dominated spaces, too, thus corroborating Lefebvre's description of late capitalist space. And in accord with Lefebvre's evaluation of urban planning, the spatial design of Battery Park City suppresses this contradiction by substituting an image that presents the area's abstract space as, instead, natural, traditional, diverse, and functionally integrated with the entire city. Public art collaborations and the discourse that validates them also assume these ideological tasks. Paramount among their methods is the assertion that the spaces they produce are useful. "It seems," says a public artist at Battery Park City,

that there are archetypal needs that are met regularly in different cultures— needs for protected spaces, places of distraction. I am interested in poking at these potent situations and trying to find ways of creating equivalents within our own context.[109]

The humanist myth rehearsed in this statement about universal human conditions and needs "aims," as Roland Barthes observed more than thirty years ago,

to suppress the determining weight of History: we are held back at the surface of an identity, prevented precisely by sentimentality from penetrating into this ulterior zone of human behavior where historical alienation introduces some 'differences' which we shall here quite simply call 'injustices.'[110]

Surely, within what the artist calls "our own context"—New York's social polarization, uneven development, homelessness—to posit a "need for protected spaces" that is *met* in Battery Park City can only perpetuate such injustices. To recognize this function, however, art discourse must renounce its own humanist myth, acknowledging its specificity within historical sites. For the weight of Battery Park City's past, as well as its current position within the urban structure, enables us to "know very well," just as Barthes knew about the character of work in capitalist society, that shelter in New York, "is 'natural' just as long as it is 'profitable.'"[111] Suppressing this realization, Battery Park City's "soul"—its public art and spaces—mentally released, through universalizing notions about beauty and utility, from the material conditions of the project's existence, performs the function of myth. Like the other portion of the "soul"—low-income housing removed geographically from Battery Park City—it attempts to reconcile conflicts arising between the belief that the city should serve social needs and the experience of New York's domination by business and real estate. It is hardly surprising, then, that accounts of the useful public art at Battery Park City fail to comment on major transformations in the project's social uses. No matter now much it speaks of the space's coherence, this art violently fractures the social picture. Apparently integrated and diverse, Battery Park City is homogenized and hierarchized. Represented as harmonious, it conceals domination. "Historical," it rejects time, converting the past as a product of human agency into interchangeable fragments of the city's architectural remains. "Public," it transforms public space into places where selected New Yorkers are permitted to do what a *New York Times* editorial called "their public thing."[112] In the end, Battery Park City's art and design do try to integrate the area with New York, but with a redeveloped New York—ghettoized and exclusionary.

■ A Beautiful and Useful Weapon

In the winter of 1987, Mayor Koch ordered that the evicted living in public places be examined by authorities and, if judged mentally incompetent, forcibly hospitalized. Coinciding with these events, occurring in the middle of a season that is always the most difficult for the evicted, the Clocktower, a city-owned exhibition space in lower Manhattan, displayed a proposal for a public artwork entitled the *Homeless Vehicle Project*. The exhibition included several elements combined in a format that resembled the presentational

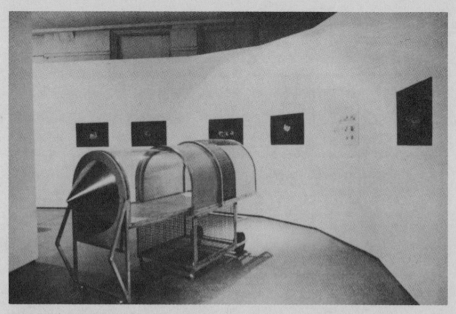

Installation of the *Homeless Vehicle Project* at the Clocktower, New York, 1988.

modes by which urban planning and architecture proposals are regularly un-veiled to the public. Its nucleus was a prototype of a stark, industrial-looking object—a vehicle designed by public artist Krzysztof Wodiczko in consultation with several evicted men. Constructed of aluminum, steel mesh, sheet metal, and Plexiglas, the vehicle aims to facilitate the survival activities of one seg-ment of the evicted population—individuals who live on the streets and survive by collecting, sorting, storing, and returning cans and bottles to supermar-kets in exchange for deposits. The device would enable this group of resi-dents to circulate more easily through the city, a mobility necessitated by their lack of permanent housing and their mode of subsistence. Besides eas-ing the job of scavenging, the cart offers a degree of shelter. Engineered so that it can expand or fold into a variety of positions, it furnishes, minimally, facilities for eating, sleeping, washing, defecating, and sitting. Sketches of the vehicle demonstrating different aspects of its operation were displayed at the Clocktower along with the model itself. Also shown were preliminary drawings revealing alterations made during the evolution of the design as the artist responded to requests from the consultants.

In a separate section of the gallery, Wodiczko simulated an outdoor urban landscape by projecting onto the walls slides depicting public spaces in New York City—Tompkins Square, City Hall Park, and the area directly outside the Municipal Building. Employing montage techniques, he then infiltrated the scenes with ghostly images, enlarged from sketches, of the vehicle being maneuvered through the municipal spaces by its potential users. The figures' spectral aspect materialized from two procedures: the drawings were printed white on black, and, blown up, their outlines became slightly blurred. By visualizing the vehicle in civic spaces, the slides thematically related homelessness to the action and inaction of local government, accusing the city not only of failing to cure the problem but, in fact, of producing it. Wodiczko's slide images also, more obliquely, associated homelessness with dispersed apparatuses of power in the city. The artist's presentation adopted an institutionalized form that embodies architecture, city planning, and urban design discourses: the visual projection of proposed objects and spatial alterations into the existing urban context in order to demonstrate their positive, benign, or, at the very least, unobtrusive effect on potential physical sites. By modifying this convention and projecting images that merged physical and social sites, Wodiczko's panorama commented on and established its divergence from the official role of environmental disciplines in New York today. Such practices engineer redevelopment, ejecting people from their homes and banishing the evicted. They also suppress the evidence of rupture by assigning social functions and groups to designated zones within the spatial hierarchy. Wodiczko's presentations, in contrast, symbolically lodged the homeless in the urban center, concretizing memories of social disruption and imagining the impact of the evicted on the city. Taped conversations between Wodiczko and evicted people, in which they discussed the vehicle's design, played continuously during the exhibition, and the gallery distributed a text containing transcripts of the conversations as well as an essay about the project, coauthored by Wodiczko and David Lurie.

Dictated by the practical needs and direct requests of men who live and

Slide Projections of the *Homeless Vehicle Project* at the Clocktower, New York, 1988.

work on the streets, the **Homeless Vehicle Project** implicitly expressed support for those people who, deprived of housing, choose—against official coercion—to resist relegation to dangerous and dehumanizing shelters. In no way offering itself as a solution, the Homeless Vehicle challenges the city's present solution—the proliferation of a shelter system not simply as a temporary adjunct to, but in lieu of, substantive construction of decent permanent housing. Questioning government housing and shelter policies does not obviate support, under crisis conditions, for the construction of low-income housing "wherever and however they can get it." It simply means that advocacy of housing and even shelters must be framed within a broad critique that voices the terms of substantive change—social ownership of housing, opposition to the rights of private property—and comprehends how policies offered as solutions frequently exacerbate or merely regulate the problem. Currently, government emphasizes "temporary" shelters, which, given the lack of new public housing construction, tacitly become permanent. Or it manufactures cumber-

some financing schemes by which a grossly inadequate number of low-income units are provided without direct public expenditure, as a means of facilitating redevelopment and, frequently, for private gain. At the same time, the city continues to channel large subsidies to business and developers. Thus, it perpetuates and disavows the relation between homelessness and the city's economic transformation. Described by one critic as "an insidious form of institutionalized displacement purporting to be humane while incarcerating thousands whose only 'crime' is poverty,"[113] the shelter system is, however, not only necessitated by restructuring and real estate development but itself participates in New York's spatial division into core and periphery areas. By increasing the visibility of the evicted, who, in reality, already inhabit urban space, the Homeless Vehicle dramatizes the right of the poor not to be isolated and excluded. Heightened visibility, however, is only the necessary, but not the sufficient, condition for this dramatization. Indeed, visibility can also be used, as it is by conservatives, to support demands for the re-

moval of the evicted. But the Homeless Vehicle reveals the evicted to be active New York residents whose means of subsistence form a legitimate element of the urban social structure. It thus focuses attention on that structure and, in so doing, not only challenges the economic and political systems that evict the homeless but subverts the modes of perception that exile them as well.

The Homeless Vehicle is, then, both practical object and symbolic articulation. In the gallery and, potentially, on the streets, it alters the image of the city. It is precisely the tension between its two functions that raises and openly confronts a troubling question, one that informs debates among the evicted and their advocates about the shelter system. Cultural practices addressing New York's environment face a similar problem: how is it possible to recognize and respond to the homelessness as an emergency situation and still not foster, as do some proposals designing equipment for the evicted, an acceptance of current conditions and concealment of their causes? The dilemma presents art with a seemingly paradoxical solution. In the very act of referring to a practical function, it must reaffirm its status as a signifying object. Yet this oscillation simply illustrates the truth, concealed by functionalist ideology, about all urban objects. Without recognizing the social construction of function—and without indicting the forces producing homelessness—practical plans to help the evicted survive on the streets are likely, no matter how well intentioned, to be tools for redevelopment. Openly complicitous, of course, are those plans sponsored by redevelopment associations themselves, groups who proffer charitable projects as evidence of redevelopment's benefits or of corporate philanthropy. A sleekly presented proposal sponsored by the Community Redevelopment Agency (CRA) of Los Angeles, exhibited in 1986 at the New York Storefront for Art and Architecture's important *Homeless at Home* exhibition, epitomizes this tactic. Observing that Los Angeles's Skid Row lies within the CRA's 1,500-acre Central Business District Redevelopment Project, the CRA announced a plan to direct a portion of the tax revenues generated from the new development and rising property values for programs to aid the inhabitants of Skid Row, "recognizing," as the proposal's text phrased it, "that skid rows will always exist" and seeking to "reduce the impact of Skid Row on the adjacent downtown area." Primarily, these projects try to shelter the redeveloped city from the adverse effects of the homelessness it causes and, simultaneously, to counteract the system's legitimation crisis by presenting homelessness as a transhistorical problem.

The *Homeless Vehicle Project* also proposes a way to alleviate some of the worst aspects of evicted peoples' lives, but in doing so, it strengthens, rather than reduces, their impact on the central business district. The project's critical force, then, springs from the interaction between its practical and signifying purposes, a reciprocity emblematized in the design of the vehicle, which, on the one hand, recalls Bauhaus functionalism and, on the other, resembles a weapon. It thus becomes a tool used against the apparatus of redevelopment. Instead of rendering the evicted invisible or reinforcing an image of them as passive objects, the Homeless Vehicle illuminates their mobile existence. Instead of severing or cosmeticizing the link between homelessness and redevelopment, the project visualizes the connection through its active insertion into the transformed city. It facilitates the seizing of space by homeless subjects rather than containing them in prescribed locations. Consequently, instead of restoring a surface calm to the "ascendant" city, as reformist plans try to do, it disrupts the coherent urban image, which today is constructed only by neutralizing homelessness. As a result, the Homeless Vehicle legitimates the evicted rather than the dominant spaces that exclude them, symbolically countering the city's own ideological campaign against the poor. In a minor, yet exemplary, gesture in this crusade, Mayor Koch, as we have seen, tried to eject the homeless from Grand Central Terminal by aiming against them the weapon of functionalization. The terminal's objective function, he insisted, is to serve the needs of travel, and it is impeded by the stationary homeless. The Homeless Vehicle retaliates by announcing a different function for the urban environment—the fulfillment of the travel needs of the evicted. It foregrounds a collateral system already built by these residents to support their daily lives. Yet the vehicle does not simply pit one use or group against another. It subverts the ideology of utility, silencing the city that seems to speak for itself—the instrumental city—by disrupting the city's silence on the subject of social needs. For the Homeless Vehicle's function, far from general or inevitable, is clearly a socially created scandal. The work strikes at the heart of the well-managed city, an image that today functions for the needs of profit and control.

At Battery Park City, collaborative public art helps build this image under the guises of utility, beauty, social responsibility—a rapprochement between art and life. But the Homeless Vehicle, too, is useful and collaborative. For this project, a skilled professional has applied sophisticated design principles to an object of everyday life, which, intruding upon space, practices a mode of urban design. But these superficial similarities only underscore profound differences. Responding to an emergency, the Homeless Vehicle is quick and impermanent. Implicit in its impermanence is a demand that its function become obsolete, a belief in the mutability of the social situation that necessitates it. Battery Park City appears to stabilize this situation, but such stationary and monumental spaces become the target of the Homeless Vehicle. Whereas Battery Park City art employs design to enforce dominant social organization, the Homeless Vehicle uses design for counterorganization, reorganizing the transformed city. The shelter system, peripheralization of low-income housing, deterritorialization of the poor—these aspects of contemporary spatial relations are fashioned by Battery Park City art, which, producing the privileged spaces of the central city, retains its own privilege as an object outside the political realm. It converts social reality into design. The Homeless Vehicle, a vehicle for organizing the interests of the dominated classes into a group expression, employs design to illuminate social reality, supporting the right of these groups to refuse marginalization.

In the essay accompanying the exhibition of the *Homeless Vehicle Project,* Wodiczko and Lurie stress the significance of collaborative relationships between professional designers and users of the vehicle. "Direct participation of users in the construction of the vehicle," they explain, "is the key to developing a vehicle which belongs to its users, rather than merely being appropriated by them."[114] Countering the technocracy of design, they seem to be referring to the distinction between a vehicle planned specifically by and for the evicted and the adaptation by the evicted of supermarket shopping carts. It is only through the collective production of objects by their users, Lurie and Wodiczko suggest, that people might resist the domination of their lives. Yet the Homeless Vehicle's substitution of an actively produced object for an appropriated one suggests the need for a more sweeping change—the possessions by users of their living space. Just as it negates the abstraction of function from specific social relations, the project challenges the abstraction of the city from its inhabitants. At the same time, however, it suggests that even under current circumstances the act of production is, in fact, not confined to those who manufacture the city, but already includes those who use and appropriate it.

Appropriating the space of the city—reclaiming space for social needs against space organized for profit and control—and diverting it, in a manner similar to what the situationists called *détournement,* from its prescribed functions, the Homeless Vehicle responds to ordinary needs and horrifying realities, yet, in a mixture of fantasy and reality that some critics find "disturbing," it offers a vision of the emancipation of the environment. "In order to change life," Lefebvre has written, "society, space, architecture, even the city must change."[115] Such a possibility will, of course, not be realized in isolated acts of détournement. Still, by upholding the "right to the city," the *Homeless Vehicle Project* corroborates Ledrut's definition of the city—"an environment formed by the interaction and the integration of different practices"—and thus anticipates the construction, not simply of beautiful or well-managed cities—they are, after all, by-products—but of a "work of life." Through this imaginative act, the project participates as well in the construction of an oppositional public sphere, one that counters the dominant relations organizing public space and permits the organized expression of social experience. The production of such a public art is, in fact, inseparable from the production of New York City as a living work. Yet the *Homeless Vehicle Project* also attests to the degree of knowledge about urbanism and the astuteness, even stealth, of operation required by public art if it is to accomplish these goals. For given its reliance on corporate and civic approval, public art, like New York itself, will, no doubt, develop unevenly.

■ Afterword

Recent developments in urban studies, including the publication of several interdisciplinary texts about postmodernism, have convinced me that the relationship between critical urban and aesthetic discourses is more complicated than it appeared when I first wrote "Uneven Development." I am especially concerned about a pronounced tendency among scholars in diverse fields—geography, art history, literary criticism, sociology—to use valuable political-economic analyses of urban redevelopment and global spatial restructuring in order to fortify what I believe is an authoritarian social theory against the challenges raised by new social theories, movements, and cultural practices. This "explanation" of society—which is seriously contested within urban studies itself—is undemocratic because it claims objective guarantees of the truth of a *total* knowledge. Thus, it denies its own condition as a representation, attempts to construct omniscient rather than situated subjects, and concomitantly, elevates its partial depiction of the world to the status of a social reality that is objective, determinate, fundamental, and total.

As I suggested in "Uneven Development," urban and aesthetic critiques paralleled each other insofar as they both initially challenged the essentialist explanations of space and art dominating their respective disciplines. Adopting social constructionist approaches to spatial and aesthetic meaning, these critical theories could be usefully combined to analyze architecture, urban planning, and other aesthetic practices within the built environment. The two fields have, however, also diverged in their elaboration of the constructionist thesis. Within contemporary film, art, literature, and criticism, perhaps the most significant event has been the emergence of feminist, postcolonial, gay, lesbian, and antiracist theories of representation. Yet, impelled by the need to respond to cultural developments, some influential urban theorists—along with equally prominent cultural critics who incorporate urban discourses— have purported to advance general theories of culture while remaining blind to such inquiries. Feeling free, despite this "omission," to assess important aspects—or even the "totality"—of contemporary culture negatively, they defend themselves against the most radical possibilities of their own encounter with cultural studies, perpetuate disciplinary specializations and hierarchies, and most important, marginalize feminist and other political discourses.

For at least twenty years, important tendencies within art practice and criticism, influenced by feminist and psychoanalytic theories of sexual difference and representation, have both elaborated and problematized the premises of materialist aesthetics as they were established within contemporary art. This process formed part of a broader and long-standing critique of radical social thought as it has been embodied in marxist traditions. Within the parameters of visual production, artists and critics explored visual images and the process of vision itself as political relations in which meaning and subjectivity are produced and reproduced through processes of subject-object differentiation. Needless to say, such investigations of subjectivity emphatically criticized aestheticist notions that universal artistic values inhere in art objects, independent of viewers and spatiotemporal context. But feminist theories have also eroded the essentialism of certain alternative formulations: on the one hand, social art history which posits that art and its viewing subject simply reflect, express, or mimic an exterior society or, on the other hand, conventional marxist interpretations of culture in which the political meaning of art is necessarily determined—in no matter now mediated a form—by an outside material realm. Both these conceptions ultimately transfer the sources of meaning from a stable aesthetic realm to one of social orhistorical essences.

In contrast, important branches of contemporary art explore visual representation as a social relation *in the first instance,* one whose specific meaning, although never isolated from other practices, can also not be referred back to objectively existing prior foundations—natural, social, or historical. And just as this aesthetic investigation asserts the autonomy of specific political practices (a relative autonomy in another sense, however, in that the very identity of a practice comes into existence only through discursive relations), so does it view different forms of social relations—sexual difference, for instance—as primary rather than epiphenomenal. Ultimately, such ideas question the meaning of "the social" itself, introducing doubt into any theory that removes meaning from contingency by constructing a model of society in which all practices and relations—their identities essentialized—are hierarchically unified by being grounded in a single, governing foundation. By abandoning fundamentalist totalizations and unitarian epistemologies, these social theories "weaken" what Ernesto Laclau has called "the absolutist character" of any political thought that claims to emanate from a stable, exterior position from which "society" can be known definitively as a distinct object (Ernesto Laclau, "Politics and the Limits of Modernity," in *Universal Abandon: The Politics of Postmodernism,* ed. Andrew Ross [Minneapolis: Univ. of Minnesota Press, 1988], pp. 63–82).

Against these increasingly complex formulations of "the social" and, specifically, of the social character of art, influential scholars combining urban and aesthetic discourses—David Harvey and Fredric Jameson are principal examples—have recently employed "the production of space" concept in order to defend classical marxism's hegemony over radical social thought, attempting to strengthen, rather than transform it, by producing a "historical-geographical materialism." (See Harvey, *The Condition of Postmodernity: An Enquiry into the Origins of Cultural Change* [Oxford and Cambridge, Mass.: Basil Blackwell, 1989] and Jameson, "Postmodernism, or the Cultural Logic of Late Capitalism," *New Left Review* 146 (July/August 1984), pp. 53–92, and "Marxism and Postmodernism," *New Left Review* 176 (July/August 1989), pp. 31–45.) Defending the adoption of a totalizing perspective and, therefore, marxism's hierarchical relations of difference with other theories, these authors relegate—explicitly or implicitly—all other explanations of social relations of subordination to secondary or competing positions. Committed to explanations of society and culture based on the deterministic relation between a foundation and what it founds, they break with the notion of spatial form as naturally or technologically produced only to fix the meaning of space—and all dimensions of culture—in the economic structures of its existence: the logic of capital.

These writers depart from the premise that the fragmenting effects produced by spatioeconomic restructuring under late twentieth-century capitalism conceal the underlying unity of global capital (a crucial statement, though one that frequently leads to overestimations of capital's totalizing effects). Since, however, within their broader social theory, culture merely expresses the postmodern "experience" of restructuring, these writers assess *all* fragmentation negatively: it is *always* an operation that conceals new forms of oppression and exploitation. Such an evaluation is disastrous because it refuses to acknowledge other kinds of fragmentation, such as that produced by voices challenging the notion of objective social coherence as itself an imperialist fantasy. In raising this challenge, such voices question the forms of power exercised by modern Western thought: abstract universalism and assumptions of unitary, unfragmented subjectivity. Because orthodox marxism maintains that the ultimate basis of any coherent emancipatory politics is—of necessity—class consciousness and struggle, it identifies all those that insist on the nonsubordinated specificity and difference of their struggles or who challenge the power of universalization as *fragmenting* forces by definition and, hence, complicit with capitalism's concealment of political "realities." Overidentifying with the totalizing ambitions of the system it criticizes, this position produces escalating casualties: new social theories and movements which insist that there are different starting points of political analysis and that the integration of movements must be articulated rather than assumed; specific-issue movements that resist unity as a basis of struggle; theorizations of new objects of *primary* political analysis—language, subjectivity, knowledge, vision; aesthetic practices that contest authoritarian representations and images by exploring the construction, hence uncertainty, of meaning and subjectivity in representation by refusing to "reveal" an underlying, deeper, social reality "behind" images; and spatial discourses such as feminist and psychoanalytic analyses of vision as a process structuring and structured by relations of sexual difference. Of course, it is no accident that those who claim to perceive social reality as an objective totality refuse such intellectual currents (often failing to even comprehend how they erode the basic assumptions of traditional marxism); it is precisely these currents that identify coherent perceptions as the fictions of a particular kind of subjective vision that, disavowing its partial and mediated condition, is motivated not, as its defenders contend, by objectivity or explanatory "adequacy," but by desire and fantasy.

Their faith in the existence of such coherence has, therefore, led some urban scholars not only to reject recent cultural developments but, in so doing, to deprive their field of the very tools it could use to amplify its own analysis of the built environment as a social product. Instead, establishing a closure in the analysis of space at the level of political economy, they purport to consider the "image of the city" while ignoring—indeed denouncing—all recent work on the politics of images. Simultaneously, they abdicate responsibility for the politics of their own representation of society. Against those who utilize spatial analyses to address social relations other than class or to consider the spatial construction of subjectivity, they level the charge of "political escapism." For a brief preliminary examination of the tendency I describe within urban-aesthetic discourse, see my "Men in Space," *Artforum* (February 1990), pp. 21–23.

I am grateful to Robert Ubell for countless conversations during which many of the ideas in this article were discussed, and to Lynne Tillman, whose valuable suggestions were incorporated into later versions of the essay.

1. Peter Marcuse, "Neutralizing Homelessness," *Socialist Review* (January/March 1988), p. 83. Marcuse's premise—that the sight of homeless people is shocking to viewers and that this initial shock is, subsequently, counteracted by ideological portrayals—assumes that responses to the presence of the homeless in New York today are simple, direct, almost "natural." It thus fails to recognize that current experience of beggars and "vagrants" by other city residents is always mediated by already-existing representations, including the naming of such people as "the homeless" in the first place. The form and iconography of such representations not only produce complex, even contradictory, meanings about the homeless—the object of the representation—but also, in the act of constituting the homeless as an image, construct positions in social relations. It is necessary to alter these relationships as well as the content of representations of the homeless. Despite its limited understanding of representation— a subject which, however, it importantly raises—Marcuse's description of official attempts to neutralize the effects of homelessness and the author's own, largely successful, efforts to counteract these neutralizations are extremely valuable. This is especially true now, when encouraged by the final years of the Koch administration, the media seem determined to depict the homeless as predators, to encourage New Yorkers to refuse donations to street

beggars, and to create the impression that city services exist to serve the needs of the poor and homeless.
2. *New York Ascendant*, report of the Commission on the Year 2000 (New York: Harper and Row, 1988) p. 167.
3. David W. Dunlap, "Koch, the 'Entertainer,' Gets Mixed Review," *The New York Times*, 19 May 1988, p. B4.
4. Raymond Ledrut,"Speech and the Silence of the City," in *The City and the Sign: An Introduction to Urban Semiotics*, ed. M. Gottdiener and Alexandros Ph. Lagopoulos (New York: Columbia Univ. Press, 1986) p. 122.
5. Henri Lefebvre, "Space: Social Product and Use Value," in *Critical Sociology: European Perspectives*, ed. J. W. Freiberg (New York, Irvington Publishers, 1979), p. 293.
6. Manuel Castells, *The City and the Grassroots: A Cross-Cultural Theory of Urban Social Movements* (Berkeley and Los Angeles: Univ. of California Press, 1983), p. 302.
7. For a more complete definition of "exclusionary displacement," see Peter Marcuse, "Abandonment, Gentrification, and Displacement: The Linkages in New York City," in *Gentrification of the City*, ed. Neil Smith and Peter Williams (Boston: Allen & Unwin, 1986), pp. 153–77.
8. Attila Kotányi and Raoul Vaneigem, "Elementary Program of the Bureau of Unitary Urbanism," in *Situationist International Anthology*, ed. Ken Knabb (Berkeley: Bureau of Public Secrets, 1981), p. 65.
9. Ibid.

10. Neil Smith, *Uneven Development: Nature, Capital and the Production of Space* (Oxford: Basil Blackwell, 1984), p. 54.
11. Jean Baudrillard, "The Ideological Genesis of Needs," in *For a Critique of the Political Economy of the Sign* (St. Louis: Telos Press, 1981), pp. 63–87.
12. Ibid.
13. "Remarks by Mayor Edward I. Koch at Awards Luncheon of the American Institute of Architects," 18 May 1988, p. 7.
14. For a discussion of one example of this process, see Rosalyn Deutsche, "Krzysztof Wodiczko's *Homeless Projection* and the Site of Urban 'Revitalization,'" *October* 38 (Fall 1986), pp. 63–98; reprinted in *The Critical Image*, ed. Carol Squiers (Seattle: Bay Press, 1990), pp. 88–120.
15. Alexander Kluge, "On Film and the Public Sphere," *New German Critique*, nos. 24–25 (Fall/Winter 1981–82), p. 212.
16. An especially patronizing depiction of the public as consumers of mass spectacle appeared in a 1980 *New York Times* editorial about New York's public space. "New Yorkers," the editorial began, "love parades, festivals, celebrations, demonstrations and entertainments, particularly when such occasions bring large numbers of them together outdoors." The conflation of political demonstrations (rallies in Union Square were cited as a historical example) and patriotic celebrations (the 1976 Bicentennial celebration, for one) and the reduction of both to an opportunity to enjoy

the weather ("The finer the weather, the greater the urge to gather, the sweeter the siren call of causes") were employed to support the use of public funds to create public parks for a luxury redevelopment project—Battery Park City. Needless to say, by the end of the editorial any reference to political demonstrations had been dropped. "What better place for New Yorkers to do *their public thing?*" the editorial concluded ("A Public Plaza for New York," *The New York Times,* 16 June 1980, p. A22, emphasis added).

17. Craig Owens, "The Yen for Art," contribution to a discussion entitled "The Birth and Death of the Viewer: On the Public Function of Art," in *Discussions in Contemporary Culture,* ed. Hal Foster (Seattle: Bay Press, 1987), p. 18.

18. Ibid., p. 23.

19. For a discussion of the notion of "the urban" that informs art history, see Rosalyn Deutsche, "Representing Berlin: Urban Ideology and Aesthetic Practice," in *The Divided Heritage: Themes and Problems in German Modernism,* ed. Irit Rogoff and MaryAnne Stevens (Cambridge: Cambridge Univ. Press, forthcoming).

20. See Douglas Crimp, "Serra's Public Sculpture: Redefining Site Specificity," in *Richard Serra/Sculpture,* Rosalind Krauss (New York: Museum of Modern Art, 1986), p. 53.

21. Ibid., pp. 53–55.

22. Raymond Ledrut, *Les images de la ville* (Paris: Anthropos, 1973), p. 28.

23. Eric Gibson, "Public Art and the Public Realm," *Sculpture* 7 (January/February 1988), p. 32.

24. Douglas C. McGill, "Sculpture Goes Public," *The New York Times Magazine,* 27 April 1986, p. 45.

25. Nancy Princenthal, "On the Waterfront: South Cove Project at Battery Park City," *Village Voice,* 7 June 1988, p. 99.

26. Nancy Holt, quoted in McGill, "Sculpture Goes Public."

27. Robert Jensen, "Commentary," in *Architectural Art: Affirming the Design Relationship* (New York: American Craft Museum, 1988), p. 3.

28. See Gibson, "Public Art and the Public Realm."

29. Kate Linker, "Public Sculpture: The Pursuit of the Pleasurable and the Profitable Paradise," *Artforum* 19 (March 1981), p. 66. Linker's article recognizes the functions of the new public art in raising the economic value of its sites but, perhaps because it was written at an early stage in the contemporary redevelopment process, does not address the social consequences of this function.

30. Quoted in McGill, "Sculpture Goes Public," p. 63.

31. Ibid., p. 67.

32. Quoted in Nancy Princenthal, "Social Seating," *Art in America* 75 (June 1987), p. 131.

33. Ibid.

34. McGill, "Sculpture Goes Public," p. 66.

35. Diane Shamash, "The A Team, Artists and Architects: Can They Work Together," *Stroll: The Magazine of Outdoor Art and Street Culture,* nos. 6–7 (June 1988), p. 60.

36. John Beardsley, *Art in Public Places: A Survey of Community-Sponsored Projects Supported by The National Endowment for the Arts* (Washington, D.C.: Partners for Livable Places, 1981), p. 81.

37. Michael Brenson, "Outdoor Sculptures Reflect Struggles of Life in the City," *The New York Times,* 15 July 1988, pp. C1, C28.

38. Beardsley, *Art in Public Places,* p. 90.

39. Kay Larson, "Combat Zone," *New York,* 13 May 1985, p. 118.

40. Neil Smith, "Gentrification, the Frontier, and the Restructuring of Urban Space," in *Gentrification of the City,* pp. 18 –19.

41. Jonathan Barnett, *An Introduction to Urban Design* (New York: Harper & Row), p. 46.

42. For critiques of traditional urban studies, see, among others, Manuel Castells, *The Urban Question: A Marxist Approach* (Cambridge, Mass.: MIT Press, 1977); M. Gottdiener, The Social Production of Urban Space (Austin: Univ. of Texas Press, 1985); Peter Saunders, *Social Theory and the Urban Question* (London: Hutchinson, 1981); Edward W. Soja, "The Spatiality of Social Life: Towards a Transformative Retheorisation," in *Social Relations and Spatial Structures,* ed. Derek Gregory and John Urry (New York: St. Martin's Press, 1985), pp. 90–127.

43. Gottdiener, *The Social Production of Urban Space,* p. 264.

44. Smith, *Uneven Development,* p. 77.

45. Summaries of these debates and of the history of spatial theories are included in Gottdiener, *The Social Production of Urban Space;* Edward W. Soja, "The Socio-spatial Dialectic," *Annals of the Association of American Geographers* 70 (1980), pp. 207–25; Saunders, *Social Theory and the Urban Question.*

46. Lefebvre, "Space: Social Product and Use Value," p. 285.

47. Ibid., p. 286.

48. For a discussion of the international urban hierarchy, see R. B. Cohen, "The New International Division of Labor, Multinational Corporations and Urban Hierarchy," in *Urbanization and Urban Planning in Capitalist Society,* ed. Michael Dear and Allen J. Scott (London and New York: Methuen, 1981), pp. 287–315.

49. Smith, *Uneven Development*, p. xi.

50. Ernest Mandel, *Late Capitalism* (London: Verso, 1975), p. 102.

51. For explanations of the "rent gap," see Neil Smith and Michele LeFaivre, "A Class Analysis of Gentrification," in *Gentrification, Displacement and Neighborhood Revitalization*, ed. J. John Palen and Bruce London (Albany: State Univ. of New York Press), 1984, pp. 43–63; and Smith, "Gentrification, the Frontier, and the Restructuring of Urban Space."

52. Lefebvre, "Space: Social Product and Use Value," p. 286.

53. Ibid., p. 290.

54. Henri Lefebvre, *Le droit à la ville* (Paris: Anthropos, 1968).

55. Manuel Castells, "From Urban Society to Urban Revolution," in *The Urban Question*.

56. Henri Lefebvre, *La production de l'espace* (Paris: Anthropos, 1974), p. 420 (translated in M. Gottdiener, "Culture, Ideology, and the Sign of the City," in *The City and the Sign*, p. 215).

57. Edward W. Soja, "The Spatiality of Social Life: Towards a Transformative Retheorisation," pp. 90–127.

58. Walter Benjamin, "Theses on the Philosophy of History," in *Illuminations*, trans. Harry Zohn (New York: Schocken, 1969), p. 257.

59. Claudia Gould, "Mary Miss Covers the Waterfront," *Stroll: The Magazine of Outdoor Art and Street Culture*, nos. 4–5 (October 1987), p. 55.

60. Robin Karson, "Battery Park City: South Cove," *Landscape Architecture* (May/June 1988).

61. Albert Scardino, "Big Battery Park City Dreams," *The New York Times*, 1 December 1986, p. D1.

62. Nancy Princenthal, "On the Waterfront," *Art in America* 75 (April 1987), p. 239.

63. John Russell, "Where City Meets Sea to Become Art," *The New York Times*, 11 December 1983, sec. 2, p. 1.

64. Ibid., p. 31.

65. Ibid.

66. Winston Williams, "Finally, the Debut of Wall Street West," *The New York Times*, 25 August 1985, sec. 3, p. 1.

67. Paul Goldberger, "Public Space Gets a New Cachet in New York," *The New York Times*, 22 May 1988, p. H35.

68. Paul Goldberger, "Battery Park City Is a Triumph of Urban Design," *The New York Times*, 31 August 1986, p. H1.

69. Meyer S. Frucher, quoted in Martin Gottlieb, "Battery Project Reflects Changing City Priorities," *The New York Times*, 18 October 1985, p. B1. Gottlieb's article is the only account in the *Times*'s extensive coverage of all aspects of Battery Park City's present state that raises critical questions about the project's social history and conditions.

70. Michael deCourcy Hinds, "Vast Project Heads for '93 Finish," *The New York Times*, 23 March 1986, p. R18.

71. Quoted in Gottlieb, "Battery Project Reflects Changing City Priorities," p. B2.

72. Ada Louise Huxtable, "Plan's 'Total' Concept Is Hailed," *The New York Times*, 17 April 1969, p. 49.

73. Alexander Cooper Associates, *Battery Park City: Draft Summary Report and 1979 Master Plan*, 1979, p. 67.

74. Huxtable, "Plan's 'Total' Concept Is Hailed," p. 49.

75. Maynard T. Robison, "Vacant Ninety Acres, Well Located, River View," in *The Apple Sliced: Sociological Studies of New York City*, ed. Vernon Boggs et al. (South Hadley, Mass.: Bergin & Garvey Publishers, 1984), p. 180.

76. David K. Shipler, "Battery Park Plan Is Shown," *The New York Times*, 17 April 1969, p. 49.

77. Ibid.

78. Ibid.

79. David K. Shipler, "Lindsay Will Get Housing Demands," *The New York Times*, 30 June 1969, p. 28.

80. Robison, "Vacant Ninety Acres," p. 189.

81. *The New York Times*, 17 April 1969, p. 49.

82. David K. Shipler, "Lindsay Reverses Stand on Housing," *The New York Times*, 15 August 1969, p. 33.

83. Ibid.

84. "Battery Park City Is Given Approval," *The New York Times*, 10 October 1969, p. 55.

85. Jack Rand, letter to the editor of *The New York Times*, 4 August 1969, p. 34.

86. Battery Park City Annual Report, 1972, "Amendments to the Master Lease."

87. Ibid.

88. Robison, "Vacant Ninety Acres," p. 183.

89. Ibid., p. 192.

90. Edward Schumacher, "13 Years Later, Battery Park City's an Empty Dream," *The New York Times*, 26 October 1979, p. B3.

91. Ada Louise Huxtable, "Is This the Last Chance for Battery Park City," *The New York Times*, 9 December 1979, Sec. 2, p. 39.

92. For critical analyses of urban fiscal crisis, see William K. Tabb, *The Long Default: New York City and the Urban Fiscal Crisis* (New York and London: Monthly Review Press, 1982); Eric Lichten, *Class, Power and Austerity: The New York City Fiscal Crisis* (South Hadley, Mass.: Bergin & Garvey Publishers, 1986); Michael D. Kennedy, "The Fiscal Crisis of the City," in *Cities in Transformation: Class, Capital and the State*, ed. Michael Peter Smith (Beverly Hills: Sage Publications, 1984), pp. 91–110; John Shutt,

"Rescuing New York City, 1975–78," in *Urban Political Economy and Social Theory: Critical Essays in Urban Studies,* ed. Ray Forrest, Jeff Henderson, and Peter Williams (Hampshire, England: Gower Publishing, 1982), pp. 51–77; Manuel Castells, *City, Class, and Power* (New York: St. Martin's Press, 1972); M. Gottdiener, "Retrospect and Prospect in Urban Crisis Theory," in *Cities in Stress: A New Look at the Urban Crisis,* ed. M. Gottdiener (Beverly Hills: Sage Publications, 1986), pp. 277–291.

93. Peter Marcuse, "The Targeted Crisis: On the Ideology of the Urban Fiscal Crisis and Its Uses," *International Journal of Urban and Regional Research* 5 (September 1981), pp. 330–55.

94. "Last Chance for Battery Park City," editorial, *The New York Times,* 17 November 1979.

95. Richard J. Meislin, "Attempt to Revive Battery Park Plan Is Readied by Carey," *The New York Times,* 28 October 1979, p. 1.

96. Ibid.

97. Annmarie Hauck Walsh, *The Public's Business: The Politics and Practices of Government Corporations,* A Twentieth Century Fund Study (Cambridge. Mass.: MIT Press, 1978), p. 4.

98. Michael Goodwin, "Construction of Battery Park City Is Now Scheduled to Begin in June," *The New York Times,* 16 May 1980, p. B4.

99. Alan S. Oser, "Battery Park City: The Newest Prestige Address," *The New York Times,* 18 April 1982, sec. 8, p. 7.

100. Ibid.

101. Alexander Cooper Associates, *Battery Park City: Draft Summary Report and 1979 Master Plan.*

102. David K. Shipler, "Battery Park City Plans Scored and Praised at Public Hearing," *The New York Times,* 17 July 1969, p. 50.

103. "Battery Park City," leaflet from Battery Park City Authority.

104. Paul Goldberger, "A Realist's Battery Park City," *The New York Times,* 9 November 1979, p. B4.

105. "Esplanade Recalls Old New York," *The New York Times,* 3 July 1986, p. C3.

106. Alexander Cooper Associates, 1979 Master Plan, p. 18.

107. Ibid.

108. Brian Sullivan, Pratt Center for Community and Environmental Development, quoted in Gottlieb, "Battery Project Reflects Changing City Priorities," p. B2.

109. Claudia Gould, "Mary Miss Covers the Waterfront," p. 54.

110. Roland Barthes, "The Great Family of Man," in *Mythologies* (New York: Hill and Wang, 1972), p. 101.

111. Ibid., p. 102.

112. "A Public Plaza for New York," see footnote 16.

113. Theresa Funiciello, reply to letters, *The Nation,* 18 June 1988, p. 876.

114. David Lurie and Krzysztof Wodiczko, "Homeless Vehicle Project," The Clocktower, 1988; reprinted in *October* 47 (Winter 1988), pp. 53–63.

115. Henri Lefebvre, "The Everyday and Everydayness," *Yale French Studies,* no. 73 (1988), p. 11; translation of "Quotidien et Quotidienneté," *Encyclopaedia Universalis.*

■ Utopia Spurned:

Ricardo Bofill and the French Ideal City Tradition

Tony Schuman

Over the past twenty years, Catalan architect Ricardo Bofill's Taller de Arquitectura has built a series of public housing projects in France notable for
their monumental scale, neoclassical form, and sophisticated prefabricated
concrete construction. The rationale for this application of civic scale and
aristocratic imagery to domestic purpose is Bofill's contention that contemporary life will invert the form and symbolism of the historic city by thrusting
everyday life onto center stage, thereby "exalting" the lives of the working-
class inhabitants. To evaluate the significance of Bofill's proposition as a
vision for human society, his work is discussed in the context of three earlier
French utopian projects in the form of ideal cities: Ledoux's Saltworks and
Ideal City at Chaux, Godin's Fourierist *familistère* at Guise, and Garnier's Industrial City project and Public Works in Lyon. The design integrity of these
three projects derives from the synthesis of form and content that enables
them to endure as historical examples, carrying forward a message about
their respective societies as revealed through architecture. Bofill's work represents a transposition of the social program of the ideal city, centered on
public life and the city, into a private world emphasizing the family and the
home. His formal symbols do not challenge us to think about the future. Instead, they offer us refuge in an idealized past, dressing up the status quo
with dazzling images that promote a false consciousness.

■ Introduction: Form and Content

*The urban design of our era will take the structure, if not the dimension, of
the historical city into account. It will, however, invert the symbolic values.
Everyday life will take the center of the stage, while the public edifice and
facility will recede into the background.*[1]

1. Ricardo Bofill, Spaces of Abraxas,
Marne-la-Vallée.
(Tony Schuman)

With these words, Catalan architect Ricardo Bofill explains the formal and symbolic intent of Spaces of Abraxas (Les Espaces d'Abraxas), a monumental housing complex designed by his Taller de Arquitectura for Marne-la-Vallée, a new town just east of Paris. Completed in 1983, the work consists of nearly six hundred subsidized apartments arranged in a semicircular nine-story Theater separated from a nineteen-story Palace by a nine-story triumphal Arch, the whole executed with elaborate prefabricated elements of polychromatic concrete (fig. 1). Abraxas is the second and boldest in a series of French projects by the Taller—starting with the Arcades by the Lake housing and the Viaduct housing (Les Arcades du Lac and Le Viaduc) at Saint-Quentin-en-Yvelines in 1972 and continuing to current projects in Montpelier and Paris. All of these are attempts to imbue domestic architecture with urban scale and civic meaning. In each instance, the built works and textual explanations reveal, beyond a preoccupation with architectural form itself, a didactic intent to induce "civilized behavior and social participation"[2] and to exalt daily life by placing ordinary activity in extraordinary settings.

In elevating housing design to paradigmatic urban dimensions and linking it to a broader set of social intentions, Bofill places this work within a rich French tradition of "ideal city" proposals. It is a comparison he invites through written and visual references to Ledoux, Fourier, and Le Corbusier, among others. With these forebears Bofill shares a philosophical intent to link built form with an ameliorative vision of human society. In pursuing this goal through a limited public housing program, which includes no shops, workplaces, or social institutions, Bofill imputes to formal imagery alone the power to transform people's lives. That he pursues this goal at all distinguishes Bofill from many of his contemporaries, broadly grouped under the "postmodern" label, who also employ historical motifs to give new allure to conventional building programs. At the same time, however, there is a serious question as to whether Bofill's formal approach is adequate to his social purpose: can daily life be exalted by a dazzling set of historical images when the fundamental structure of that life remains unchanged and unheralded?

To evaluate the significance of Bofill's design intentions, it is instructive to review earlier efforts to express social visions in built form. For this purpose I have selected three French utopian projects that take the form of ideal cities: Claude-Nicolas Ledoux's Saltworks and Ideal City at Chaux, Jean-Baptiste Godin's Fourierist familistère at Guise, and Tony Garnier's Industrial City project and Public Works in Lyon. Beyond their common cultural heritage, the three projects share a desire to use architecture and urban planning and design to edify and improve the daily lives of ordinary people; all include housing as a principal programmatic element; and all exist today as full or partial built realizations of the original projects, thereby allowing on-site inspection of the works themselves. My visits to these projects over the past few years have brought to life the history book accounts, elucidated these projects' syntheses of program, plan, and imagery, and urged an assessment of their relevance to contemporary work such as Bofill's.

■ Ledoux at Chaux

Claude-Nicolas Ledoux (1736–1806) lived on the cusp of history in two respects: he was witness both to the triumph of the Enlightenment over the ancien régime with the French Revolution and to the incipient rise to prominence of the industrial over the feudal agricultural economy. The conflicting values of old and new in both the social and productive spheres are evident in his masterwork, the Royal Saltworks at Chaux, built between 1773 and 1779 while he served as architect to the king under Louis XV and Louis XVI. Dismissed from the post at Chaux for the "turbulent" character of his work, as well as its "extravagant expense," Ledoux continued to work under the king's aegis, constructing a series of toll-gate *barrières* at the gates to Paris between 1785 and 1789. Perceived by the French people as symbols of their oppression under the monarchy, these gate houses were largely responsible for Ledoux's imprisonment in 1793 after the fall of the Bastille. While in prison Ledoux expanded the Saltworks scheme into a proposal for an Ideal City at Chaux, which was published in 1804 under the title *Architecture considered in relationship to art, custom, and legislation.*

For over a thousand years, salt had been extracted from underground springs at the nearby town of Salins. By 1773, however, the local supply of wood used to evaporate the water to extract the salt had been exhausted, and a decision had to be made whether to haul wood to Salins or to transport the water to another site. It was Ledoux, in his new post as inspector general of the Jura Saltworks, who proposed to bring the water from Salins to Chaux, which constituted at that time the second largest forest in France. This was accomplished through a seventeen-kilometer aqueduct constructed of hollowed logs fed by gravity along the 114-meter drop in elevation. With the elaborate pumping apparatus still located at Salins, Ledoux had a simple program at Chaux: sheds for processing the salt, workshops for the blacksmiths and vat-makers, administrative offices, residences for the workers and director, and a guardhouse to incarcerate salt thieves (salt, being the principal means of preserving food before refrigeration, was a valuable commodity). The striking innovation of the program was Ledoux's decision to combine the elements in an idealized urban plan.

Ledoux laid out the Saltworks originally in a semicircular plan (fig. 2), later

2. C.-N. Ledoux, Royal Saltworks, Chaux.
(Editions Combier Macôn)

3. C.-N. Ledoux, Royal Saltworks, director's house, Chaux.
(Tony Schuman)

expanded to a full circle in the Ideal City project. The entry building contained administrative offices and the guardhouse. This was flanked by two
curving wings of dormitories for the workers, organized by craft in separate
pavilions. On axis with the entry building was the director's house, which
served as the focal point of the composition, occupying the central position
on the diameter of the semicircle. The salt sheds share this prominence,
stretching out laterally from the director's house. A semicircular wall surrounds the compound, leaving space for vegetable gardens behind the workers' dormitories. When Ledoux later expanded the Saltworks plan into his
Ideal City, he completed the circle with the addition of a variety of civic buildings, which included church, stock exchange, houses of culture, and an iso-

morphic phallus-shaped building called an *oikema,* where the sexual needs of the workers were to be accommodated.

The symbolism of the plan was circumscribed, quite literally, by the ideal of the Enlightenment—the age of light, the age of reason. Images of light, and of the sun in particular, abound in works of the period—the paintings of David, the fantasies of Boullée.[3] Beyond the symbolism of the sun itself as the manifestation of the Enlightenment, the pure geometry of the plan was significant in its own right. Simple and strict geometries were proposed in writings just prior to the Revolution as the appropriate symbols of the perfect society. Ledoux himself wrote, "The circle and the square—these are the alphabet that authors use in their best works."[4]

The vision of society embodied by these symbols was one of equality, represented by the equal sides of the square and the inherently equal radii of the circle. Within this framework, society may be expressed as either an independent equality—a collective organism without differentiation by rank or class—or as a dependent equality, marked by a benevolent hierarchy. It is clearly the latter view to which Ledoux subscribed, as manifest in the central position given to the director's house. This compromise in the ideal of equality is not surprising given the patronage Ledoux enjoyed from the king.

The imagery of the buildings themselves, as distinct from the site plan, reveals a second set of concerns: the acknowledgment and celebration of the dawn of industry. The plan, of course, is still of interest here, for it is altogether noteworthy that Ledoux chose to endow an industrial enterprise with a formalistic building complex. Consistent with his vision of a new social order based on dependent equality, it is the director's house that is most articulated with traditional symbols of respectability. For this building, Ledoux invented a hybrid column of alternating circular and square sections to signal the formal entry. The columns are surmounted by a restrained pediment and pyramidal mansard roof (fig. 3). The walls of the director's house are, with the exception of quoins at the entry and corners, flush ashlar masonry, a style they share with both the salt sheds and the workers' quarters, thereby suggesting the underlying equality of the participants in the enterprise. The plainness of the wall surfaces was also another symbol of the new age: no

4. C.-N. Ledoux, Royal Saltworks, workers' pavilions, Chaux. (Tony Schuman)

decoration, no luxury, no ornament, for these were the discredited symbols of the decadent society against which the Revolution was waged (a theme which reappears, significantly, in both the Soviet Union and Germany after the fall of the czar and the kaiser).

The salt-processing pavilions that flank the director's house, and that thereby become part of the central focus of the composition, bear elements that link these pavilions to the critical parts of the complex and to the surrounding countryside as well. The quoined, arched entries echo the formality of the director's house; the pitched roofs reflect the vernacular style of the region; and the extraordinary carved stone urns from which spout thick, salty water also relieve the flat surface of the workers' dormitories. The roofs are the one gesture toward regionalism in the Saltworks and help place it as a transitional step from an agricultural to an industrial economy. The carved spouts, which constitute the sole projections on the planar wall surfaces, reinforce the link between the production process and the producers themselves, the workers (fig. 4).

In all, the Saltworks may be read as a paean to industry, construed by Ledoux as the new basis of society. "(Industry), mother of all resources without which nothing can exist save misery," Ledoux exclaimed, "you expand the influence which gives life; you brighten the arid deserts and the melancholy forests."[5] Industry, for Ledoux, was to be the centerpiece of the new city, a city marked by an architecture that scorns decoration while exalting idealized order. The Saltworks may be identified straightforwardly as one of the first attempts to create an industrial architecture that links production facilities to workers' housing. It may also be read as a project aimed at restructuring the world along principles of order, centrality, and hierarchy—an attempt to act on people through architecture to inspire and transform the world.

■ Godin at Guise

If the Neoplatonic principles and formal symbolism of the Ideal City at Chaux may be seen as a cerebral creation whose impact on its occupants must have been problematic, the familistère (a communal living and working experiment) at Guise is more concrete. Jean-Baptiste Godin (1817–1888), the blacksmith turned entrepreneur who launched the experiment in 1859, was also a child of the intellectual fathers of the Enlightenment—Diderot, Voltaire, Rousseau— and an advocate of the grand revolutionary principles of liberty, fraternity, and equality. He was, moreover, deeply impressed by the socialist ideas of the Revolution of 1848. But his work owes its primary debt to the early nineteenth-century utopian theorist Charles Fourier, whose ideas Godin had encountered in a newspaper article in 1843. Fourier rooted the principles of the Enlightenment in a singular theory he called "passional attraction," a theory of the development of human civilization based both in behavioral analysis and cooperative enterprise, concepts that prefigure in many respects ideas of both Marx and Freud.

In his *Theory of Four Movements*, published in 1804, Fourier propounded a vision of human society that would supersede what he saw as the crass commercialism of his day to reach a state of universal harmony. This evolution would be propelled by a natural human inclination toward twelve basic passions: the five senses plus four "affective" and three "distributive" passions. While Fourier saw cooperative enterprise based on profit-sharing as critical to his system, the primary vehicle to encourage and assist the transformation of human behavior was the creation of a physical environment that would promote "passional" association among equals through spontaneous

5. Charles Fourier, phalanstère or social palace dedicated to humanity. (Centre de Creation Industrielle, Centre Georges Pompidou)

encounters. His spatial unity of organization was the phalanx, an industrial and agricultural community in a rural setting of specified size. The main building of each phalanx was to be the *phalanstère,* a series of landscaped courtyards enclosed by wings from a central building (fig. 5). All parts of the building were to be served by wide, continuous "galleries of association," three stories high, designed to encourage spontaneous meeting and weld together the social and emotional lives of the community. To reinforce this communal aspect, members of the community shared dining and sanitary facilities; only sleeping quarters continued to respect the privacy of the family.

The form of the phalanx was drawn from the Palace of Versailles in an effort to place "the equivalents of wealth" before the working inhabitants of a "social palace." The image of Versailles, while certainly a more recognizable symbol than the abstract geometry of Chaux, has to be seen as a timid attempt to gain acceptance for a radical set of social ideas by cloaking them in the grandeur of the past. At best, the effort may be seen as an effort to expropriate the perquisites of royalty for the working class, a gesture that would remain without meaning in the absence of Fourier's social and economic innovations.

In this light, it is significant that Godin, in building what remains the most complete and faithful rendering of Fourier's social theories, emphasized the behavioral aspects of spatial planning over the formal imagery. When Godin undertook to construct his phalanstère, which he called a familistère, the iron-works that he founded had been in operation for thirteen years. Already a suc-

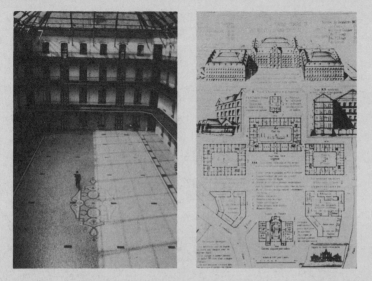

6. J.-B. Godin, familistère central pavilion, Guise. (Tony Schuman)

7. J.-B. Godin, familistère, Guise. (Centre de Creation Industrielle, Centre Georges Pompidou)

cessful enterprise as a leading manufacturer of stoves and other heating appliances, the foundry's economic success had two important effects on the new community at Guise: it assured the economic viability of the undertaking, and it led to a concentration on the residential and service components. Thus, with the workplace already in operation, Godin commenced construction in 1859 with the first of three residential units that he envisioned as a social palace for his workers. The term *familistère* with which he labeled these structures conveys the emphasis on family dwelling, as distinct from the more encompassing *phalanstère,* as Fourier called his new community under one roof.

Godin's "palaces" differed in two basic respects from Fourier's phalanstère. First, the locus of human association was not a linear gallery but a central, glass-roofed courtyard around which the family units were grouped (fig. 6); second, the dwelling units were self-contained residences that included a kitchen and living room (although sanitary facilities were still shared). The only element in the site plan recalling Versailles is the positioning of the three courtyard buildings in the form of two flanking pavilions that create a forecourt in front of the central unit (fig. 7). Each building has a separate, central entrance and is linked to the others by diagonal passages at the corners. The outlying buildings, which contain other services and facilities, are not disposed to create a formal ensemble but evoke, rather, the feel of a small village.

Godin placed at the disposition of his workers an extraordinary range of social, cultural, educational, and recreational services and facilities. Many of these, such as a pension system and medical and disability insurances anticipated France's public social services by some years. Others, such as a covered swimming pool and theater, were made available for the first time to people of modest means. Additional facilities such as game rooms, meeting halls, and a bandshell reflected Godin's encouragement of recreational and cultural activity by his workers. These activities included a chorus, an orchestra, and numerous sporting and social clubs. The three realms in which his innovations were most striking are education, cooperative purchasing, and worker involvement in management. In education, Godin provided not only an elementary school but also an infant care center incorporating avant-garde pedagogical theories of child development: play structures, for example, were carefully designed to assist motor development. Secondary and adult education classes combined book learning with practical exercises. The cooperative shops for food and clothing, located on the ground floor of the familistères, offered favorable prices to Godin's workers using special company scrip. These shops were so successful that they led to friction with the townspeople, whose wares were undersold and who did not themselves have access to the Godin commissaries.

It was with regard to worker involvement in management that Godin placed his highest hopes and offered his most far-reaching proposals. Starting with the issuance of stock certificates in the company, Godin wished to see the enterprise evolve toward worker self-management. While this ultimate goal was never reached, the foundry did become, in 1880, a cooperative production association, a status it enjoyed until it was taken over in 1968 by the giant French conglomerate, Le Creuset. In all his efforts, Godin involved his workers in various deliberative bodies within the company. Notably, he insisted on equal participation for women, sharing Fourier's belief that "in any given society the degree of women's emancipation is the natural measure of the general emancipation."[6]

The familistère and ironworks at Guise have to be rated among the most successful of utopian experiments. The cooperative community survived for more than a hundred years. It was successful both economically and socially during its time: families remained in the familistère for several generations, and the workers, after Godin's death, erected a statue to his memory in the forecourt of the pavilions. Today, although some buildings have fallen into disuse—the public baths and pool, the slaughterhouse and butcher shop—others are still in continuous use: the school, theater, library, the foundry itself, and notably, the housing. When the foundry was taken over by Le Creuset in 1968, the housing passed into municipal ownership, to be operated as social (public) housing on both a rental and cooperative ownership basis. There are still families who have resided in the familistère for over fifty years.

The form of the familistères themselves has been criticized for the panopticon-like qualities of the central courts, where the circulation system makes everybody's comings and goings a matter of public record. But these great halls contained no surveillance tower, no company spy watching for misbehavior. The eyes on the court belonged to peers, and one can imagine the courts functioning as they were intended—arenas bubbling with social interaction, highlighted by two great annual assemblies for Work Day and Children's Day. In any event, one had only to shut the door to the apartment unit to retreat into the sanctity of the family.

Yet the utopia at Guise was a limited one in two respects: it was thoroughly dependent on the benevolent vision of its founder, and thus was an enlightened corporate version of utopia; and it failed to suscitate similar experiments in the surrounding town and region, thus remaining an isolated, miniature model for the new society. These shortcomings are at the heart of the distinctions made by Friedrich Engels in his pamphlet *Socialism: Utopian and Scientific.* Society cannot be transformed by the force of a limited example, he argued, however nobly conceived. That transformation can only be accomplished, in Engels's brief, by the class-conscious action of the work force acting as a class in its own self-interest.

■ Garnier in Lyon

If the utopian experiments at Chaux and at Guise were restricted by their reliance on symbolic geometry and psychological theory, which produced in each case a small, self-contained model for society, Tony Garnier (1869–1948) had the breadth of vision to posit the city itself as the spatial unit for his uto- pian vision. Raised in a radical workers' quarter in the French textile center of Lyon and further politicized by his studies at the Beaux-Arts in Paris during the time of Jaurès and the Dreyfus affair, Garnier developed his project for an Industrial City while a *prix de Rome* laureate at the Villa Medici. On his return to Paris in 1904, Garnier exhibited the project as supplementary material along with a more conventional study he had executed to fulfill the expecta- tions of classical and Renaissance studies placed on Rome Prize winners. Programmatically, the Industrial City offered by Garnier has two underlying premises: it is an industrial city, and it is a socialist city. The former consider- ation is indicated by his emphasis on transportation, hydroelectric power, and sufficient land to allow for expansion, as well as by the thoughtful attention given to matters of hygiene (ventilation, sunlight, vegetation) and construc- tion technology (reinforced concrete). His socialist beliefs are revealed in the banishment of private property and walls, the absence of churches, army barracks, and police or court buildings, and in the prominence given to the assembly complex containing union meeting rooms and a great public hall.

Garnier shared with Fourier a belief in the inherently cooperative nature of humankind as well as a belief in the essential satisfaction to be found in work. But it is his belief in the civilizing capacity of the city itself that distin- guished his vision. This is particularly represented by his emphasis on the public arena. While the most formal expressions of this value are found in the assembly building and the civic buildings that surround it at the core of the city—a museum, library, theater, stadium, and pool—it also pervades each district of his city. Although Garnier organized his city functionally into sepa- rate zones for industry, residence, public services, and hospitals, each dis- trict was conceived as a miniature city in itself. Whereas Fourier encouraged human association to occur most frequently within the architecture of his phalanstère, Garnier saw these contacts as occurring informally along the streets, paths, and gardens of his wall-less neighborhood, where all unbuilt space was to be public parkland. Where Fourier saw space as shaping human consciousness to lead the way to greater harmony, Garnier proposed a framework for a new society that will exist after the accouterments of bourgeois power have been swept away in favor of a syndicalist social organization managed directly by the workers. In this context, the realm of the city becomes the locus for the free exercise of power, and the concept of public space recaptures the meaning (if not the form) of the old town square and public hall: a vital source of information, exchange of ideas, and direct, participatory democracy.

In retrospect, it is easy to criticize Garnier's rigid division of the city into separate zones both as vitiating the dynamic life of the city and as impeding a framework that links living, working, and civic functions together as the continuous web of daily life. Indeed, this is the substantial criticism leveled at Le Corbusier's city planning proposals, which were strongly influenced by those of Garnier. That Garnier was aware of the values represented by older, multifunctional cities is demonstrated by his inclusion of an old medieval town in his drawings for the Industrial City, which was designed for an imaginary site in southeast France. In this light, it seems clear that the idea of separate zoning issued from his concern for hygiene—the isolating of the hospital and manufacturing districts—and his foresighted grasp of the rapid explosion of urban growth brought by industrialization. His emphasis, within each district, was on natural amenities (another theme developed by Le Corbusier) and on the open quality of the city in social terms.

While the Industrial City project remains a theoretical proposition, Garnier had the good fortune to find in Edouard Herriot, the mayor of Lyon, a sympathetic champion. Under Herriot's sponsorship, Garnier was commissioned to execute a series of public works. Between 1909 and 1928, the city of Lyon built Garnier's designs for a slaughterhouse and cattle market, an olympic stadium, a municipal hospital, and a residential district known as the Quartier Etats-Unis. Of these constructions, it is the Grange-Blanche hospital, now named after Herriot, that offers the most complete demonstration of

8. Tony Garnier, Grange-Blanche hospital, Lyon. (Tony Schuman)

Garnier's architecture. Laid out on a gently sloping site, it was conceived as a series of free-standing pavilions separated by small gardens and a network of narrow roads in a simple grid (fig. 8). For functional purposes, the pavilions are linked by underground passageways.

Although the hospital does have a primary entrance and gate house, there is no formal hoopla to the scheme, no grand axes, no central building. The visual focal point is the twin chimneys of the heating plant. The design of the pavilions themselves is restrained and classical; Garnier, as a Beaux-Arts product, believed in a kind of perennial architecture, where unchanging formal considerations could be put in the service of a variety of social needs. He was more concerned with the human scale and open feeling of the ensemble than with architectural detail and contented himself on that score with simple, repetitive elements like a modest cornice or trellised entry. His priority of program and plan over detail was shared by Mayor Herriot in these words:

A monument to be built appears to me like a problem to be solved. First one must establish the intellectual lines of the work, define the needs it must fulfill, subordinate the appearance of the vessel to the needs of what is to be contained. We have had enough of Renaissance façades and mock Louis XVI pavilions.[7]

Of the slaughterhouse-market complex "de la Mouche," also laid out as a miniature city, only the central market hall remains, but this building must

9. Tony Garnier, market hall, Abattoir de la Mouche, Lyon. (Tony Schuman)

10. Tony Garnier, market hall, Abattoir de la Mouche, Lyon. (Tony Schuman)

be counted among the major achievements of modern architecture. The vast hall—eighty meters wide and more than two hundred meters long—bears a tiered metal roof supported by a sweeping procession of twenty-one three-hinged metal arches (fig. 9). The front and rear entry walls are of reinforced concrete with enormous stepped windows over a ground level base of entry doors (fig. 10), a device that imbues this service structure with civic meaning.

Shared Visions

The three projects—Ledoux's at Chaux, Godin's at Guise, and Garnier's in Lyon—share a belief in the perfectibility of human society and in the role of architecture as intrinsic to this transformation. Each is concerned with extending a progressively more encompassing franchise to the workers who run the industrial apparatus, which, in turn, is seen as the vehicle to progress. As a group, they indicate an evolution toward higher, more complete, and more direct forms of democracy. In each instance, the nature and emphasis of the formal symbolism, program, and site planning are conditioned by their individual social visions. These in turn are influenced both by the historical moment of their creation and by the personal background of their creators. Thus, Ledoux supports his vision of a dependent democracy with a formal plan relying on geometric symbols of Neoplatonic ideals; his is a moralizing view of human society, a statement of what ought to be. Godin centers his vision of a cooperative society on a radical new building type, the familistère, which relies on the buildings' plan and section to encourage the personal interaction of its inhabitants; his is a behavioral view of human society, a statement of what can be. Garnier bases his vision of a socialist democracy on the civilizing force of the city itself; his is a political view of human society, a statement of what will be.

The design integrity of these three projects derives from their synthesis of form and content. Each offers a physical form for industrial society at different stages of growth—Ledoux at its birth, Godin at its adolescence, Garnier at its maturity. Each imagines a set of social relationships to be symbolically and experientially reinforced by architecture. Thus even where the purely formal aspects may be questioned as didactic propositions, their grounding in social structure lends a certain authority. Conversely, even where the moral, psychological, or political theories might be viewed as old-fashioned, eccentric, or extreme, their expression in built form helps to clarify their meaning. It is this synthesis that enables the three projects to endure as historical examples, carrying forward a message about their respective societies as revealed through architecture.

■ Bofill at Marne-la-Vallée

In the light of these powerful works—in program, plan, and form—what can we learn from Bofill's Spaces of Abraxas? What can it tell us about the way we see ourselves and our society and how architecture is used to explicate this vision? To begin with, we are not dealing here with a utopian program but a single-purpose building complex—housing—separated even from the corner store by a huge parking garage that lies between the housing and the town core of shops and services. The new town of Marne-la-Vallée is a linear series of five villages linked by auto and rail lines. Although there is some commercial and office space in the village centers, this new town, like the others, is primarily a dormitory suburb. Thus the concept of the new town itself represents a retreat from the historical utopian vision, which centered on public life and the city, into a private world emphasizing the family and home.

Indeed, the Taller is quick to argue that their work here is not a utopian project:

Far from utopia, in a state more like pessimism, we sought to construct a realistic model capable of explaining to the public and to our colleagues, that even if the utopia of 1968 had vanished, it was still possible to make a better, more rational architecture, capable of creating communal spaces.[8]

Despite this expressed pessimism, which presumably refers to the restricted funds and bureaucratic impediments in public housing construction and, possibly, to the continued need for subsidized housing at all (the rebellions of 1968 having failed to erase class distinctions in French society), the Taller attempts to overcome limitations of budget and program. "Daily life should not be banalized," Bofill contends, "but exalted to become rich and meaningful."[9]

In architectural terms, this apparent contradiction between pessimism and exaltation is resolved by reducing construction costs through the application of rationalized construction technology in the form of progressively more sophisticated prefabricated concrete techniques. Peter Hodgkinson, the Taller's lead architect for the Viaduct and Arcades by the Lake housing at Saint-Quentin-en-Yvelines, justly observes that this project "opened up a

11. Ricardo Bofill, Arcades by the Lake, Saint-Quentin-en-Yvelines. (Tony Schuman)

12. Ricardo Bofill, Spaces of Abraxas, detail of palace. (Tony Schuman)

13. Ricardo Bofill, Antigone, Montpelier. (Tony Schuman)

second-generation postwar epoch of industrialization in the building trade—architectural industrialization both in plan (crane movement) and in panel design (composition)."[10] The evolution of these precast panels—from the monochromatic components with terra cotta cladding at Saint-Quentin-en-Yvelines to the polychromatic and integrally colored (by mixing oxides with the cement) components at Marne-la-Vallée to the on-site panel production at Montpelier (figs. 11, 12, 13, respectively)—is certainly one of the Taller's most striking achievements, giving them credibility with engineers and building contractors as well as cost-conscious housing developers.

If the production technology addresses one paradox, the formal expression to which it is turned introduces a more difficult one, for what gives the Taller's work in France its special character is the use of classical elements—columns, pediments, cornices, and so on—as the basis for the precast panels. The choice of this formal language stems from an assumption that French neoclassical architecture and urbanism of the eighteenth century remain as viable models for late-twentieth-century design, surviving a two-century time warp and transcending categories of class as well. For in counterposing an image of nobility to the banality of the *grand ensembles*—the first generation of French postwar housing estates built according to the tenets of the modern movement—Bofill poses the second paradox: the proletarian aristocrat.

In his desire to ennoble the lives of his working-class tenants and cooperative owners, Bofill has opted for a set of images meant to recall the glory that was Rome (or, at least, Versailles). The inhabitants of Marne-la-Vallée have been placed in an elaborate stage set, which Bofill has executed deliberately and literally. The semicircular Theater defines a tiered amphitheater (fig. 14) that looks through the (proscenium) Arch (fig. 15) at the giant Palace as backdrop. Tall slots, or "urban windows," in the Theater and Palace align axially with the Arch to provide a theatrical succession of vistas through the complex toward the countryside beyond (fig. 16). But while this architecture has already been used to good effect as a backdrop for at least one recent film *(Brazil)*, its appropriateness as a setting for everyday life is more problematic.

The quite secondary consideration given to the routines of ordinary living is evident in the way the unit plans are distorted to fit the precision of the for-

14. Ricardo Bofill, Theater, Spaces of Abraxes, Marne-la-Vallée. (Tony Schuman)

15. Ricardo Bofill, Arch, Spaces of Abraxas, Marne-la-Vallée. (Tony Schuman)

16. "Urban windows," Spaces of Abraxas, Marne-la-Vallée. (Tony Schuman)

17. Ricardo Bofill, Theater, Spaces of Abraxes, Marne-la-Vallée. (Tony Schuman)

18. Ricardo Bofill, ground floor plan, Spaces of Abraxes, Marne-la-Vallée. (*Progressive Architecture*)

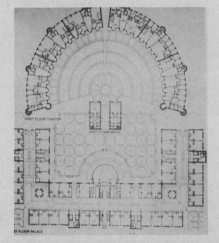

mal scheme. The mirrored glass "columns," which lend formal elegance to the interior façade of the Theater (fig. 17), result in awkward floor plans for the units inside (fig. 18). The bays fall haphazardly, sometimes in the living room, sometimes a bedroom, on occasion a public hall; here, in the center of the room; there, off to one side. Walls in adjoining units have been skewed to accommodate the intrusion of the bays. While the cooperative apartments in the Theater all have through ventilation, the rental units in the Palace are deep, with dark recesses toward the blank interior wall.

In its public space, the project is an all-or-nothing proposition: either the epic drama of the whole population in the civic-scaled amphitheater, or the minidramas of six hundred private family lives. There are no spaces of intermediate scale designed to encourage spontaneous neighboring at different levels of association. Even the community space on the ground floor of the Palace is remote from the action in the amphitheater. It might be argued, in support of Bofill's life-as-theater metaphor, that even daily life around the house has its share of spectacle, if not drama: the various routines of washing and drying clothes, cleaning the car, children at play. But these activities have been banished from Bofill's stage, the cars to a parking garage and the children to a rudimentary set of swings *outside* the Theater. Thus, while claiming to celebrate everyday life, Bofill effectively holds it in low esteem.

This contradiction between the experience of daily life and the setting for it offered at Marne-la-Vallée follows from Bofill's inversion of the symbolic form of the classical city, where housing constitutes a neutral ground against which public monuments are set in relief. With the Spaces of Abraxas, housing becomes an iconographic object. Bofill defines the Palace as "a monument to everyday life . . . conceived and composed in space after the rules of classical art. The transformation of space and, to a certain extent, of time, will condition and exalt the life of its inhabitants."[11] As a monument, Abraxas is most successful when viewed from a distance, as an object in the landscape on the approach from Paris. It looms as a landmark, a point of reference, a symbolic entry point for the new town. Imagine, however, the surprise of the casual traveler to find that this monumental classical complex contains not the town hall and civic center but public housing! This inversion of architectural symbolism, beyond the practical shortcomings of the plan, raises some disturbing questions about the use of formalism to convey meaning in architecture: Can civic architecture—in scale and symbol—be appropriated for domestic use? Can working-class life be transformed through the visual trappings of the aristocracy?

Bofill himself is highly conscious of the ambiguity of meaning carried by architectural form. As he acknowledges:

The new formal language which architecture is using is still incoherent and lacks the precision to express or clarify its ideas or clarify projects which are still in gestation. It is an esoteric vocabulary.[12]

Playing fast and loose with architectural syntax is most problematic when it contravenes established conventions of understanding, as in Bofill's appropriation of public scale and symbolism for domestic purpose. The gravity of this act is implicit in Suzanne Langer's appreciation of the relationship between culture and architecture:

[T]he great architectural ideas have rarely, if ever, arisen from domestic needs. They grew as the temple, the tomb, the fortress, the hall, the theater. The reason is simple enough: tribal culture is collective, and its domain is therefore public. When it is made visible, its image is a public realm.[13]

In proposing that people literally inhabit "monuments"—be they "columns" or the triumphal arch—Bofill proclaims that these collective symbols are no longer the province of the public realm, a heresy that suggests that contemporary society has lost its cultural coherence. More ominous is the corollary that it is only in retreating from the public realm, from the world of production and civic action that forms the wellspring of social well-being, that the richness and exaltation of life is to be found. Despite its massive scale, Abraxas calls to mind the insularity of the suburban house, with its "home as castle" ideology.

In this retreat, moreover, the form and image of domestic life provided for the inhabitants of Abraxas do not promote their development through social interaction, but simply exhort them to higher self-esteem "conditioned" by the majesty of the surrounds, a disturbing echo of the reference to B. F. Skinner in the Taller's earlier Walden 7 project. The inhabitants of Abraxas are apparently meant to identify themselves with a Roman emperor (or French king) and use this enhanced self-image to achieve greater satisfaction in their lives at the workplace and in the community. While it may indeed be preferable to awake in a pseudo-palace than in a typical public housing slab, it is unlikely that the power of architectural imagery can transform the reality of low-paid industrial or bureaucratic routine. Bofill has put the cart before the horse. "It is not the consciousness of men that determines their social being," Marx argued, "but, on the contrary, their social being that determines

19. Ricardo Bofill, Walden 7,
San Just (Barcelona).
(Tony Schuman)

their consciousness."[14] In promoting form over content, Bofill may be accused
of inducing false consciousness.

If one takes seriously Bofill's aspirations to a socially progressive architecture, there is a sad irony in this critique. As a bearer of the emblem of the
Catalan spirit of rebellion and cultural nationalism as well as the idealism of
the sixties generation, Bofill's own history of social activism includes jailings
under the Franco regime. His hero, Antonio Gaudí, is valued not only for his
romantic architecture of Mediterranean light and geological form but for his
political integrity as well. The Taller, itself, over which Bofill presides as in-
spirational leader, includes philosophers, poets, and political activists as well
as talented groups of designers in Barcelona and Paris.

The ideological contradictions of the Taller stem from two parallel concerns that take precedence over social content: formalism and the role of the
architect. "Morphology is our proper domain," Bofill asserts, "as the knowledge of formal problems and the inherent laws of form."[15] In the early days of

the Taller, this search for form was rooted in geometric repetition—the "City in Space" scheme for Madrid and the early Barcelona housing projects grew out of a manipulation of cubic elements (fig. 19). A 1975 doctoral thesis by Anna Bofill, Ricardo's sister and Taller associate, offered "A Contribution to the Study of the Geometric Generation of Urban and Architectural Forms."

In this context, the transition from the Spanish practice to the projects in France must have felt like a homecoming for the Taller, a return to the land of the neoclassical order. Hodgkinson describes the first housing at Saint-Quentin-en-Yvelines as representing "our theory that all architecture had been invented, our job being only to compose according to Platonic rules."[16] This support for an eternal architecture, however, is at odds with the Taller's stated belief in a culturally relative formal expression:

Whatever epoch concerns us, we consider it of great importance to discover the intrinsic reasons for the changes in architecture and their formal manifestations. Architecture, as a cultural phenomenon, is capable of producing an avant-garde system of symbolic expression. It thus develops a specific language in each epoch. Today, this language is concerned with the town.[17]

While the contemporary reaction to the urbanism of the modern movement has occasioned a renewed appreciation of traditional urban form ("the town"), it is not so evident what "intrinsic reasons" of the age impel this attention. Does the town acquire new meaning in contemporary society? If the town retains its "old" meaning as the public arena for social participation, why is this quintessential democratic activity symbolically removed in Bofill's work to the privacy of the domestic world?

The philosophical musings of the Taller tantalize like their architecture. They pose a series of provocative ideas that play on our sense of history (both architectural and social) and imply a bold new direction for socially responsible architecture. The failure to clarify the implications of these gestures lies in the identification of social objectives as only one among many determinants of design—along with construction cost, building technology, bureaucratic negotiation, and political maneuvering—all of them subservient to the pursuit of architectural form. The content of these social objectives,

moreover, is left to the benevolent imagination of the architect, whose em-
powerment is the overriding goal of the Taller. As Hodgkinson divulges:

*The one all-important theme ever constant in the development of the Taller
is the relationship between work and power. The architect has passed
from divine creator to a supplier of service, in many countries even to a
servant. . . . The architect must get above this barrier to impose his knowledge, humanism, and universality on the administrators, politicians, and
bankers."*[18]

■ Conclusion: Utopia Spurned

In Bofill's brief, then, the path of social progress lies through the superior
vision of the architect, a viewpoint that recalls Ledoux, whose paean to the
profession asks rhetorically, "Is there anything unknown to the architect, he
who is as old as the sun?"[19] There are other parallels to Ledoux, not the least
of them Bofill's success at becoming architect to the French "king," in the
person of former president Valéry Giscard d'Estaing, whose support was instrumental in securing the Taller's first commissions in France. Notably, Bofill
has been more successful than Ledoux in negotiating the shifting sands of
French politics, winning major new contracts under the socialist government
of François Mitterand. In this regard, the Taller's success may be attributed to
the notoriety of their early work, their mastery over construction technology
and building costs, and a highly sophisticated public relations effort.

The debt to Ledoux is evident in formal terms as well, from the conifer
crown atop the Theater at Abraxas to the semicircular form of the Theater
itself. But where Ledoux's linking of regional vernacular with classical form is
intended to give a new image to a new industrial society, centered on labor
and production, Bofill's symbolism lacks programmatic clarity. This contrast
is particularly clear in the treatment of the semicircular open space that
serves as a central element in both schemes. At the Saltworks, this area is
used for unloading the shipments of lumber that fuel, literally and figuratively,
the whole enterprise. At Abraxas, on the other hand, it is hard to imagine

what level of domestic activity might animate the arena to the point of justifying its civic scale and architectural embellishment.

This tenuous link between form and content also impairs Bofill's interpretation of Fourier's "social palace." Unlike Godin's realization of Guise, where the architecture is meant to assist the inhabitants in their climb up the social ladder by encouraging cooperative effort through social interaction, Bofill subordinates substance to style. Compare, for example, the scale of the glass-roofed courtyards at Guise with the arena at Abraxas. Here, as in the shopless "streets" at Saint-Quentin-en-Yvelines, Bofill relies more on the inhabitants' interpretive powers than on their daily lives.

While the visual record identifies a historical and philosophical debt to both Ledoux and Fourier, Bofill's relationship to Tony Garnier presents a stark contrast. Although both men share a fascination with the technological possibilities of reinforced concrete and a belief in the Beaux-Arts doctrine of the eternal appropriateness of classical form, they draw opposite conclusions from this aesthetic premise. For Bofill, it opens the door to an endless refinement of these forms, a posture analogous to Mies's devotion to a technologically based architectural vocabulary. For Garnier, the acceptance of the classical canon marks an end to formal exploration in favor of a discourse on the city viewed as an arena for the exercise of democratic power. Garnier sees urban housing as part of that neutral ground against which the true public monument—the cultural facilities and assembly halls—can emerge to symbolize the collective will. Against this vision one can almost hear Bofill inverting Herriot's dictum: "A problem to be solved is a monument to be built."

In an essay written for the exhibition he shared with Leon Krier at the Museum of Modern Art in New York, Bofill expressed contempt for the idea of utopia. "These utopias [in the technological or social writings of the 1960s] destroy geniuses and masters. In the 1970s, architecture begins to concentrate on itself again. Architects rediscover the pleasure of creation, and their craft."[20]

This defense of traditional architectural formalism, unfettered by the burden of transforming society in the process, would appear to oppose design integrity to social intent, Ledoux notwithstanding. Yet Bofill is surely not suggesting that we have reached a state of social development where each individual is already "exalted" by the quality of his or her everyday life. Rather, he appears to be arguing for a window-dressing architecture that will not, or cannot, transform the underlying social structure and that is, therefore, to be evaluated within its own terms of reference. Because Bofill offers no discussion of how he imagines people will actually use the Spaces of Abraxas, we are left to rely on the imagery alone to convey the social meaning of the work.

What are we to make of the symbolism itself? On a general level, the very fact that so much attention and money have been lavished on social housing carries a message that people of modest means are valued in French society, a message that increases in significance in comparison with the paltry resources devoted to public housing in the United States.[21] But this message can be, and has been, carried by a wide range of architectural styles and *partis*. One must ask: Why Rome? Why the distant past to give form to contemporary life? When Ledoux invented new form for his Ideal City, he was using it to symbolize a new social and economic program. Bofill is using an old form to dress up the status quo. The message is that our own age has no coherence, no grandeur, no form of its own. In the midst of wide confusion and debate about what contemporary society stands for, there is a corollary confusion about what it looks like. But instead of seeking an architecture that helps us discover, understand, and transform the meaning of daily life, Bofill offers us refuge in the values of the past. Abandoning the ideal city project of provoking our thinking and engaging our participation in looking toward the future of human society, Spaces of Abraxas sends us looking backward. And we are tempted to conclude, somewhat sadly and anticlimactically, "We have seen the past, and it doesn't work."

1. Ricardo Bofill, quoted in Barry Bergdoll, "Subsidized Doric," *Progressive Architecture* (October 1982), p. 74.

2. Ricardo Bofill, quoted in Christian Norberg-Schulz, "Form and Meaning," in *Ricardo Bofill: Taller de Arquitectura*, ed. Yukio Futagawa (New York: Rizzoli, 1985), p. 11.

3. For a discussion of the imagery of the French Revolution, see Jean Starobinski, *1789: Les Emblèmes de la Raison* (Paris: Flammarion Press, 1979).

4. C.-N. Ledoux, quoted in Starobinski, *Les Emblèmes de la Raison*, p. 51. All translations from the French are by the author.

5. C.-N. Ledoux, quoted in Michel Parent, *Les Salines Royales d'Arc et Senans* (Paris: Dermont Press, 1973), unpaginated.

6. Charles Fourier, cited by Friedrich Engels in *Socialism: Utopian and Scientific* in Marx and Engels, Selected Works (New York: International Publishers, 1970), p. 406.

7. Edouard Herriot, quoted in Leonardo Benevolo, *History of Modern Architecture,* vol. 1 (Cambridge, Mass.: MIT Press, 1978), p. 340.

8. Bofill, in *Ricardo Bofill: Taller de Arquitectura* (Rizzoli), p. 120.

9. Bofill, quoted in "Subsidized Doric," p. 74.

10. Peter Hodgkinson, "A Personal Point of View," in *Taller de Arquitectura: Ricardo Bofill* (London: Architectural Association, 1981), p. 8.

11. Bofill, in *Ricardo Bofill: Taller de Arquitectura* (Rizzoli), p. 120.

12. Ibid.

13. Suzanne Langer, *Feeling and Form* (New York: Charles Scribner's Sons, 1953), p. 97.

14. Karl Marx, *Preface to a Contribution to the Critique of Political Economy* in Marx and Engels, *Selected Works* (Moscow: Progress Publishers, 1973), p. 503.

15. Bofill, in *Ricardo Bofill: Taller de Arquitectura* (Rizzoli), p. 21.

16. Hodgkinson, "A Personal Point of View," p. 7.

17. Bofill, in *Ricardo Bofill: Taller de Arquitectura* (Rizzoli), p.121.

18. Hodgkinson, "A Personal Point of View," p. 9.

19. C.-N. Ledoux, quoted in Michel Gallet, *Ledoux et Paris,* "Cahiers de la Rotonde 3" (Paris: Ville de Paris, Commission du Vieux Paris, 1979), p. 51.

20. Ricardo Bofill, *Ricardo Bofill and Leon Krier: Architecture, Urbanism, and History* (New York: Museum of Modern Art, 1985), p. 11.

21. Although this paper is focused on architectural imagery and utopian visions rather than housing policy, it is worth bearing in mind that Bofill's Spaces of Abraxas are, in fact, public housing (which the French call "social" housing). Social housing is home to a full 25 percent of the French population and is a primary arena for experimentation in architecture; many of France's leading architects have produced works for this sector. There are important lessons here for housing policy in the United States, where less than 2 percent of the population lives in public housing and where this housing has been produced, for the most part, in an atmosphere unsympathetic to the notion that quality housing is a public responsibility.

Contributors

Margaret Crawford
teaches at the Southern California Institute of Architecture, Los Angeles.

Mike Davis
teaches at the Southern California Institute of Architecture, Los Angeles.

Rosalyn Deutsche
teaches at The Cooper Union, New York City.

Kenneth Frampton
teaches at Columbia University, New York City.

Diane Ghirardo
teaches at the University of Southern California, Los Angeles, and is visiting
professor at the Southern California Institute of Architecture.

Vincent P. Pecora
teaches at the University of California, Los Angeles, and is visiting professor
at the Southern California Institute of Architecture.

Tony Schuman
teaches at the New Jersey Institute of Technology, Newark.

Ferruccio Trabalzi
teaches at the Southern California Institute of Architecture, Los Angeles.